RAUNDS FURNELLS

The Anglo-Saxon church and churchyard

RAUNDS AREA PROJECT

RAUNDS FURNELLS

The Anglo-Saxon church and churchyard

RAUNDS AREA PROJECT

Andy Boddington

with
Graham Cadman, Rosemary Cramp,
David Parsons, Terry Pearson, Faye Powell

and contributions by
John Evans, Tony Gouldwell,
Diana Sutherland, Paul Woodfield

ENGLISH HERITAGE
1996
ARCHAEOLOGICAL REPORT 7

First published 1996 by
English Heritage, 23 Savile Row,
London, W1X 1AB

ISBN 1 85074 520 X

A CIP data record for this book is available from
the British Library.

In Figures 1 and 2, the grid is the National Grid taken
from Ordnance Survey mapping with the permission
of the Controller of Her Majesty's Stationery Office,
© Crown Copyright

In Table 2, the alignments quoted are based on the
National Grid taken from Ordnance Survey mapping
with the permission of the Controller of Her Majesty's
Stationery Office, © Crown Copyright

Editors: Kate Hughes (consultant), Margaret Wood
(English Heritage)
Layout design: Helen Colman (consultant), Karen
Guffogg and Andrew McLaren (English Heritage)
Cover design: Andrew McLaren (English Heritage)

Contents

List of illustrations

List of tables

Microfiche contents *(inside back cover)*

Preface

It is with pleasure that we introduce this volume which is the first to appear from the fruitful long-term partnership between English Heritage and Northamptonshire County Council in the Raunds Area Project.

The Raunds Area Project is a large-scale archaeological investigation designed to trace the evolution of the landscape in an area of forty square kilometres in eastern Northamptonshire. The project sprang from a convergence of circumstances in the later 1970s. Northamptonshire County Council had identified certain priority areas in the county (in a Northamptonshire County Council Occasional Paper, Foard 1979). One such area lay around the village of Raunds in the middle Nene valley east of the town of Higham Ferrers.

No sooner had the value of the Raunds area been recognised than it became clear that extensive and unavoidable destruction of archaeological evidence would take place in both the villages and the surrounding countryside as a result of quarrying, road building, and housing development. Assessment showed an exceptional wealth of potential, for example in a group of prehistoric barrows near Stanwick, a Saxon and Norman manor in north Raunds.

The possibility of investigating the interlocking relationships of different periods of human activity over a long timespan within a particular area was agreed to be an outstanding opportunity and a project was designed to pursue archaeological research in a rescue context. The project was not site-specific but rather about settlements, in space and time, and about the fields between the settlements which were to be an integral part of the study. The objective was no less than to investigate the origins and development of settlement and the evolution of the countryside from prehistoric to late medieval times by combining extensive field survey of the landscape with intensive recording by excavation of selected sites.

Early in the life of the project the Saxon and Norman origins of Raunds itself were investigated. Excavation at Furnells revealed a Saxon and Norman manorial group including a wealthy homestead, a church, and a cemetery. It is the cemetery which is described and analysed in this volume. The Furnells settlement is in turn grouped with nearby sites which together will be published as *North Raunds*, the second volume in the series.

This volume and those which follow contain the results of fieldwork, allied with the intensive study of the artefacts and environmental evidence, encompassing nearly two decades of endeavour and involving the collaboration of English Heritage, Northamptonshire County Council and also the private sector and universities, in the case of this site the universities of Bradford and Durham, and the Open University. The Raunds Area Project is important because the evidence embraces much that is normal, routine and typical of ancient settlements – enclosures, manor houses, cemeteries, villas, tenements, roads, farms, and fields. One of the exciting challenges in interpreting the results, however, has been that they do not readily fit our preconceptions.

The Raunds Area Project is a great step forward in landscape and settlement studies and its results will teach us about our origins and help to shape future studies into the next millennium.

Geoffrey Wainwright
English Heritage

Alan Hannan
Northamptonshire County Council

Acknowledgements

Andy Boddington

The excavation and post-excavation were financed by the Historic Buildings and Monuments Commission (formerly Inspectorate of Ancient Monuments, DoE), the Manpower Services Commission and Northamptonshire County Council. We are grateful to Ideal Homes (Thames) Ltd (formerly Combem Homes, formerly Bruce Fletchers) for access to the site and for material and financial aid. Particular thanks are extended to Mr Roy Mason, the site agent at Churchfields (the name reflects the archaeological discoveries rather than the original field name, which was Furnells). Among the many project staff and volunteers, special mention should be made of Andy and Pat Chapman who contributed valiantly to the excavation and post-excavation of the graveyard. Merry Morgan advised on the recording of the cemetery. My colleagues Graham Cadman, Glenn Foard, Alan Hannan and Terry Pearson have together provided the academic, archaeological and administrative environment within which the excavation took place. The importance of the site was only realised through the endeavours of David Hall and the Northamptonshire Field Group.

In the course of writing, this text has broadened from a mere technical description toward a comprehensive interpretation. Discussions with Faye Powell and Dr Keith Manchester were invaluable in placing the skeletal material in context; Keith Manchester has also supplied additional pathological identifications. The statistical analysis of the graveyard commenced as an undergraduate dissertation at the School of Archaeological Sciences, University of Bradford. Here I must thank Arnold Aspinall, John Haigh and Rick Jones for their help, advice and discussion. At Durham the invaluable help and advice of Professor Rosemary Cramp and Sue Gill encouraged my thoughts on the graveyard to mature. Details of the graveyard interpretation have been greatly enhanced through discussion with Bill White, Neil Garland and Rob Janaway. David Parsons has done much to elucidate the liturgical and social context of the church and contributed to the summary of sequence in chapter 5.

Computing analyses were for the most part carried out at the Computer Centre, University of Durham, principally using SPSSG. The skeletal osteometrics were calculated using SPSSG at the Northamptonshire County Council Computer Section. Further analysis and text processing took place under the auspices of the Academic Computing Service, Open University. Figure 59 was generated with UNIRAS. Figures 90, 92, 83, 85, and 86 were drawn by Dorrie Orchard, Figure 97 by Andy Chapman and Dorrie Orchard, Figure 94 by Andy Chapman, Christopher Addison-Jones and Dorrie Orchard, and Figures 63 and 88 by Andy Chapman. Figure 3 is based on a drawing by Christine Addison-Jones. Figures 1, 2, 4, 6, 38, 39, 66, 67, and 68 were drawn by Joanna Richards. The remainder of the line drawings were by Andy Boddington. Fig 62 was photographed by David Hall. Figs 91, 93, 95, 96, 98, and 100 were photographed by Tom Middlemass and are the copyright of Professor Rosemary Cramp.

Faye Powell

My gratitude goes to Andy Boddington for his never-failing encouragement and support. His cooperation was remarkable and his rapid, efficient use of the computer provided all the osteometric statistics. I thank him, also, for the use of his life tables (Tables 42–45). I thank all those at the Northamptonshire Archaeology Unit involved in the Raunds project, in particular Graham Cadman, who delivered many boxes of bones and provided much information with good grace. I would like to thank Dr Keith Manchester for his specific diagnoses of the lepers (burials 5046 and 5256) and his comments on burial 5218. He currently has custody of the material in the Department of Archaeological Science, Bradford University. Present and former members of staff at the Ancient Monuments Laboratory were helpful. In particular, Roger Jones expended great effort in conjunction with the Water Data Unit, Reading, to make the figures in the osteometric section 'computer readable'. His comments in the initial discussion stages, with regard to statistical analyses, gave much food for thought. Janet Henderson provided much technical advice, as did Keith Manchester, on difficult pathologies, including the cranial cuts. Justine Bayley must receive particular thanks for her support, advice and comments throughout the project. Last, but most definitely not least, Bob Powell deserves much credit for constant encouragement and faith, as well as putting up with cramped living conditions and 'skellies' under his bed!

Tony Gouldwell

Thanks are due to Miss J Virdee for assistance with flotation procedures, Miss Y Burrows for help with flotation and examination of the residue fossils, and Miss N Avory and Mr B D Custerton who devoted part of their practical class time to picking out charcoal from the flot. Mr G C Morgan gave helpful advice on some of the charcoals, for which gratitude is expressed.

Diana Sutherland

The thin sections were prepared in the Geology Department of Leicester University under the direction of Dr J D Hudson, who has given valuable comments.

Summary

The Anglo-Saxon settlement at Raunds Furnells was established in the sixth century. During the late seventh century the buildings were enclosed by ditches and by the late ninth or early tenth century the settlement had gained a small church erected to the east of this enclosure. In the tenth century ditches were cut to define a graveyard and a chancel was added to supplement the original single-celled structure. Burial commenced immediately adjacent to the church and after a period of overspill from the initial zone, expanded south and east until after two centuries all the enclosed graveyard area was in use. By the late eleventh or early twelfth century the tiny church had been replaced by a larger building. This second church may have been shortlived; certainly burial in the graveyard seems to have ceased shortly after its construction. Later in the twelfth century, or perhaps the thirteenth, the second church was converted into one of the principal buildings of a manor house. The main buildings of the manor house originally lay further west and were moved on to the former graveyard only during the fourteenth or fifteenth centuries. The manor buildings themselves became disused by the late fifteenth century and since that date the site has remained under pasture until the recent development for housing.

Within the first church it has been possible to identify a *sacrarium*, a clergy bench and the position of the altar. The door was in the south wall. A wooden structure, tentatively interpreted as a belfry, stood against the west wall. Analysis of the graveyard has proved particularly fruitful, generating a range of interpretations concerning demography, health, graveyard development and burial practice. The graveyard can be shown to have developed in a series of zones. The central and earliest zone lay adjacent to the church; this zone was dominated by a plot within which lay a decorated grave cover and at the head of which may have stood a stone cross. This may have been a 'founder's' grave. The graveyard subsequently expanded to the north, east and south. Most burials, however, were interred in earth graves; some were in wood coffins, more rarely in stone coffins. Most had stones arranged around the grave to provide the body with protection and support. During the later use of the graveyard infants were interred in the 'eaves-drip' zone adjacent to the church walls.

Résumé

L'occupation anglo-saxonne de Raunds Furnells date du sixième siècle. Au cours de la dernière partie du septième siècle les bâtiments furent entourés de fossés et à un moment quelconque avant la fin du neuvième, ou le début du dixième siècle l'occupation fut pourvue d'une petite église érigée a l'est de l'enclos. Au cours du dixième siècle on creusa des fossés pour délimiter un cimetière et on ajouta un choeur pour compléter l'édifice original qui se composait d'une seule partie. Les premières inhumations se situaient tout contre l'église puis, après une période au cours de laquelle elles dépassèrent la zone initiale, elles finirent par s'étendre vers le sud et l'est, si bien que, deux siècles plus tard, l'ensemble du cimetière délimité par les fossés se trouvaient utilisé. Vers la fin du onzième, ou au début du douzième, siècle la minuscule église avait été remplacée par un bâtiment plus important. Il se peut que cette seconde église n'ait pas subsisté très longtemps; il semble en tout cas évident qu'on a mis fin aux inhumations dans le cimetière peu après sa construction. Plus tard, au douzième ou peut-être au treizième siècle, la seconde église fut convertie et constitua un des bâtiments principaux d'une demeure seigneuriale. A l'origine, les bâtiments principaux de ce manoir se trouvaient plus a l'ouest et ce n'est qu'au cours du quatorzième ou du quinzième siècle qu'on les déplaça pour les mettre sur le site de l'ancien cimetière. Les bâtiments du manoir furent eux-mêmes abandonnés avant la fin du quinzième siècle et depuis cette date le site est resté en pré jusqu'au récent projet de construction d'habitations.

Dans l'enceinte de la première église on a pu identifier un *sacrarium* – récipient destiné a recevoir les débris liturgiques –, un banc pour les membres du clergé et la position de l'autel. La porte avait été percée dans le mur sud. Une structure en bois, un beffroi est une possibilité d'interprétation, se dressait contre le mur ouest. L'étude du cimetière s'est avérée particulièrement fructueuse, elle a engendré une serie d'interprétations concernant la démographie, la santé, l'évolution du cimetière et les coutumes funéraires. On a pu démontrer que le cimetière s'était développé en une série de zones. La partie centrale, la plus ancienne, se trouvait adjacente a l'église, elle était dominée par un emplacement contenant une dalle funèbre décorée et à la tête duquel s'était peut-être dressée une croix en pierre. Il se peut que cela ait été la tombe d'un 'fondateur'. Ultérieurement, le cimetière s'étendit vers le nord, l'est et le sud. La plupart des inhumations, toutefois, se faisaient dans des tombes en terre; certains corps avaient été placés dans des cercueils en bois ou, plus rarement, dans des cercueils en pierre. Dans la plupart des cas des pierres avaient été disposées dans la tombe pour protéger et soutenir le corps. A la fin de la période d'utilisation du cimetière, les enfants en bas-âge étaient enterrés dans la partie sous les 'gouttières', tout contre les murs de l'église.

Traduction: Annie Pritchard

Zusammenfassung

Die angelsächsische Siedlung bei Raunds Furnells entstand im sechsten Jahrhundert. Gegen Ende des siebten Jahrhunderts wurden die Bauten von Graben umgeben; am Endes des neunten oder zu Beginn des zehnten Jahrhunderts stand an der östlichen Seite dieser Umfriedung bereits eine kleine Kirche. Im zehnten Jahrhundert wurden zur Abgrenzung eines Friedhofs Graben ausgehoben, und der ursprünglich einzellige Bau wurde durch einen Altarraum vergrößert. Zunächst wurden die Toten unmittelbar neben der Kirche beigesetzt, doch dieser Umkreis erwies sich im Lauf der Jahre als zu klein; allmählich griff die Bestattungszone in südlicher und östlicher Richtung um sich, so daß zwei Jahrhunderte darauf die gesamte umfriedete Begräbnisstätte in Gebrauch war. Ende des elften oder Anfang des zwölften Jahrhunderts hatte ein größeres Gebäude die winzige Kirche ersetzt. Diese zweite Kirche bestand vielleicht nur vorübergehend; jedenfalls scheinen bald nach ihrer Errichtung keine Beisetzungen im Friedhof mehr stattgefunden zu haben. Im Verlauf des zwölften bzw. im dreizehnten Jahrhundert wurde die zweite Kirche zu einem der Hauptgebäude eines Herrensitzes umgestaltet, dessen wichtigste Bauten sich ursprünglich weiter westlich befanden und erst im vierzehnten, bzw. fünfzehnten Jahrhundert in den Bereich des ehemaligen Friedhofs verlegt wurden. Ende des fünfzehnten Jahrhunderts kamen die Bauten des Herrenbesitzes außer Gebrauch; das Gelände ging im Weideland über und wurde erst kürzlich für Wohnbauten erschlossen.

In der ersten Kirche konnten ein *Sacrarium* (eine Altarstätte zur Aufbewahrung von Heiligtümern), eine Bank für die Geistlichen und die Orientierung des Altars identifiziert werden. Die Tür befand sich an der Südwand. An der Westwand stand ein hölzerne Bau, eventuell ein Glockenturm. Besonders aufschlußreich war die Untersuchung des Friedhofs, die zu allen möglichen Interpretationen über dessen Ausgestaltung, Demographie, Gesundheit, Friedhofserweiterung und Bestattungspraxis Anlaß gegeben hat. Der Friedhof erweiterte sich nachgewiesenermaßen in einer Folge von Zonen.

In der zentralen, ältesten Zone unmittelbar neben der Kirche nahm ein Grundstück mit einem verzierten Grabdeckel, an dessen Kopfende vielleicht ein Kreuz angebracht war, die dominierende Stellung ein. Möglicherweise handelt es sich dabei um das Grab eines 'Gründers'. Später breitete sich der Friedhof nach Norden, Osten und Süden aus. Die meisten Toten wurden in der Erde begraben; manchmal in Holzsärgen, verhältnismäßig selten in Steinsärgen. Zumeist wurden zur Sicherung und Stützung des Leichnams Steine um das Grab gelegt. Später wurden Kinder im Bereich der Traufe neben der Kirchenmauer begraben.

Übersetzung: Gerry Bramall

1 Introduction

Raunds is a small town on the south side of the Nene Valley in East Northamptonshire (Fig 1). In recent centuries, its economy had been based on making boots and shoes. Inevitably, with the decline of this industry within the United Kingdom, the settlement has increasingly become a dormitory town, with some light industry. The population now numbers about 7000. The landscape of the Raunds area is gently undulating arable land based on a mixed geology of clay, limestone and gravel.

Archaeological interest in the area was stimulated by the imminence of warehouse and housing development adjacent to and within the present settlement. These expansion and infill projects threatened known earthwork sites. In the river valley below the village, gravel extraction and road improvement threatened further known sites of prehistoric, Roman and medieval date. The excavation conducted at Raunds Furnells between 1977 and 1984 was the first response to these threats. The quality of the data revealed led to a detailed examination of archaeological survival in the Raunds area. As a result, the Raunds Area Project was established in 1985 to investigate the development of the Raunds landscape, primarily through response to rescue threats but additionally with field, archival and analytical research programmes (Fig 1; Foard and Pearson 1985). The project is jointly managed by the Northamptonshire Archaeology Unit and English Heritage.

Raunds Furnells (NGR 999733) lies north-west of the present village (Fig 2). Attention was first drawn to this site when the trial trenches excavated by David Hall during 1975 uncovered fine decorated grave covers of late Anglo-Saxon date in association with burials and medieval stone walls. Full-scale excavation commenced in October 1977 under the direction of Andy Boddington; in October 1979 the excavation became the responsibility of Graham Cadman who directed until its completion in 1984. In response to the discoveries in the trial trenches, the impetus of the excavation was directed initially at the total excavation of the church and graveyard. This was soon found to underlie a medieval manor house which was also excavated during this initial phase. From 1980 attention shifted westward of the graveyard enclosure to examine the earlier manor house and its underlying sequence of buildings and enclosures (Fig 3).

This volume has been much delayed in publication. In a small part, this delay has been due to the time required for completion of excavations at Raunds Furnells and analysis of the phasing of graveyard and manor. The major contribution to the delay has, however, arisen from my own departure from the Northamptonshire Archaeological Unit in 1979 and my somewhat sporadic

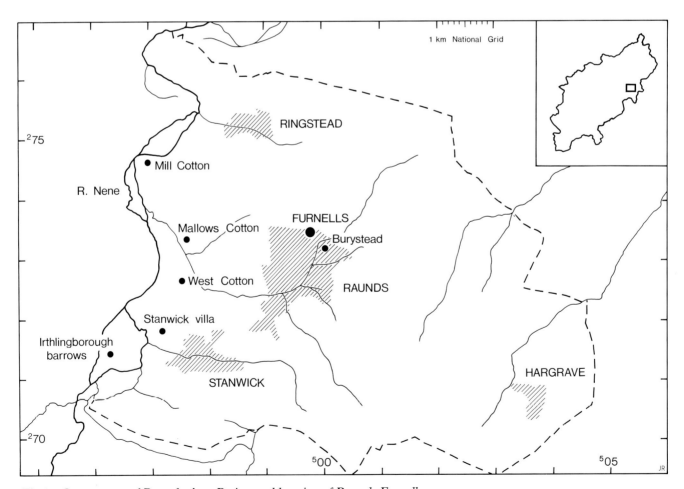

Fig 1   Survey area of Raunds Area Project and location of Raunds Furnells

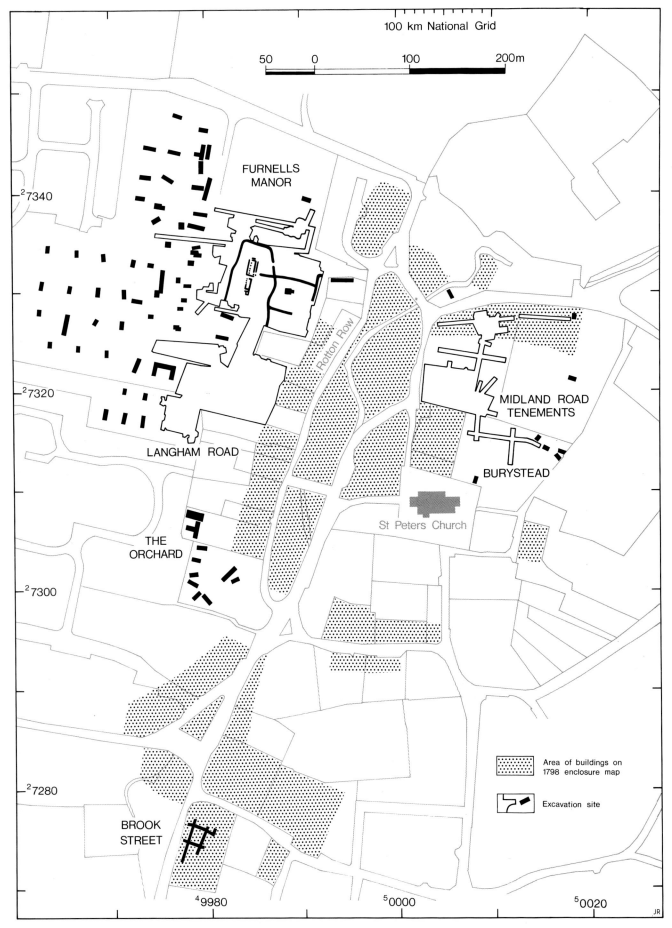

Fig 2   North Raunds: Location of site

association with the project thereafter. The immediate consequence of the delay is that some contributions to the text were written some time ago. In particular, Faye Powell's text was completed in 1982, David Parsons' in 1985. Terry Pearson's text was completed in 1990.

The overall structure and sequence of the site will be fully discussed in a second report (Audouy forthcoming; hereafter *North Raunds* forthcoming) along with a further exposition of the dating and selected artefactual evidence. This volume, which will take a comprehensive view of the origins and development of North Raunds, will place the church and churchyard in the context of village and manorial development. The church and graveyard, however, are presented in this separate volume to take account of the special character of the graveyard in terms of both excavation and analytical techniques. Throughout, authorship is by Andy Boddington, with the exception of those sections individually attributed to other authors. The text draws heavily on the contribution of all the specialists and the Furnells excavation, post-excavation and Area Project teams; the responsibility for the interpretation here does, however, rest with Andy Boddington alone.

The record archive

Commenced in 1977, the excavation and post-excavation of the church and cemetery divided its data sets and analytical levels along the lines of the Frere report (DoE 1975) with a modification of Level III to create Levels IIIa and IIIb. Level IIIa comprises a set of analytical pro-formas and post-excavation drawings, while Level IIIb is an extensive analytical text describing and interpreting the site by structural and phase component. That text is collating and analytical rather than summarising in its form; summary and expanded interpretation are reserved for this volume, which forms the Level IV or the Report Digest (DoE 1982). Technical appendices and the burial catalogue are provided on microfiche but the sheer volume of processing and text generated by this complex and extensive site has dictated that it is more appropriate to lodge the analytical (Level III) text as an archived reserve rather than to distribute it with this volume. The arrangement of Levels IIIa, IIIb and IV has proved both versatile and practical in terms of processing the raw site data and has allowed a comprehensive compilation dictated by site structure to be followed by an integrated synopsis moulded within a broader academic framework.

At the site level (Level II) record units were allocated unit numbers and described under standard and published procedures (Boddington 1978). The units were collated at Level IIIa into a hierarchical set of phases comprising groups and structural phases. Briefly defined, they are:

Unit numbers (no prefix) are stratigraphic units wherever possible and arbitrary records otherwise.
Groups (prefix **G**) are features and may range from a single layer through to a wall with its cuts, fills and construction material. For any set of units forming a group, the unit number of the earliest stratigraphic unit is taken as the group number (for example, G700 – the floor of the first church nave).

Structural phases (prefix **SP**) are created by drawing together those groups which have a structural coherence in terms of plan and interdependence of function. These might include buildings, pit groups, ditch networks or grave groups (for example, SP3 – the first church nave).
Periods (prefix **P**) are chronologically rather than structurally determined. These provide a view of the site in terms of broad units of landscape use and development and provide a basis for chronological comparison with other sites.

A summary of the structural phases used in this paper is given in Table 1 (see Chapter 2). Note that the numbers reflect the order of field recording, not chronological order.

The structural phases for the graveyard and church were allocated in the following manner. Most of the graveyard is stratigraphically isolated from the church and boundaries; here the graves might be of any date during the working life of the church. Closer to the church, some stratification is present and phasing of graves can be determined. To cope with this variation in the precision of phasing, the graveyard as a whole is encapsulated inside SP20. Within SP20 certain graves can be equated with church phases; these are labelled with the relevant church phase (SP4 or SP5) though for more general statements and analysis they are regarded as part of SP20. While the phasing of the graveyard in relation to external events has proved difficult, it has been possible to phase the graveyard development internally using non-stratigraphic evidence. It can be shown that it developed in a series of successive zones (Zones 1–5; Table 3). These zones are in effect subsets of SP20.

A meticulous procedure was adopted for recording the burials (Boddington and Morgan 1979). Slightly oblique photographs were taken of each burial from a height of *c* 4m. Each grave had been suitably marked with tags of known separation and coordinate location, enabling rectified and scaled photographs to be produced. Plans of the burial were drawn in the post-excavation stage from these photographs, as only the grave cut and structural items were drawn in the field. From these field plans, and the photographic data, a basic three-level 1:20 atlas was compiled of burial cut, body posture and structural arrangements. Normally the lowest stratigraphic unit number within a group is used as the group number; graves are an exception to this procedure and for ease of identification the burial unit number has been used. Each burial unit number was allocated from the series 5000–5999 which was reserved exclusively for skeletal material. To facilitate the structural and statistical analysis of the graveyard, the grave and its occupant were classified according to various structural and osteological components. The catalogue will be found in Microfiche 2.

For clarity the various numerical values cited in the text are given in brackets in a standardised form: (number of observations/number of possible observations/ the ratio of observations to possible observations expressed as a percentage). Hence (26/363/7) indicates that of 363 instances in which observations were possible, 26 or 7% possessed the relevant attribute. Note that while the remains of 363 burials were recovered, not all could be assessed for all analyses due to differing survival conditions. Hence the number of observations is often less than 363. For example, there are 191 adults, but only 182 survived in sufficiently good condition for sex classification. Of these, 82 were judged to be female and 100 to be male. Hence the statement that 45% of adults were female indicates 45% of 182 adults (82/182/45), not 45% of 191.

Small finds numbers are given in square brackets, for example [300], while sample numbers are given in diagonal brackets, for example, <129>. Age and sex details for burials are given in the form (burial number/sex/age range), for example (5128/M17–25), a male aged between 17 and 25 years.

Enquiries regarding the excavation artefacts and archive should in the first instance be addressed to:

Northamptonshire Archaeological Archive
Central Museum
Guildhall Road
Northampton NN1 1DN

PART I   AN ANGLO-SAXON CHURCH AND CHURCHYARD

2 The church and churchyard

Raunds Furnells lies at a height of *c* 58m OD close to the head of the narrow valley of Raunds Brook, a minor tributary of the Nene which flows some three kilometres distant (Fig 1). On the opposite side of the valley, just 260m away and at a height of *c* 61m OD, stands the parish church of St Peter (Fig 2). The geology underlying the village is a mixture of limestone, sandstone and clay. The site of Furnells itself is situated on a range of geology including Blisworth clay, Blisworth limestone, cornbrash and a red loam deposit. The north edge of the churchyard was over upper and lower cornbrash though the majority of the churchyard area was located on Blisworth clay.

The Furnells site was continuously occupied from the sixth to the late fifteenth centuries. For full details of the non-ecclesiastical structures the reader is referred to the second Raunds volume (*North Raunds* forthcoming; see also Cadman 1983). By the late seventh century the site had buildings arranged regularly within a rectangular enclosure which had an eastern entrance. The buildings were replaced and the enclosure modified over the succeeding centuries, developing by the eleventh century into what may be presumed to be the Domesday manor of Burgred (Fig 4; Cadman and Foard 1984). By the late

ninth or early tenth century the site had gained a small church set outside the east entrance of the enclosure.

The church was constructed adjacent to, but outside, the manor house complex (Fig 4). It is difficult to determine the nature of the activities east of the manor enclosure prior to the construction of the church, particularly in view of the extensive disturbance by the graveyard. It does appear, however, that during the ninth century the area of the future church was largely unused. Late in the ninth or early in the tenth century this area was cleared for the churchyard.

While an integral part of the late Saxon manorial complex, the church was established outside the 'inner court'. Analysis of the topography of the site from the late seventh to the late thirteenth centuries shows that it was set south of a long-lived access route leading from the east and ending at the manor house. The relevance of this location is explored more fully in Chapter 6.

The church was a short-lived phenomenon (SP3; Fig 7). A span of 200 years saw the church expanded, firstly by the addition of a chancel (SP4) and then through a complete rebuilding (SP5; Fig 8). The church was established without a graveyard but, at about the time of the addition of the chancel, ditches were cut to define a

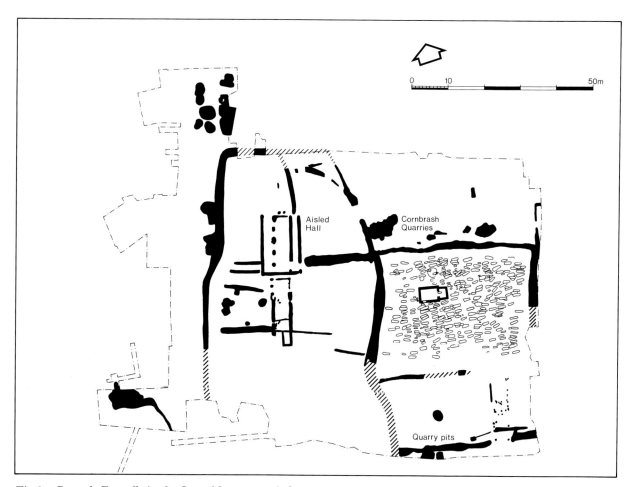

Fig 3   Raunds Furnells in the Saxo-Norman period

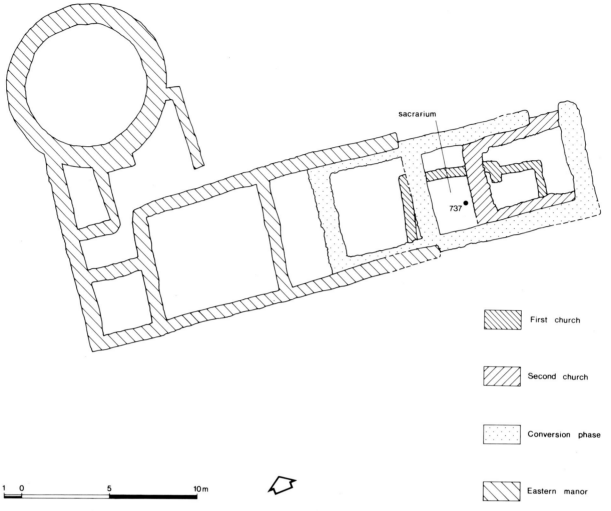

First church

Second church

Conversion phase

Eastern manor

Fig 4   Relative position of the churches and the medieval manor

churchyard enclosure about 40m by 30m across. Within this enclosure the graveyard expanded in a series of stages (SP20; Fig 7). The initial graveyard lay close to the church itself with the nearest graves 2.5m from the church walls (Zone 1). Subsequent overspill to the west and east (Zones 2 and 3) was followed by the infilling of the north-east and south-east corners of the graveyard plot (Zones 4 and 5). During this expansion the area adjacent to the church walls was brought into use, firstly for adult burials (Zone 1A), then for infants (Zone 1B). While the adults were buried to within 1m of the church walls, the infants were buried right up to the wall. Overall, at least 363 people were interred in the graveyard and it is probable that the cemetery served a population of about 40 people (p 67).

The first church came into the 'field church' category, minute even by Anglo-Saxon standards, but was promoted, along with its owner, when it acquired burial rights at the beginning of the tenth century (p 65; Barlow 1979, 187). A modest increase in size allowed it to accommodate a slightly larger congregation. The second church was, in relative terms, much bigger though it did not reach the size of some comparable eleventh-century churches (such as St Mark's, Lincoln; Gilmour and Stocker 1986). In its village context, however, it was well suited to congregational use as a potential parish church. This potential was not realised but the reasons for this

situation cannot be deduced from the archaeology of the church itself. The medieval parish church is on the opposite side of the valley.

During the late twelfth or thirteenth century the church was converted into a manorial building (SP6) which was subsequently partially incorporated into the late medieval manor house. Before, or at the time of, the conversion of the church the graveyard ceased to be used and eventually its existence was forgotten.

Table 1   Summary of structural phases

Period	Structural phase	Description
Late Saxon	SP2	Pre-church levelling
Late Saxon	SP3	The first church, single cell
Late Saxon	SP4	Addition of chancel to SP3
Late Saxon	SP20	Graveyard
Late Saxon	SP5	Second church
	SP6	Conversion of second church into manor building

The phasing nomenclature used within this report is detailed in Table 1. An explanation of the use of periods (numbers prefixed by P), structural phases (SP), groups (G) and units (no prefix) has been given in Chapter 1. The burials as a whole have been allocated to SP20, which is contemporary with church phases SP4 and

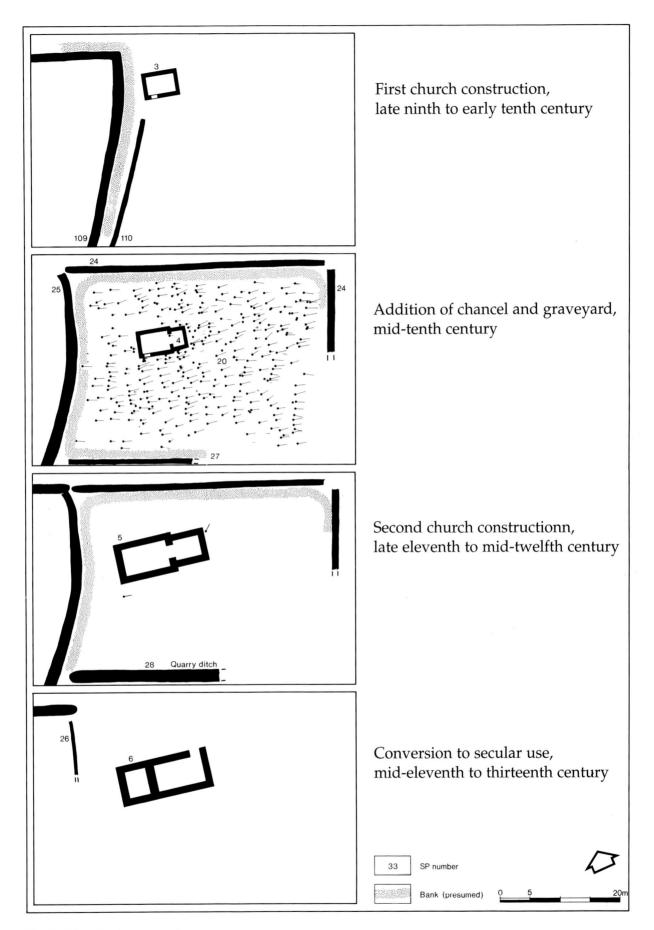

First church construction,
late ninth to early tenth century

Addition of chancel and graveyard,
mid-tenth century

Second church constructionn,
late eleventh to mid-twelfth century

Conversion to secular use,
mid-eleventh to thirteenth century

33   SP number

      Bank (presumed)   0   5   20m

Fig 5   The church construction sequence

Fig 6   Relative positions of first and second churches

SP5. Most burials could not be closely phased, though many of those close to the church could be shown to be contemporary with SP4. These are generally referenced as phase SP4, though when the graveyard as a whole is considered they are included within SP20.

The first church

Established in the late ninth or early tenth century, the first single-celled church (SP3) was constructed of cornbrash rubble bonded with ginger mortar. The aggregate for this mortar may have been derived from the red loam deposits south of the churchyard (p 100). At least some of the rubble building stone was extracted from quarry scoops to the north of the churchyard, while the finer masonry was also of local Blisworth or 'Barnack' limestone (pp100–1). The door was set in the west part of the south wall; it was provided with a wooden frame and had a width of approximately 1m.

A chancel was added, and the nave provided with a new floor, probably before the Norman Conquest (pp19–21). This chancel was designed to provide extra space for the clergy and included a bench against its east wall. At least one infant was buried under the new chancel arch behind the altar, which was retained in its original position. The plastering of the internal walls of the chancel and the external walls of both nave and chancel was also new at this phase. The raw material for the plaster may have been derived from the same quarries as the mortar. Quoins and building blocks, some of non-local 'Barnack' limestone, recovered from the second church foundations (p 98), suggest that part of the church, perhaps the chancel arch, was built of a higher quality stone. A fragment of architrave (Fig 88), also of 'Barnack' limestone, demonstrates that some dressed stone was used in the otherwise rubble-built structure.

Within the single cell church, debris from a fire was collected and placed in a pottery vessel set in the floor west of the altar, perhaps during the consecration of the church (p 62). The vessel was probably used first as a *sacrarium* and thereafter as a piscina (p 62). The altar itself was positioned against or near the east wall. Two wooden posts supported a bellcote on the gable of the west wall (pp 64–5).

The first church at Furnells is of the greatest interest for the light it sheds on liturgical and social aspects of ecclesiastical life in the tenth and eleventh centuries (pp 58–66). The *sacrarium* in the early church is one of only two or three British examples of the ablution drain/reliquary pit group of features otherwise so well attested on the continent. The feature consists of a plain pot with a complex and potentially significant history (Fig 69). Before its burial beneath the church floor, it appears to have been used for wax processing, though the suggestion that this use had an ecclesiastical rather than a secular purpose depends entirely upon inference. Once inside the church, however, it became a repository for sacred material and perhaps finally a piscina for the disposal of ablution water.

The altar stood over the *sacrarium* or to its east. With the addition of the chancel, facilities for a clergy bench were provided. The altar, possibly with canopy, was perhaps west of the chancel arch at this point. These alterations must have been associated with, and may even have been made necessary by, changes in liturgical practice (pp 63–4).

The second church

After the majority of burials had been interred, the first church building was demolished and replaced by a larger church. This was on a similar orientation (Fig 6) and overlay some of the earlier graves. The mortar from the demolished first church was spread around as a levelling

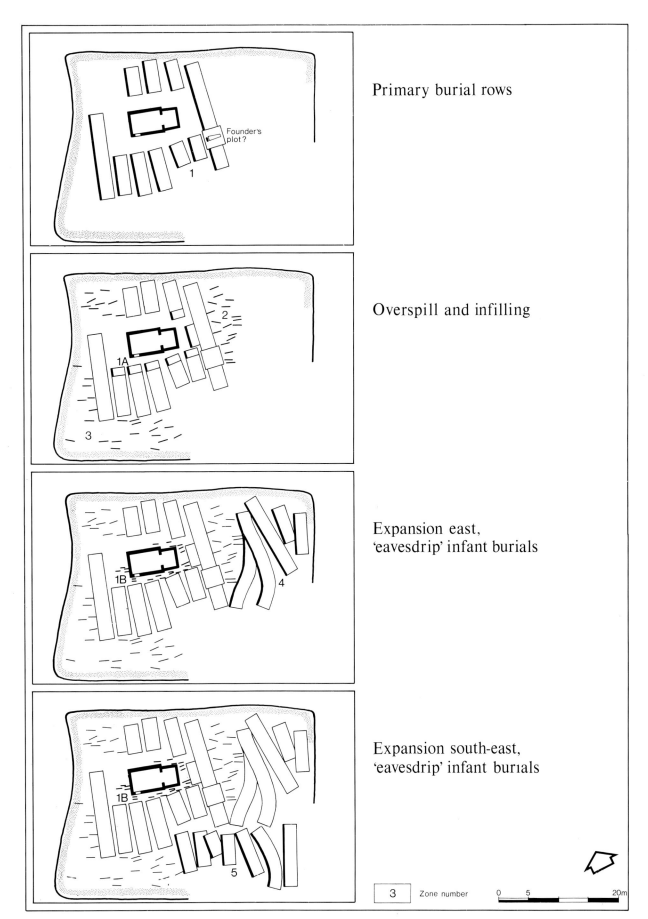

Primary burial rows

Overspill and infilling

Expansion east, 'eavesdrip' infant burials

Expansion south-east, 'eavesdrip' infant burials

Fig 7   The expansion of burial areas within the churchyard

Fig 8   The churches and central churchyard viewed from the north

deposit and the stone was reused as foundation material for the new church.

A 266% increase in area was provided by the new building. This was largely devoid of surviving internal features except for a vertical post at the west end of the nave which might be tentatively interpreted as a bellcote support (p 25). The pitched stone foundations were surmounted by horizontally bedded walls with quoins reinforcing the angles of the structure. No mortar was used and megalithic and ashlar stone was absent, except perhaps for the door frames. A churchyard cross was broken up and trimmed, perhaps to form part of a door jamb ([302/7]; p 105). The unstratified soffit may have been part of the chancel arch of this church, while the fragment of hood moulding, recovered from a later context, may have been part of the head of a piscina ([303], p 99; [132], p 98).

The chancel arch of the new church was close to that of its predecessor (Fig 6). The alignment of the church was swung by a few degrees to the north during reconstruction. The corners were only approximate right angles, leading to the new nave being misaligned with the chancel. This small difference of alignment between nave and chancel probably reflects casual surveying and construction methods and is not of liturgical or other significance (p 25). The alignment of the church in relation to the topography of the site generally is, however, of significance. Both the church and its burials are orientated at an angle to the rest of the site and the adjacent Rotton Row; their alignment was closer to, though not quite, true east (92°–94°) indicating a desire for correct orientation of the building and burials.

The impact of the new building on the graveyard sur-

face was dramatic, entailing clearance of the grave mounds, markers and crosses adjacent to the church and the instigation of a new 'generation' of burials in the churchyard. Those individuals previously fortunate enough to be buried in stone coffins appear to have been summarily reburied in pits. The occupants of other disturbed graves had their bones either discarded or sealed beneath the new foundation (p 28). Nevertheless, surprisingly little disturbance was caused to the existing burials by the construction of the second church itself, only about 13 burials being affected.

The conversion phase

Early in the twelfth century the church and graveyard ceased their ecclesiastical functions and the second church was converted to apparent secular use (SP6, Fig 21). Whether a chapel was incorporated into this new building to continue, in a revised form, the ecclesiastical use of the building cannot be determined from the available archaeological evidence.

The conversion of the second church entailed the demolition of the chancel and the extension of the nave walls eastwards to meet the line of the east chancel wall. Later robbing removed all the east wall, except its foundations, hence it is not possible to determine whether the east wall of the chancel was retained or completely rebuilt. A new wall was built across the original nave, 4.2m from its west end. This created two rooms 4.6m wide, the east room being 8.0m long.

A key issue here is the length of use of the second church. Was it a long-lived and decaying building in need of reconstruction or was it a short-lived building

Table 2 Summary of characteristics of the churches

Phase	Construction	Dimensions (external)	Alignment [1]	Features
First church nave (SP3)	Cornbrash rubble foundations and walls. Walls mortared. Blisworth and 'Barnack' quoins. 'Barnack' architrave. Wood framed door in south wall. Dressed architrave. Stone floor?	Length 8.1m Width 3.5m	96°	Burnt floor area, *Sacrarium*, Altar, Bellcote?
First church chancel (SP4)	As above. Chancel plastered internally. Nave and chancel plastered externally. Stone floor in nave. Earth floor in chancel.	Length 2.0m Width 2.8–3.0m	95°	Piscina, Altar, Clergy bench, Bellcote. Burial in chancel arch.
Second church (SP5)	Unmortared cornbrash, Blisworth and ironstone foundations and wall. Foundations pitched courses, wall flat-bedded. Stone framed door (location not known). Earth and small rubble floors. Decorated arch soffit.	Length 15.2m Chancel 4.5m Nave 5.6m	94° (nave) 91.5° (chancel)	Bellcote? Piscina?

1 *The alignments quoted are based on the Ordnance Survey Grid.*

converted to a new use after its principal ecclesiastical functions were stripped away from it? There is modest evidence that the church was in a state of disrepair prior to conversion. While the new wall across the nave was keyed into the south wall, it cut through the north wall and returned east (Fig 22). This demonstrates that the north-east corner of the church nave was rebuilt while the south-east corner was reused. This asymmetrical relationship in what was essentially a conversion from one symmetrical building to another is, however, the only hint that any part of the church was in disrepair. Such is the paucity of ceramic evidence that it is difficult to assign a length of use to the second church. The lack of burials near the church which also cut through the demolition deposits from the first church suggests that burial could not have continued long after the demolition of the first church.

Another key issue is the function of the converted building. The increase in ground floor area gained by the new building, less than 5 sq m, hardly seems to justify the scale of the rebuilding and, given this limited gain, it might be argued that the principal reason for conversion was the insertion of a first floor and that the conversion may have been designed to create a first floor hall (in some respects similar to that at Boothby Pagnell; Wood 1965). Whether the new building continued the ecclesiastical use of the site through incorporation of a chapel cannot be determined.

The churchyard

The church was positioned on the edge of a ridge from which the ground fell away southwards and eastwards (Fig 59). This position would have provided an unobstructed view of the building from the village area to the east and south-east. The west wall of the first church (SP3) was constructed over the backfilled ditch of the manorial enclosure (SP110; Fig 5). It is probable that only that part of the ditch which lay beneath the church was initially backfilled, the southern part of the ditch remaining open. The inner enclosure ditch remained in use (SP109). Most probably this inner ditch had an external bank and the high level of residual pottery in the fill seems to support this interpretation (p 73). Certainly the close proximity of a structure (SP101) to its inner edge indicates that it did not have an internal bank. If

Table 3 Summary of churchyard zones

Zone	Description
Central zone	Area *c* 20m by 20m centred on church
Zone 1	Primary zone centred on church
Zone 1A	Graves within 1.5–2.5m of church walls
Zone 1B	Graves within 1.5m of church walls
Overspill zones	East and west of central zone
Zone 2	Irregular rows east of Zone 1
Zone 3	Irregular rows west of Zone 1
Eastern zones	Last areas of churchyard brought into use
Zone 4	North-east area of churchyard
Zone 5	South-east area of churchyard
Outer zones	Zones 2–5

such a bank existed it would seem that the west wall of the church stood directly against it.

The original churchyard did not have ditched boundaries, neither were there any burials. There is, however, some indication that the 'church plot' was marked by posts (p 14).

Analysis of the relationship of the church, its associated stratification and the adjacent graves suggests that burial commenced with, or shortly after, the addition of a chancel to the church (SP4, Fig 5). In particular there were no burials beneath the chancel; neither was there space to the west of the church prior to the relocation westwards of the manorial enclosure ditch. The row and zone organisation of the graveyard, discussed at length on pp 53–7, also demonstrates that the cemetery was laid out around the chancel.

The graveyard developed in a series of clearly defined intakes of land within the bank and ditch of the enclosure (Figs 7 and 66; p 53). The church lay central to the primary zone (Zone 1) which was laid out with well ordered rows. The zone contained graves with wooden and stone coffins (p 42), decorated grave covers (p 45) and freestanding crosses (p 46). Graves were dug to within 1.5m of the church walls. At the east edge of the primary zone a decorated cover stood in its own plot and may have had a fine decorated cross at its head (p 51–2). This may have been a 'founder's' grave (p 67). After an undetermined period, as the zone became full, burials overspilled beyond the periphery of the area

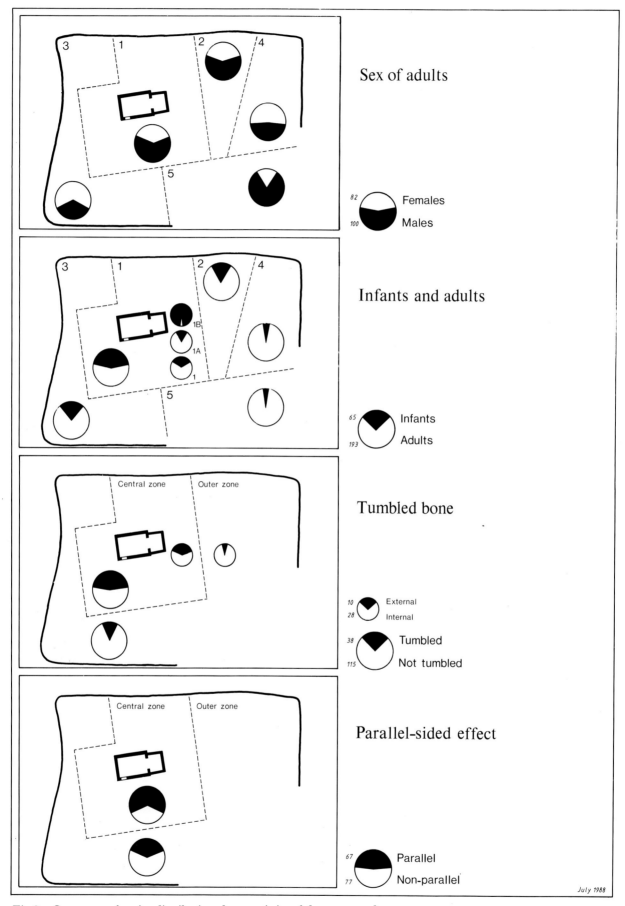

Sex of adults

Infants and adults

Tumbled bone

Parallel-sided effect

July 1988

Fig 9   Summary of major distribution characteristics of the graveyard

Fig 10   The first church (opposite)

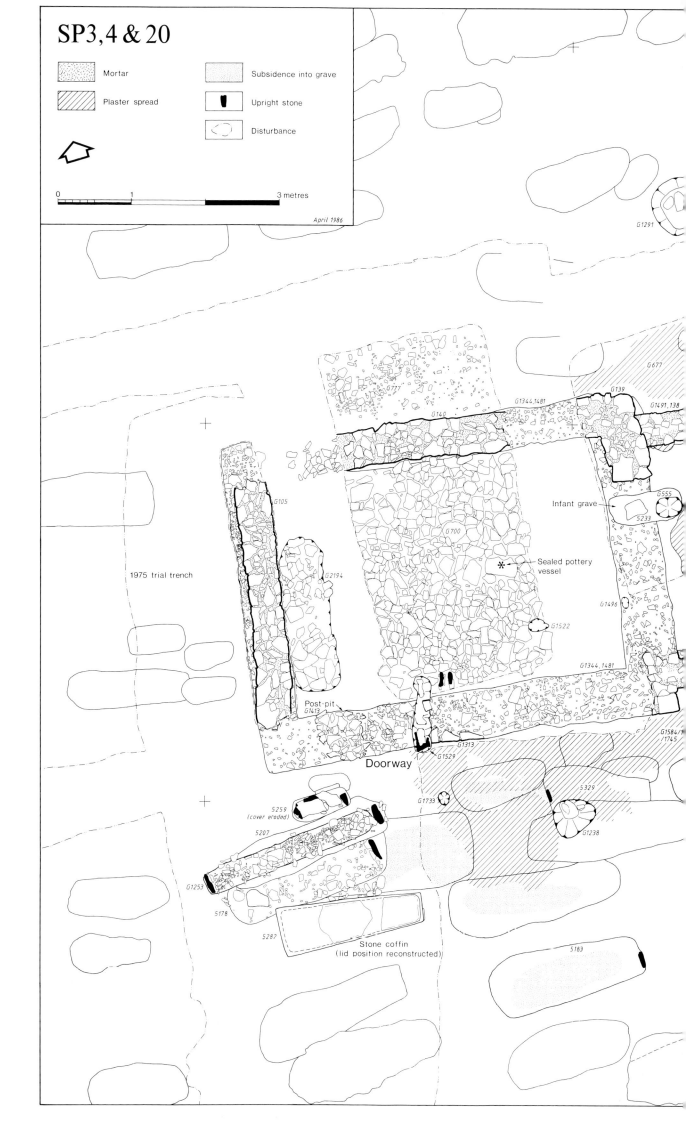

SP3, 4 & 20

Mortar

Plaster spread

Subsidence into grave

Upright stone

Disturbance

0   1   3 metres

April 1986

G1291

G677

G139

G140   G1344,1481   G1491,138

G105   G1491,138

1975 trial trench   G700   Infant grave   G555
                                                                  5233
          G2194   *   Sealed pottery
                                    vessel

                                    G1496

                                    G1522

                          G1344,1481

Post-pit   G1584/1
G1413   /1745

          G1313
Doorway   G1529   G1733   5329

5259
(cover eroded)   G1238

5207

G1253

5178

5287
          Stone coffin   5183
          (lid position reconstructed)

Recut of SP3 post-hole

5274

G1765

5345

G766

5258

G1668

5257

G1384

5279

G1702

G123

G1623

1411

G550

G569

Pitched stone
surface

Plaster face

G1491,1410

G1491, 141

1229

5300

5280 [305]

5000

Abandoned grave
G1011

1975 trial trench

Base for cross?

5283 [300]

Abandoned grave
G1512

5316

G2432

where they were placed rather haphazardly without any attempt to form orderly rows (Zones 2 and 3). Encroachment toward the church walls also occurred. A higher proportion of females than males were displaced to the west (Zone 3); this in turn led to a higher than expected predominance of males in the primary zone (Fig 9). Even within Zone 1 males were concentrated to the south of the church and females to the north.

Subsequent to this overspill the north-east corner of the graveyard was laid out with rows adapted to the almost triangular-shaped area that remained (Zone 4). Two multiple burial plots have been identified in this zone (p 50). Finally, rows of graves were laid out in the south-east area (Zone 5). Infants were almost entirely absent from this zone. Combining the totals of infants and children around the church with those in the eastern zones (4 and 5) produces a demographically balanced population. This provides strong, but circumstantial, evidence that infant burial beneath the 'eaves-drip' of the church was an innovation contemporary with the eastern zones (p 55). It is probable that the early zones continued to receive burials after the new areas were

opened. The concentration of infants around the church suggests that Zones 4 and 5 were contemporary with the first church and that the majority of the burials were associated with the first and not the second church building.

Burial at Furnells was generally accompanied by considerable attention to the protection of the corpse within the grave. Some burials were in coffins, others beneath covers. A distinctive feature of the graveyard is the marvellous variety of stone arrangements (p 38). Of these, some stones were simply intended to prop up the head, no doubt to impart a more dignified pose and to prevent stone and clay being thrown directly on to the face. The more complex stone arrangements which covered most of the body may be seen as extensions of this protection, but might also be seen as designed to prevent disturbance by subsequent interments.

Careful interpretation of the posture of the burial within the grave and the location of each bone has revealed systematic patterns. These differentiate the burials into groups according to whether they were 'parallel' or 'non-parallel' (p 35), whether their bones were 'tumbled' or not, and whether this tumble was 'external' or 'internal' (p 36). The tumbled bone phenomenon, in which bones are dislocated by the stresses induced during the decay of the body, probably reflects the use of coffins rather than shrouds and an extended time delay between death and burial. Parallel burials have their limbs tight to the trunk of the body and, it is argued, were more likely to have been in coffins and/or tightly wrapped in shrouds. Non-parallel burials, which had their limbs less tightly arranged, were more likely to have been buried without coffins and in clothing.

Where stratigraphic relationships between the church and the adjacent burials could be established, the burials invariably predated the second church. Analysis of the surviving external layers reveals that few burials can be assigned to the second generation of churchyard burial which commenced with the building of the second church (p 55). Most burials are sealed by layers associated with the use or demolition of the first church; some

Table 4 Burial phasing and zoning

Phase	Burials	
	No	%
First church chancel (SP4)	48	13.2
Possibly SP4	12	3.3
Possibly second church (SP5)	2	0.5
Unphased	301	83.0
Zone 1	116	32.2
Zone 1A	25	6.9
Zone 1B	30	8.3
Zone 2	22	6.1
Zone 3	37	10.3
Zone 4	76	21.1
Zone 5	54	15.0
Central zone (1, 1A & 1B)	171	47.5
Overspill zone (2 & 3)	59	16.4
Eastern zone (4 & 5)	130	36.1

The majority of unphased burials are arguably SP4

Table 5 Summary of characteristics of graves

Characteristics	Percentage of all graves	Comments	Page
Reburials	2%	Mostly from stone coffins	27
Burials within church		One infant beneath first church chancel arch	21
Disturbance of skeleton by later graves	10%		50
Skeletons with crushed bones	42%	Disproportionally affects infants and elderly	32–3
Skeletons with decayed bones	10%	Mostly ribs and vertebrae	34
Supine burials	100%	No prone burials	35
Parallel-sided skeletons	20%	Posture conferred by tight shrouds or coffins	35, 48
Non-parallel skeletons	23%	Buried in loose shrouds or clothing	48
Tumbled bone	27%	Bone movement due to decay of corpse (numbers for aged 6 years or over)	36, 37
Internal bone tumble	20%	May occur in coffins or under covers	48
External bone tumble	7%	Probably resulting from delayed burial	48
Grave goods	0%	No shroud pins or other non-residual objects	48
Stone arrangements (all types)	55%	Very varied; ranging from simple pillows to cists	38–45
Stone head pillows	30%	More frequently provided for men	39
Stone coffins		About six, one *in situ*	43
Wood coffins		Some indirect evidence	42
Stone covers		Two *in situ*	45
Stone crosses		Three, none *in situ*	46
Marked graves	11%	Vary from covers to posts and slots	46
Charcoal deposits in grave	15%	No 'charcoal' beds but thin and scattered traces of charcoal	37

Fig 11 The first church after addition of the chancel (opposite)

cannot be related to these deposits but none can be shown to cut them or to cut the surfaces associated with the second church. Of those burials within the stratified area, 67% can be shown to be contemporary with, or probably contemporary with, the first church chancel (SP4). Some 30% are unphased and just two burials can be argued to be of second church date (p 55). The lack of burials close to the second church walls, particularly on the south and east sides, does suggest that – even if graves were being dug elsewhere in the churchyard – the life of the second generation of churchyard burial was short. Indeed, it remains uncertain if there were burials during this phase at all.

The churchyard boundaries

A group of large postholes can be assigned to the first phase of the church predating burial in the churchyard (Fig 10). The posts seem to delineate the east and south sides of a plot within which the church stood. Sporadic pit activity continued outside this area until the graveyard was established. The postholes were not evenly spaced; each is rather different in character and has a different arrangement of stone packing and recuts. The presence of mortar in many of their fills confirms their association with the church rather than any pre-church phase. One posthole continued in use during the graveyard period (G3031); the others are cut by graves. The posts appear to define a space without creating a continuous barrier to access. If they were linked in any manner at all, it is unlikely that they formed a continuous fence. More probably they are evidence of a series of independently erected wooden posts set around the edge of the plot. The character of these posts must remain a matter for speculation (p 11).

The subsequent boundaries of the graveyard were composed of a series of ditches. The west side of the enclosure was created by recutting the manorial enclosure ditch (SP109, G1293) 5m further west (SP25, G2365; Fig 5). Demonstrably, this relocation of the boundary was prior to the commencement of burial west of the church. Inferentially, it predated burial in the graveyard generally. Ditches were also cut to delimit the north and south edges of the graveyard (SP24, SP27). It is not clear whether the east ditch was cut specifically as a boundary for the graveyard or whether it was dug to delineate the rear of plots along Rotton Row. In either case, it eventually constrained the easterly spread of graves.

Excavations of the south ditch revealed two phases: the first (SP27, G69), contemporary with the first church chancel (SP4), was a small ditch extending from the west ditch to a point c 16m from the east limit of the graveyard. After construction of the second church, this partial or eroded boundary was replaced by a larger ditch which extended along the entire south edge of the graveyard. This was cut into the top of a large linear quarry ditch 2.0–3.5m wide and 1.5–2.0m deep. The quarry had extracted Blisworth limestone, in all probability destined for the walls and foundations of the second church (SP28, p 22, 100).

Encroachment of non-ecclesiastical structures into the churchyard after the end of burial was slow. Initially it was confined to an enigmatic structure in the northeast graveyard, which disturbed two burials (SP66/67;

North Raunds forthcoming). This intrusion is dated to the twelfth century. It was not until the fourteenth or fifteenth century that a new manor house was built over the west graveyard. This utilised the east room of the converted church and elsewhere has shallow foundations, hence did not disturb any burials. Further constructions for this eastern manor complex were outside the limits of the former graveyard. This left the church and churchyard essentially undisturbed until the present century, despite its conversion to secular use nearly eight centuries before.

The date of the church and churchyard

For the purposes of this volume the Furnells site can be simplified into four principal components:

- The church buildings
- The burials
- The churchyard boundaries
- The manor house complex

The sequence of development illustrated in Figure 5 arises from study of the stratigraphic links between these components and the dating of each component from pottery and radiocarbon evidence. The dating evidence is considered more fully on p 72. Here the synchronisation of events in the churchyard area will be considered along with the broad outline of the dating scheme.

The interaction between the church and the manor complex occurs principally at the east boundary of the manor house enclosure (Fig 3). Here the smaller outer ditch (SP110) is partially infilled prior to the construction of the first church. Subsequently the larger ditch (SP109) is shifted west (SP25) to accommodate the graveyard. This sequence – with its associated pottery fragments, the *sacrarium* vessel in the first church (p 58), and the radiocarbon dates for the burials in the churchyard – provides dating evidence for the construction of the church and the foundation of the graveyard. A date of the late ninth or early tenth century is proposed for the foundation of the church.

Stratigraphic evidence and reasoned argument (p 65) suggest that burial begins after the foundation of the church, probably with the addition of the chancel. Dating for the chancel period (SP4) is, however, problematic and restricted to a limited group of sherds which suggest a tenth-century date (p 77). The inception of burial can also be dated from the backfilling of the inner manorial enclosure (G1293, SP109) and the soil deposited during the levelling of the graveyard area. The pottery from these deposits confirms a tenth-century date, probably at least the second quarter of that century.

Any modest confidence over the date of the first church cannot be extended to the second church (p 82). The apparent contamination of the context with medieval pottery weakens the utility of a small assemblage of sherds. Three Lyveden sherds which might be dated to the thirteenth century were recovered from the foundation of the second church but their location within the foundation was not recorded. The rebuilding of this wall during the conversion phase (SP6) and the subsequent robbing of the wall during the medieval period are a potential source of this contamination.

In these circumstances radiocarbon dates from the first church and churchyard provide our best evidence for dating the use of the graveyard and the construction of the second church (Table 24). The 1σ probabilities of the calibrated dates are plotted on Figure 72 (with the exception of the unacceptably early seventh/eighth-century date for burial G5266). These eight dates confirm the tenth/eleventh-century use of the graveyard but inevitably cannot date the beginning or end of burial with precision. A date for the construction of the second church between the late eleventh century and the mid-twelfth century seems probable. This is supported by the late eleventh-century date assigned to a fragment of soffit of an arch ([132], p 98) and the post-1100 date attributed to the hood moulding which might have derived from a piscina ([303], p 99).

Difficulties over the dating continue with the conversion of the second church and the end of burial. The phasing shown in Figure 5 presents a tentative view that the end of the second church is contemporary with the end of burial rather than later. In structural terms the extensive rebuilding entailed in the conversion might follow some time after the cessation of burial in the churchyard, particularly as few burials seem to be associated with the second church and the second generation of churchyard burial. Away from the buildings, the churchyard boundaries provide another potential source of dating. It would appear that with the demise of the churchyard the north boundary ditch was largely filled in, and the west (manorial) ditch was filled and recut as a minor gully, while the east ditch continued in use. The absence of significant quantities of thirteenth-century pottery in the churchyard boundaries (Table 32) suggests they were infilled during the twelfth century, with the exception of the south boundary ditch which was not filled in until the thirteenth century, though this infilling was prior to the expansion of the converted building into the eastern manor complex (SP7–9). A twelfth-century date for the end of burial in the churchyard would therefore seem likely. The very limited quantity of pottery from the converted building and its associated surface would appear to agree with this date but there is too little material and the conversion could conceivably be as late as the thirteenth century, that is, some time after the end of churchyard burial.

The approximate dating for the church and churchyard sequence can be summarised as:

Late ninth – early tenth	First church (SP3)
Mid tenth	Chancel of first church (SP4)
Mid tenth	Beginning of burial (SP20)
Late eleventh – mid twelfth	Second church (SP5)
Late eleventh – mid twelfth	End of burial (SP20)
Mid eleventh – thirteenth	Conversion of church (SP6)

3 Description of the churches

The evidence for the single cell first church (SP3)

It is remarkable, considering the six centuries of manorial development that followed, that the first church survived reasonably intact (Figs 10, 11, and 17). True, 45% of its floor area had been removed by two later foundations: one the foundation of the chancel arch for the second church (SP5, G499) and the other a foundation of post-church date (SP6, G137). But, apart from this, the walls, floor and internal features were undisturbed.

Prior to the construction of the church the ground was partially levelled (SP2) leaving a residual slope from north to south of 0.5m over the width of the building, and just 0.1m over its length. During construction, the north part of the internal area was lowered to reduce the residual slope to *c* 0.15m across the internal width.

The church was constructed of cornbrash limestone rubble. The cornbrash outcrop to the north of the churchyard had been quarried at various periods (Cadman and Audouy 1990) and these quarries may well have been the source of stone for this church. One such quarry has been dated to 900/950–1100/1150 (SP73; *North Raunds* forthcoming). This may have supplied stone for the chancel and perhaps also for some of the graves.

Fig 12   The first church viewed from the west

The foundation of the building was 0.35–0.43m wide and was set in a narrow, vertical-sided, flat-based construction trench (G1344). The south side of this trench was generally lower, reflecting the lower ground level on that side. The foundation was composed of two layers of cornbrash limestone. The lower layer was constructed of two or three rough courses of cornbrash limestone rubble, the stones of which were generally 0.06–0.20m across and set in clay (G1344, 1621). In contrast (Fig 15) the overlying and thicker layer – 0.3m deep compared to 0.1m – is constructed of quite small cornbrash limestone fragments, rather less than 0.12m across, in a matrix of sand and clay (G1344, 1481). The top of the south foundation was 0.15m lower than the top of the north foundation, reflecting the slope of the pre-construction levelling. At the south-west corner of the foundation an additional layer of larger cornbrash limestone fragments reinforced the surface in the area of the doorway.

The lowest course of the walls survived along the entire length of the west side (G105) and along much of the north side (G139), but barely at all on the south side (G1414). Here it had been removed by the south nave wall foundations of the second church (SP5). The walls were built of medium to large flat cornbrash limestone fragments which were up to 0.25m across in the core of the wall face, with generally larger stones up to 0.4m across at the face. Throughout, the cornbrash limestone was rough hewn, without tool marks and bonded with a ginger mortar (for details of the mortar, see p 100). Only the north-east external angle of the nave survived (G139). There was no quoining evident, though quoinstones were recovered from the second church foundations and these no doubt derived from this building (p 98). The walls survived to a maximum height of 0.18m. Their original height could not be determined, though the quantity of mortar debris associated with the demolition of the church suggests they were probably more than mere dwarf walls (p 21).

There was clear evidence for a door in the south wall. It was hung on a large post set in a posthole (G1413) cut into the foundations; in contrast the opposite side of the door was relatively slight (Figs 10 and 14). A slot cutting into the south wall of the church evidently held three upright posts (G1529). The form of the slot and the arrangement of packing stones suggests that this side of the door frame was formed by two rectangular posts, each *c* 0.1m by 0.2m. The third post lay within the interior of the church and had a circular postpipe, 0.12m in diameter. This may have been part of a non-structural frame to the doorway or of a short internal screen.

A shallow slot positioned directly opposite the south door slot cut into, and protruded either side of, the north wall foundation (G1527, 0.72m long by 0.25m by 0.06m deep; Fig 10). The slot was sealed below the wall and was presumably a wooden slat removed before the overlying wall was constructed; its purpose is obscure. Against the north wall a posthole with an oval postpipe (0.11m by 0.16m; G1524) was directly opposite the interior post of the south wall door slot (G1529).

There was little evidence for the nature of the initial

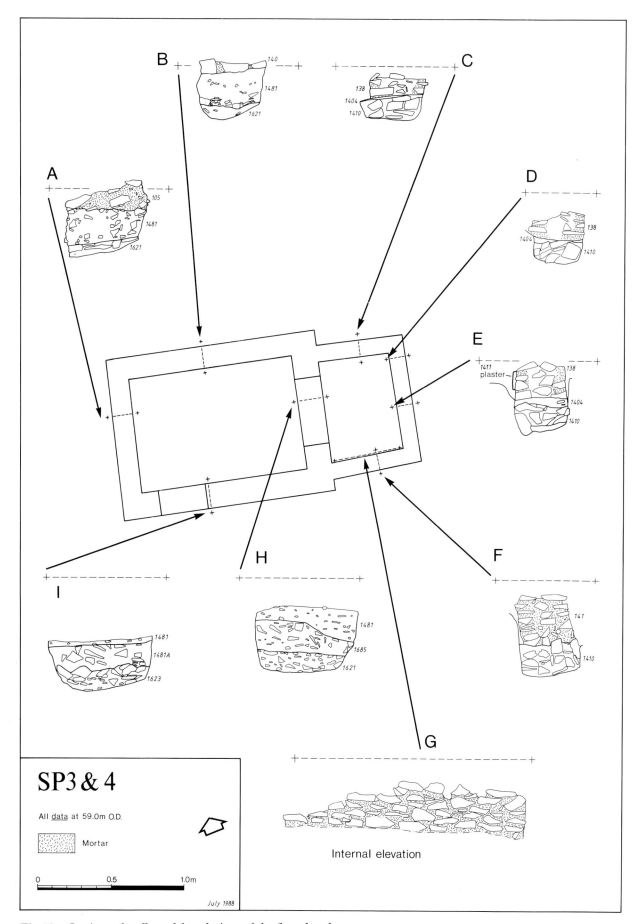

Fig 13 Sections of walls and foundations of the first church

Fig 14   The first church doorway viewed from the north

Fig 15   The first church foundation, showing difference in construction between top and lower courses of foundation

floor. Two areas of stone (G763, G765) might suggest that a stone floor was present prior to that laid in the chancel phase (SP4, G700).

Within the interior of the church two features predominated, a stone foundation against the west wall and a part-buried pottery vessel on the central axis.

An elongated pit against the west wall of the nave contained large fragments of cornbrash limestone, apparently packing for two posts (G2194, Fig 11). The approximate dimensions of the north post, 0.4m north – south by 0.3m east – west, could be discerned from the stone arrangement. The other post was situated 0.8m to the south. This arrangement has been interpreted as the base for a bellcote (p 64).

In the east part of the nave a layer of burnt soil with ash, 2–10mm thick, spread across the central axis. At the centre of the burning a complete pottery vessel of St Neots type ware was set in a small pit (G745, diameter 0.3m, depth 0.12m; Fig 10). The lack of fire damage to the upper part of the pot indicates that it was placed in this position after the fire. A dark grey silty-clay deposit with *c* 15–20% charcoal filled the lower two-thirds of the vessel. This was of a similar character to the burnt deposit around the vessel (for analysis see p 97) and may have been scraped from the burnt area. The internal base of the pot was covered with a burnt residue containing honey, sugars, and tartaric acid (see p 96). The charcoal and silt fill was sealed by the broken fragments

of the top of the pot which were covered with a light brown clay. This clay was present on the broken edges of the pot and had filtered into the fill below, so that the clay formed about 70% of the deposit at the top of the fill top but only 5% at its base. The burnt layer (G742) surrounding the vessel comprised the incinerated top of the pre-construction levelling layer (G2294) with some additional ash. This suggests that the burning predated any church floor and it seems probable that the fire was contemporary with the construction of the church. Of course, any floor may have been removed prior to the burning but this seems unlikely. The small areas of surviving stone floor (G763 and G765) may have originally extended over the burnt area to the lip of the pot which protruded 65mm above the surface. These stone areas are potential fragments of the first floor of the first church.

A layer of scattered limestone fragments, extending for some 8m to the north-east of the first phase of the church, formed a pre-graveyard surface contemporary with the church (G1383, G1744, G1788). The absence of any plaster either on this surface or in the soil build-up above (G1715) suggests that the church was not plastered at this stage. The most detailed sequence of surfaces survives immediately north of the nave. Here the first surface was sealed by a succession of spreads of limestone rubble representing at least three surfaces (G777).

Fig 16   The sacrarium *pottery vessel* in situ

The evidence for the first church chancel (SP4)

In common with the first phase of the church, the chancel survived remarkably well (Figs 11, 17, 18, and 19). It was disturbed along its south side only by the south chancel wall foundation of the second church (SP5); this removed about 40% of the floor area.

The construction cut was similar to that of the first phase with vertical sides and with the same general slope from north to south (G1491). The foundation construction was, however, of a different character. No formal courses occurred in the foundation which was constructed of fragments of cornbrash limestone up to 0.26m across (G1491, 1410; Fig 13, C, D, E, and F). Small patches of ginger mortar clung to the limestone. This was of the same character as that which bonded the walls of the nave, demonstrating that the foundation layer was laid with stones removed from the east wall of the nave during the cutting of the chancel arch. The thickness of the foundation varied from 0.18–0.24m; it was overlaid by a levelling layer of clay with smaller fragments of cornbrash limestone forming a levelling layer 0.02–0.07m thick (G1491, 1404). The wall itself was constructed of rough-hewn fragments of cornbrash limestone, 0.10–0.20m across (G1491, 138). In contrast to the walls of the nave, the wall was bonded with mortar at the face only and had sandy clay as the matrix for the core.

The chancel wall was plastered on its internal face (G1491, 1411; Figs 13 E, and 19). This plaster was *c* 14mm thick and extended behind the stone bench (G123) into the top of the construction trench. The quantity of plaster around the church also suggests that the external surfaces of the nave and chancel walls were plastered during this phase; some plaster concentrations contained what appeared to be collapsed plaster (in G677, G1623, G1053; Fig 11).

The provision of a chancel required the making of an opening for the chancel arch through the east wall of SP3. The north respond for this survived intact to a height of one course (G139) but the south respond had been removed by the second church foundation. It is estimated that the chancel arch was originally 1.7m wide.

A stone base (G123), interpreted as a clergy bench by David Parsons (p 63), was set against the east wall of the chancel. This was constructed with a layer of rough hewn slabs of cornbrash limestone, up to 0.38m across, lining its west face and with smaller fragments infilling between the face and the wall. For the most part only one course of stone survived though there was evidence for two courses at one point. Its depth was 0.6m and it presumably continued across the entire width of the chancel.

A number of floor and occupation layers occurred within the chancel and chancel arch area. The lowest floor (G569) comprised grey-brown clay mixed with about 40% plaster. This was sealed by accumulations of mixed grey-brown sandy clay, ginger mortar and white plaster (G521, G538–9, G546, G548, G563, G568–9).

possible that the posts were tied into the wall at the top and were required to absorb the weight of the bell and cote, a task for which the wall itself may not have been structurally adequate.

The purpose of the post on the inside of the door frame, and its opposite number against the north wall of the church, is not clear. If an equivalent post existed on the west side of the door (it would have been destroyed by a later foundation) then some sort of non-structural, even decorative, framing on the inside of the door may be postulated. An alternative explanation involving both posts is that they supported short screens extending into the church. The posts would appear to have continued in use into the chancel phase.

The absence of ceramic or stone tile fragments indicates an organic roof covering, perhaps wooden shingles, though thatch is more likely in an area with a later tradition of thatched roofs.

The evidence for the second church (SP5)

The rebuilt church appeared to have been carefully positioned (Fig 6). Its south nave wall overlay that of the first church, presumably to minimise disturbance of the graves to the south, although some stone coffins and graves were disturbed during the construction operation (p 27). The foundation of this phase of the church has survived relatively undisturbed though much of the walling above had been robbed. Major disturbance to the nave area was caused by one of the 1975 trial trenches, subsequently severely eroded prior to the 1977 excavation, and a conversion phase wall (SP6). Together these removed 44% of the nave area. In the undisturbed areas of the nave, surfaces survived intact, but in the chancel they had been completely eroded during later manorial phases.

Extensive spreads of mortar sealed the graves adjacent to the church. This indicated that while the stone from the walls was reused in the second church foundation, the mortar was spread to seal the early graves and as a bed for the limestone rubble external surface for the second church (G105, G120). The demolition rubble and plaster filled several hollows where graves had subsided. The posts for at least three grave markers had been uprooted and the postholes left empty to be filled by demolition material (p 48). The foundations and surviving floors sloped southwards by 0.25m and eastwards by 0.3m, reflecting the slope of the site following the demolition of the first church.

A single continuous construction trench (G499) was cut for the foundations to a depth of 0.35–0.9m from the ground surface. The trench was particularly shallow where it encountered the south nave wall of the previous church, while in the east corners of the nave and chancel it was deeper than average. The foundation was laid to a typical thickness of 0.35m in the nave and 0.5m in the chancel. Two courses of pitched stone were laid as a foundation for the nave walls, extra courses being provided at the deeper wall angles (G499, 439). For the chancel three foundation courses were provided. The south wall had an additional fourth course. An area of large Blisworth limestone and ironstone blocks, up to 0.5m across and laid flat, reinforced the south-east corner of the chancel (G499, 482). The different character of this area of foundation should not be taken to suggest that it represented a later repair, as the construction trench had been cut to a deeper level to accommodate the extra thickness of stone beneath. This reinforcement was presumably designed to give extra strength in response to the fall of land to the south and east of this corner. There was no equivalent reinforcing elsewhere, though rough quoin stones up to 0.4m across were present at the west, north-west and south-west corners of the nave. Mortar was absent throughout the foundation except where residual deposits from the previous church were included along with reused stone. In size the stones were generally 0.1–0.3m across and, although the courses were pitched, there was no attempt to create a formal herringbone pattern.

Walls survived only in limited areas and then only to a height of one course. These were constructed of rough-hewn flat-bedded limestone fragments, up to 0.3m across, with smaller rubble in the core. In common with the foundation, mortar was not used to bond the walls and there was no evidence from any context of mortar being used in the second church construction.

About three-quarters of the stone used in the foundations and surviving walls of the church was Blisworth limestone. Much of this was probably quarried from a linear ditch along the inside edge of the south graveyard boundary (SP28, G59). This is calculated to have produced in the region of 85 cubic metres of stone. Assuming 25% wastage this would have constructed c 3m height of walls, if 30% is allowed for mortar and apertures. About 20% of the stone in the foundations and walls was cornbrash, some of this being derived from the previous building, along with a small quantity of ironstone concentrated in the chancel area. Ironstone outcrops c 250m south of the excavation, cornbrash immediately to the north of the churchyard. If it is assumed that 25% of the walls were not of Blisworth limestone then a structure 3.75m high may be postulated. As this is a little lower than might be anticipated (5–6m), an additional source of Blisworth or other stone might be assumed. A number of stones were burnt, including a quoin fragment derived from the first church ([177], p 98). When and where these stones were burnt is not clear.

For such a large structure, scaffolding posts would have been utilised. Evidence of only one such post survived. This was at the south-east external angle of the nave and was sealed by the external surface to the church (G120), confirming that it can be assigned to the construction phase of the second church. During the construction of the foundation, layers of trample were deposited in the former nave and to the east of the former chancel.

No specific evidence survived for the chancel arch and hence its width could not be determined. Neither does evidence survive for any of the door positions, though it may be argued that a recut cross-shaft had been trimmed for use as a door jamb for this phase. A fragment of arch soffit may be from the chancel arch and a piece of hood moulding might be from the head of a piscina ([303], p 99; [132], p 98).

SP6

0 1 3m

July 1988

Retained second
church walling

G33

G137

1975 trial trench

Fig 22 Conversion of the church to secular use

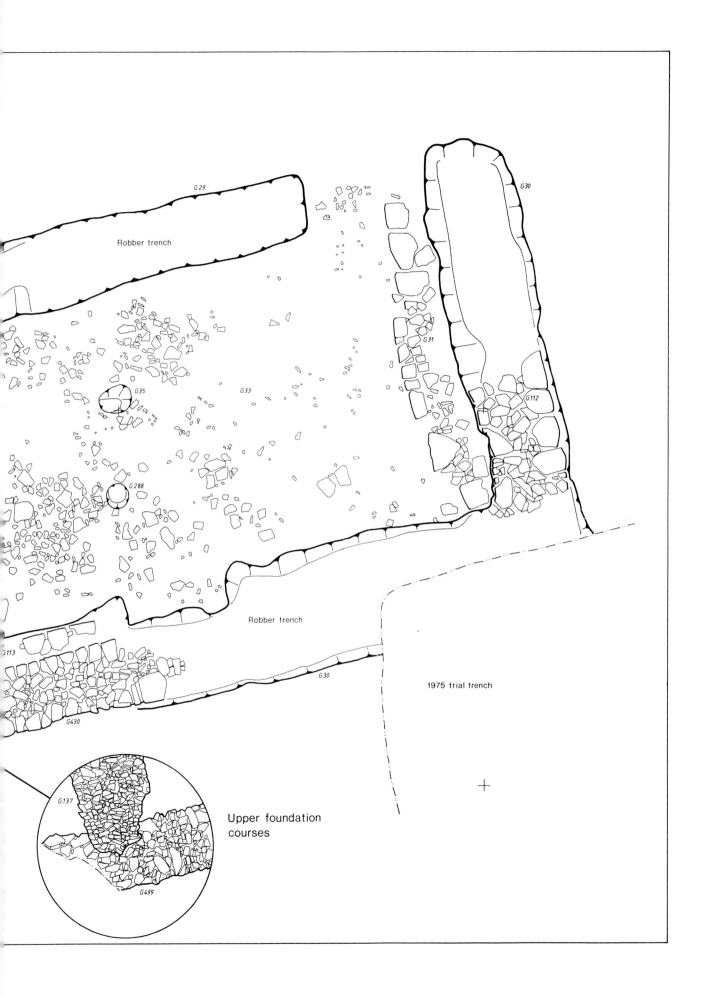

G 29

Robber trench

G30

G31

G35

G33

G112

G 288

Robber trench

G113

G30

1975 trial trench

G430

G137

Upper foundation
courses

G 499

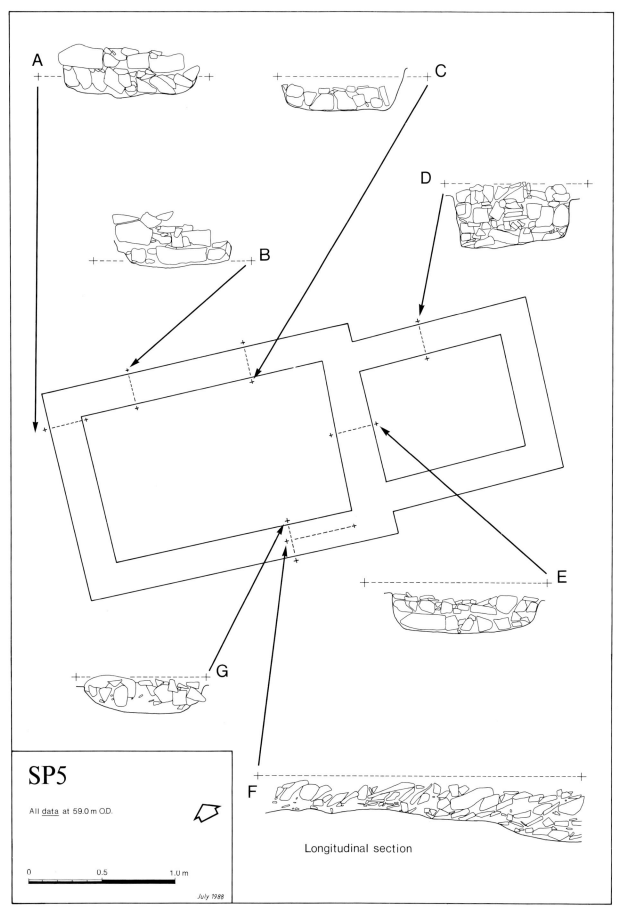

A

C

D

B

E

G

F

SP5

All data at 59.0 m O.D.

0   0.5   1.0 m

July 1988

Longitudinal section

Fig 23   Sections of the foundations of the second church

Internally the only structural feature was an oval post-hole against the west wall of the nave (G518, 0.5m by 0.45m by 0.15m deep). This contained a fragment of stone coffin as packing ([189]). While the fragment of coffin, similar to others found in the foundation, suggests that this posthole was of this phase, stratigraphically it may have been of either church or post-church date. Some indication of the weight borne by this post is given by the slumping of the adjacent floor layers into the underlying first church grave (G5287). Within the nave the floors were constructed of thin spreads of small limestone rubble in brown silty clay.

The superstructure of the second church

It is unfortunate that so little is known of the internal and structural features of the second church. There is no indication of door position. The precise trimming of a fragment of the cross-shaft ([302/7]) indicates that it was probably utilised as a door jamb but it is not known where in the building this was located. Equally, little is known of the walls above the foundation except that the lowest course was of rubble without ashlar masonry. There are no large quantities of ashlar on the site which might suggest the presence of a grander building. One decorated fragment of arch soffit is assigned on stylistic

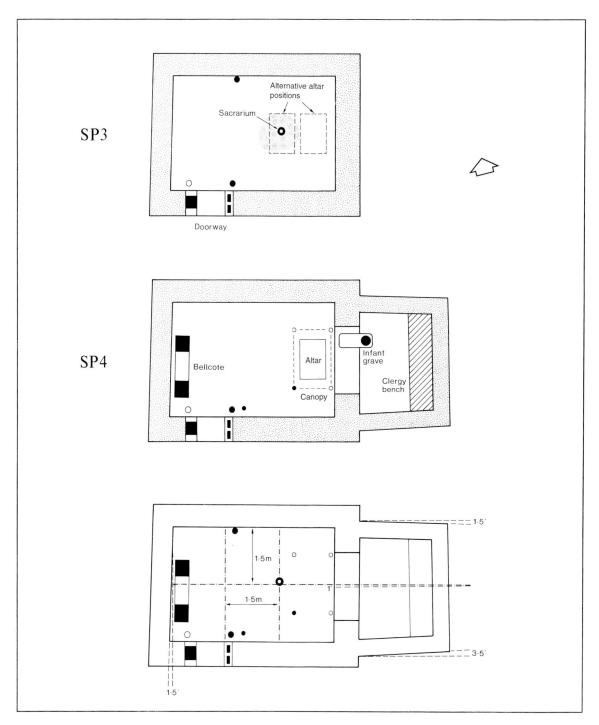

Fig 24   Interpretation and layout of the first church

grounds to this phase ([303], p 99); this may have been part of a chancel arch with an estimated diameter of 1.7m. A smaller arch fragment may be a hood moulding from above a piscina with an arch diameter of 0.6m ([132], p 98). Overall, the evidence suggests a rubble-built church, largely without ashlar, with quoins at each external angle and some decorated detail. It is likely that the quoins were of a minor rather than megalithic character. Insufficient of the walls survived to indicate if any of their courses were set in a herringbone pattern. The lack of evidence for post supports, and the trimmed cross fragment, suggest that the doors were framed with stone and not with wood as in the first church. As with the first church the absence of tiles suggests a thatched roof.

Internally the only feature, which itself is not securely phased, is the post against the west wall. This, from its position, seems unlikely to be part of a door structure. The surviving floor levels demonstrate unequivocally that there was not an equivalent earthfast post south of the church axis. Whether the post represents a bellcote similar to that suggested for the first church must remain speculation (pp 18, 64).

The plan and dimensions of the churches

The first Furnells church was very small, with an external length of just 5.5m (Table 6). No surviving Anglo-Saxon church is as small, even when the additional length of the chancel is taken into account (overall length 8.1m). Small churches are better known from excavated contexts but none is quite as small as the first church, though many are comparable with the second church (for examples see Rodwell and Rodwell 1986, fig 62). With the addition of the chancel the church was converted from a unitary to a cellular linear form (the

Table 6 Church dimensions and alignment

Dimensions [1]	First church	Second church
Total external length	8.1	15.2
Nave internal width (N–S)	3.1	4.6
Nave internal length (W–E)	4.5	7.5
Chancel internal width (N–S)	1.9	3.5
Chancel internal length (W–E)	2.6–2.7	4.7
Nave area (sq m)	13.9	34.6
Chancel area (sq m)	5.1	16.3
Total internal area	19.0	50.9
Width of foundation/wall	0.45–0.5	0.9–1.05
Alignment of axis (nave) [2]	96°	94°
Alignment of axis (Chancel) [2]	95°	91.5°

[1] Dimensions in metres   [2] Deviation from true north

terminology here is that of Taylor 1978; cf fig 720, p 970). The replacement church was cellular linear from the beginning, with an overall external length of 15m. It is rather shorter than the extant Anglo-Saxon churches, though its length/breadth ratio of 1:6 is well within the norms for Saxon churches (Taylor 1978).

There are insufficient dimensions available from Furnells to allow a statistical determination of the unit of measure originally employed when building either church. It is not possible, therefore, to determine whether the church was laid out in 'northern feet' or any other such measurement system (Huggins et al 1982). It is, however, possible to comment on the manner in which the churches were laid out. The methodology of this analysis has been closely controlled and some care has been taken to produce unbiased dimensions.

It has been suggested that the external faces of the second church chancel were laid out on the projected centre-lines of the nave walls (Huggins et al 1982). That this is not the case at Furnells is demonstrated by the angular variation observed and by the difference of 0.18m between the distance across the nave wall mid-lines and the exterior width of the chancel. To assess the likely method of layout, the width and alignment of the walls were rigorously determined using linear regression analysis. This analysis demonstrated that few right angles existed. The alignments of the walls for the first church differed from each other by up to 3.5°. Here the largest deviations may represent a deliberate, though minimal, taper to the chancel (Fig 24). In the second church variations of up to 2.5° occurred. Empirical experimentation demonstrates that such errors, although apparently small, are not likely to have occurred if a rectangular grid or a baseline had been used during the construction. In particular, it might be suggested that the chancel of the second church was laid out from the east wall rather than from a common baseline, a method resulting in an angular error of up to 2.5°. In the light of these observations also, little relevance can be attributed to the deviation in alignments between the nave and chancel of either church or between the first and second churches.

The evidence for the Furnells churches seems to indicate a casual approach to the setting out of buildings. Such imprecision has implications for the determination of metrological units. It is tempting to see the first church as being laid out with a module of 1.5m, close to 5 modern feet, 4.5 northern feet and 6 natural feet (Huggins et al 1982). The module works reasonably well for the nave of the second church but has no obvious relevance to the chancel of either period. But any interpretation of metrological unit must be more fanciful than real given the apparently informal setting out of the walls and the exact measurements given in Table 6.

4 Description and analysis of the graveyard

All 363 Furnells burials were inhumations, most surviving within their original graves (339/363/93; see p 3 for an explanation of this use of numbers). Of those skeletons or part skeletons which occurred in disturbed contexts, 11 were assigned on archaeological and osteological grounds to part burials remaining *in situ*.

Methodology

Details of the methods used to record the burials have been outlined (p 3). The excavation of the graveyard was a central priority for the initial years of excavation; accordingly, all burials were excavated to a standard level and considerable attempts were made to ensure that all the burials within the graveyard were recovered. It is certain that all surviving burials were excavated.

Faye Powell has determined the age and sex profile of the population inhumed within the graveyard. Of the 363 individuals excavated, 328 could be allocated to one of the ten age categories which range from neo-natal to 45+ years (Fig 100; Table 7). These 328 burials are used for detailed analysis of age distribution. A further 35 burials could be less precisely aged. With the exception of the two unaged burials, these burials can be used in certain age-based analyses; for example, the broader age categories of sub-adult (0–17 years), and adult (17–45+ years) (Table 7). For this reason each age analysis will have a different total number of individuals, depending upon the definition of the age category used.

The post-excavation analysis sought to classify, enumerate and correlate the attributes of each burial in order to seek significant variations in grave rite between different age, sex, area or (more problematically) status groups. For each attribute a distribution plan was computer generated and visually examined.

Schematic plots were preferred for speed of production (Boddington 1987a, fig 2). Those with patterns of visual interest were then subject to two sets of statistical analyses to determine if the pattern revealed was statistically non-random. For the first set, designed to examine general spatial trends, the graveyard was divided into 12 analytical grids, each 10m by 10m (Fig 27). Conveniently, the site survey grid forms a suitable basis for such analytical grids, the 10m divisions appropriately splitting the graveyard into areas north and south of the church and the eastings running between rows rather than dissecting them. Archaeologically, the grids chosen are of considerable use in dividing the graveyard into comprehensible sectors and, statistically, they pool together sufficient burials to allow useful analysis. On average there were 28 burials per grid square with a range from 10 to 45. A variety of techniques, particularly the F, Student's t, chi-squared and Kolmogorov-Smirnov tests, were used to examine the data for statistically significant trends and correlations. For studying spatial distribution these techniques involved taking the individual values for each square and comparing them with the pooled values from the other eleven grids; in effect ascertaining how each grid differed from the remainder of the graveyard. This form of analysis was then repeated a second time using the development zones as defined by morphological criteria (pp 53–7). The arbitrary grids form a framework for analysis of non-zonal trends such as grave depth, while the zones provide a more relevant basis for examination of demographic and grave structure.

Throughout all the analyses the significance level is taken at 5% in line with common, though arbitrary, practice (Hurst-Thomas 1976). The term 'significant', used in conjunction with the correlation or spatial analysis below, means that the observed trend or correlation is statistically non-random at a given level of significance. A trend that is not statistically significant may result either from a random, meaningless fluctuation in the data, or may represent a genuine trend whose significance cannot be demonstrated statistically due to the small numbers of observations. All statistical tests are tests of probability; there are no certain proofs in this form of analysis. Rather, for any given statement of statistical significance, it is argued that the data being analysed contain a non-random relationship. On occasions this judgement will be incorrect and a random fluctuation sufficiently large to give a non-random result will be erroneously declared significant. In the long run, out of a large number of analyses, this spurious significance will occur in one out of twenty results at the 5% level of significance, and in just one out of one hundred results at the 1% level of significance.

The survival of the graves

Not all those buried in the graveyard remained undisturbed and not all graves survived to be excavated. There is, however, little evidence to suggest extensive disturbance and loss of burials. The late medieval manor foundations did not intrude significantly into the graveyard surface, the degree of intercutting of graves was low and the construction of the second church did not have a large destructive impact. The boundary ditches did not intrude into graves, though scattered fragments of one individual were found in the west ditch (G5328). Some graves may have been lost due to surface erosion along the south edge of the graveyard, where the shal-

Table 7 Age and sex of burials and reburials

Age	In situ			Not in situ			Reburial	
	?	M	F	?	M	F	?	MF
Neonate	21	–	–	0	–	–	0	–
0 – 1	40	–	–	5	–	–	0	–
1 – 2	6	–	–	1	–	–	0	–
2 – 6	33	–	–	2	–	–	0	–
6 – 12	30	–	–	2	–	–	0	–
12 – 17	11	–	–	0	–	–	0	–
17 – 25	1	22	32	0	0	1	0	01
25 – 35	0	21	18	1	1	1	0	12
35 – 45	8	25	7	0	0	0	0	00
45+	7	26	14	0	0	0	0	21
Sub–adult[1]	160	–	–	10	–	–	0	–
Adult[1]	32	96	76	3	1	2	0	34

[1] Includes some burials which could be assigned only to the general categories of sub-adult (0–17 years) and adult (17+ years).

Fig 25 Graveyard plan: skeletal posture (opposite)

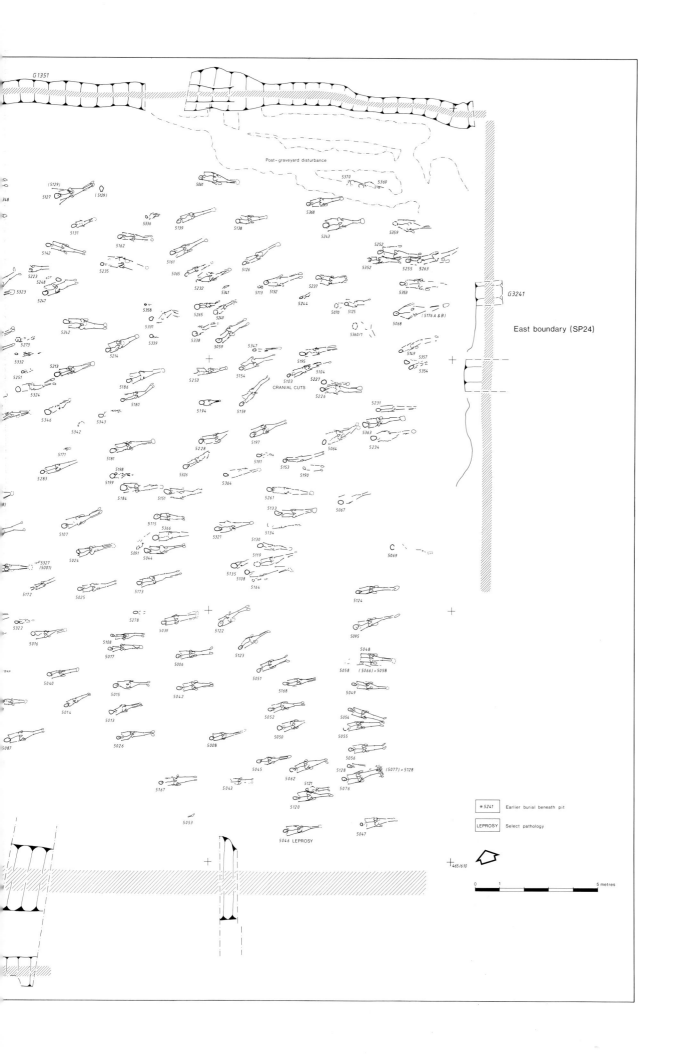

G1351

Post-graveyard disturbance

East boundary (SP24)

G3241

CRANIAL CUTS

5046 LEPROSY

*5241   Earlier burial beneath pit

LEPROSY   Select pathology

0   1   5 metres

465/610

Fig 27 Graveyard analysis grids

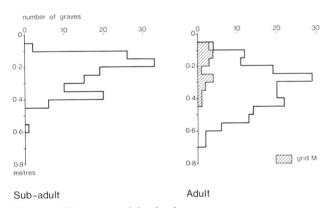

Fig 28 Histogram of depth of graves

(Fig 28). As many infant graves elsewhere in the cemetery were shallow, some infants may well have been lost from this area.

Burial and reburial

The majority of the Furnells burials survived *in situ* (339/363/93). Of those in disturbed contexts, some were reburied (7/363/2), but most occurred in later grave fills or other contexts (17/363/5). An additional 11 partial skeletons occurring in secondary contexts could be assigned on archaeological and osteological grounds to part burials remaining *in situ*. Most disturbances resulted from the cutting of new graves, though 13 graves were disturbed by the construction of the second church.

Some reburials were deposited in the disrupting grave; characteristically, only fragments of these burials tended to survive. In contrast, one group of reburials was virtually complete and had most of the small hand and foot bones present, though no bones remained articulated. These burials were in round pits and clearly result from the complete exhumation and redeposition of skeletons rather than casual disturbance. Given the presence of most of the smaller bones, it is likely that these reburials result from exhumations from stone coffins, rather than earth graves from which smaller bones are less likely to have been retrieved. Three skele-

lowness of the grave cuts indicated post-graveyard erosion; however, little human material was found in the small area of quarry ditch backfill excavated. The southeast corner of the graveyard had suffered from erosion, in particular in Grid M (Fig 27), and it might be considered that this was a contributing factor towards the absence of infants in this area. The degree of erosion can be estimated by a comparison of adult grave depths; they were reasonably constant across the north and central graveyard but were consistently shallower along the south edge; the adults of Grid M were in graves averaging just 0.2m deep while the other grids averaged 0.34m

Fig 26 Graveyard plan: stone arrangements (opposite)

tons were dumped in two large pits against the north wall of the second church; presumably these were cleared from stone coffins broken up for the church construction (5094A/M/45+, 5094B/F/45+, 5236/F/17–25). Fragments of coffins were recovered from the second church foundations (pp 22, 103). These pits were very large for the quantity of bone deposited (*c* 2m across) but no attempt was made to include the bones of any of the nine other burials disturbed by the new church. A fourth reburial lay in a small pit in the north graveyard; from the symmetrical arrangement of the bones reinterment in a sack may be inferred (5239/F/25–35; Fig 30). While this 'sack' burial may also be from the church rebuilding phase, its separate location may suggest otherwise. Ten other burials were disturbed by the construction of the second church – one completely (5163), the others to lesser degrees. The disturbed bones were either left in their original graves, or discarded; the bones of three burials were dumped in the bottom of the construction trench. Possibly at the same time, the surviving stone coffin was sealed with an inverted and repaired lid; the skeleton retrieved may not have been the coffin's first occupant (5282). It might also be speculated that the 'sack' burial (5239) was the original interment in this coffin.

Two or three apparently abandoned graves occur, all close to the church. One was abandoned after disturbance of two previous interments, the disturbed bones being neatly laid in the pit (5188, G1512), while another was abandoned after dislocation of the left humerus of

5200 (G1011). A third pit north of the church was less certainly an abandoned grave. Elsewhere disturbed bones were reburied in the disturbing grave, often in a neat arrangement. For example:

– The bones of 5128 were buried in a triangular arrangement around the feet of 5076 (Fig 32; the reburied bones of 5128 are numbered 5077 in this photograph).
– The femora of 5129 were laid in wing-like positions either side of the shoulders of 5127, with the other bones scattered alongside the burial (Fig 25).
– The disturbed bones of 5078 appear to have been packed on either side of 5118, in a manner that suggests that the latter was in a wood coffin (Fig 25).
– The skull of 5157 was used with stones to prop the body of 5156 off the grave floor. The latter is so tightly parallel-sided that it was almost certainly buried in a tightly wrapped shroud (Fig 31).

Demography

In all, 363 burials were recovered from the churchyard. This is not likely to be severely short of the total as erosion of the graveyard has been minimal. A maximum of 400 burials might be postulated, though 380–90 might be a more realistic range.

In this text the term population refers to the recovered population or, in the terminology I have defined else-

Fig 29   Reburial in pit north of the second church (5094A/M/45+; 5094B/F/45+; 5236/F/17–25)

Fig 30   Possible reburial in a sack (5239/F/25–35)

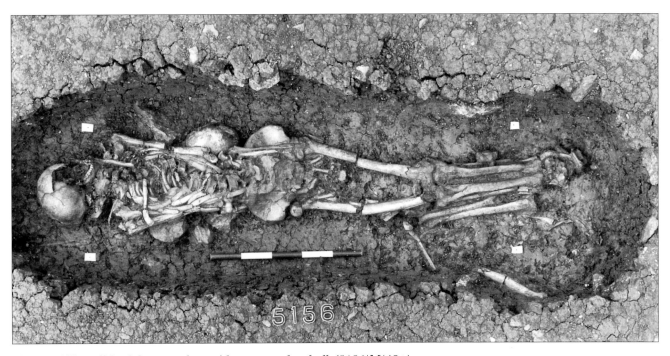

Fig 31   'Shroud' burial, propped up with stones and a skull (5156/M/45+)

where, the *assessed* population (Boddington 1987c). The *assessed* population is that part of the *contributing* population that survives to be excavated and the *contributing* population is that subset of the local population which uses the graveyard. It is not possible to determine where the people forming the contributing population lived within the late Saxon settlement; they may have lived adjacent to the manor or further afield.

A fuller discussion of the demography of the population will be found in Faye Powell's report on the skeletal evidence (Chapter 13). Here it may be noted that the range of ages is close to that expected for a pre-industrial population. Apparently no selection on the grounds of age occurred; in particular infants are quite well represented and the level of infant mortality (20%) is at the lower limits of that conventionally expected from pre-industrial populations (Weiss 1973). It may be questioned whether this mortality figure has been reduced by disturbance of infant burials within the graveyard or by disposal of infant corpses elsewhere. There is little evidence of extensive disturbance of infants within the graveyard, though some may have been lost from Zone 5 (p 55). Equally, the care invested in infant burial probably reflects concern over their proper burial and there is

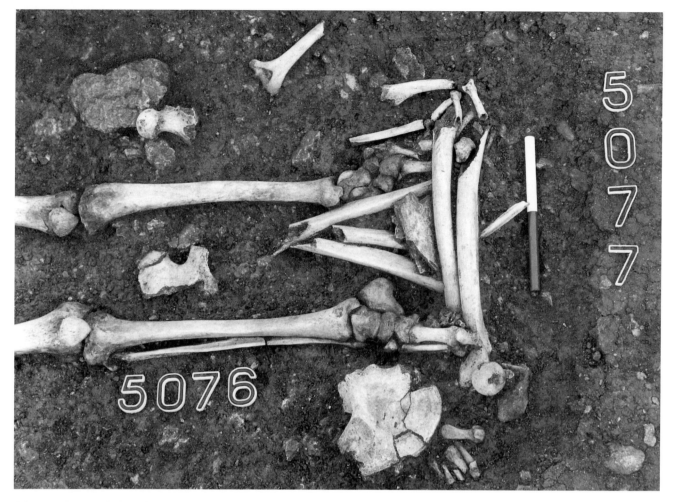

Fig 32   Reburial of adult male around the feet of a female skeleton (5128/M/Adult; 5076/F/25–35)

Table 8 Age and sex distribution

Age	Male	Female	Unsexed	All
Neonate	–	–	21	21
0 – 1	–	–	45	45
1 – 2	–	–	7	7
2 – 6	–	–	35	35
6 – 12	–	–	32	32
12 – 17	–	–	11	11
17 – 25	22	34	1	57
25 – 35	23	21	1	45
35 – 45	25	7	0	32
45 +	28	15	0	43
0 – 6	–	–	8	8
about 6	–	–	7	7
about 12	–	–	4	4
Adult	2	5	7	14
Unaged	–	–	2	2
Totals	**100**	**82**	**181**	**363**

no evidence from the archaeological or historical record for other methods of disposal of infants at this date. While no firm statement can be made, the figure of 20% infant mortality could be argued to be a little lower, but not very much lower, than the true infant mortality rate at Raunds.

More males are present than females, however (though the difference is not statistically significant).

Despite a historical tendency for osteologists to assign the male sex to burials not clearly female (Weiss 1972), the osteometric variability of the Furnells skeletons demonstrates clear sexual dimorphism (Tables 88–90) and any systematic misassignment of sex is likely to be minimal. The difference in representation of the sexes might be due to immigration of males into the contributing community or to a lower rate of survival of females into adulthood.

More difficult to assess is the accuracy of adult age determination. The ages attributed to each individual by Faye Powell are biological ages. For ancient populations, biological age does not necessarily equate directly with calendar age and there is an increasing awareness that for ancient populations biological age is a biased under-estimate of the true chronological age (Boddington 1987c). Potentially, the ages given to the Furnells burials are on average too young. Estimates of the degree of under-ageing are not easy to calculate and are not attempted here. In any event the bias is systematic and probably reasonably constant across the entire popula-tion; it will not affect any analysis of age-related burial practice.

It does, however, affect the estimation of the size of the contributing population to the graveyard, though the distortion is not of undue scale in comparison with the other errors inherent in palaeodemographic estimation (Boddington 1987c). It is possible to make a reasonably accurate estimate of the size of the contributing population. Given an average age at death of 20 years (Table 42), 400 buried individuals and a graveyard use of 200 years, then the contributing population is about 40 individuals. Of these 19 are adults. Lengthen the use of the graveyard and the population size is reduced; increase the average age at death, to correct for any underestimation of adult age, and the population size is increased; decrease the average age at death, to allow for under-representation of infants, and the population size is once again reduced. Here it is adequate to assign a size of about 40 persons to the population, noting that this is not a precise estimate.

Grave morphology

With the exception of approximately six stone coffins, only one of which remained in position, all the graves were earth cut. The subsoil was of a variable nature, ranging from Blisworth clay with little stone, to clay with heavy limestone concentrations and occasionally to cornbrash limestone bedrock. It was difficult to define the grave edges on many occasions and hence detailed analysis of grave morphology is inappropriate for this site. Some general comments on grave shape and dimension can, however, be made.

A variety of grave shapes were observed. Of note is an exceptionally wide grave, its occupant lying with slightly flexed legs against the north edge of the cut (5331/M/45+; 1.85m long by 1.1m wide by 0.32m deep). Also of unusual form is an almost circular infant grave (G5342; 0.4m long by 0.35m wide by 0.2m deep). Most graves were, however, about three times as long as they were broad and about half as deep as wide (ie proportions of approximately 6:2:1). It was not possible in most instances to discern whether the graves had rounded or rectangular ends, though in the stony soil rounded ends were no doubt the norm. On average the adult graves were 2.0m long, 0.7m wide and 0.3m deep. Erosion of the graveyard surface has probably reduced this depth. The depth of only five adult graves could be measured from the surface into which they had originally been cut; these averaged 0.44m deep. Younger people were, not unexpectedly, in smaller graves – the smallest, for neonates, having average dimensions of 0.8 by 0.4 by 0.1m.

Grave alignment

The alignment of Roman and post-Roman graves is a topic which has attracted some considerable debate in recent years (cf Rahtz 1978). In particular, attention has been focused on the solar hypothesis which postulates that the graves were aligned so that the foot end was directed toward sunrise on the day of burial. Thus with the seasonal movement of the sun the orientation of the graves would vary. From this variation it would be possible to determine for any individual the time of death as being one of two dates within the year. Such arguments have unfortunately been developed in the absence of rigorous methodological analysis and without a clear understanding of the nature of the underlying statistical distributions (Boddington 1987a; Boddington 1990).

Briefly, any attempt to align a grave on a given point or in a given direction will be subject to a limited degree of

Table 9 Body posture and bone tumble: age and sex distribution

Age	Parallel	Non-parallel	Tumbled	Not tumbled
Neonate	0	0	4	3
0 – 1	2	1	8	5
1 – 2	0	1	2	1
2 – 6	1	1	10	8
6 – 12	7	6	4	12
12 – 17	6	3	3	4
17 – 25	18	20	15	31
25 – 35	12	16	8	23
35 – 45	8	10	5	18
45 +	11	16	7	21
Males	29	34	20	55
Females	21	29	15	40
Sub-adults[1]	16	14	34	41
Adults[1]	51	63	35	96
All	67	77	69	137

[1] Some burials could be assigned only to the general age ranges sub-adult (0 – 17 years) and adult (17+ years).

Table 10 Age and sex of burials with internal and external tumble

Age	Internal tumble		External tumble	
	Male	Female	Male	Female
17 – 25	5	9	1	1
25 – 35	5	2	3	1
35 – 45	7	1	0	0
45 +	5	1	1	0
Adult	22	14	5	2

error. Small errors will occur frequently while larger errors will occur with relative infrequency. Such a distribution of errors is modelled statistically by the normal distribution (Hurst-Thomas 1976) and the normal distribution fits well both visually and statistically with the observed alignments at Furnells (Fig 33). The Furnells distribution, while not significantly different from a model normal distribution, does show a slight skew to the north, ie there are slightly more burials with their heads to the north of the mean than the model distribution predicts. This can be explained as follows. Overall the burials have an average alignment of 274° (standard deviation 14.9°). This is very close to the alignment of the first church (276°) and indicates that the intention was to align the burials with the axis of the church. The boundaries of the graveyard were not, however, aligned with the church and, although their nature makes it difficult to assign a single alignment to them, they were in the range of about 286–298°. Examination of the detailed distribution of alignments shows that the burials around the edge of the graveyard were aligned with their heads slightly more northwards than those nearest the church (Fig 66). It is obvious that, while the intention was to align all burials on the church, the banks of the graveyard proved a distraction, causing a small systematic misalignment towards the boundaries and away from the church. Hence the range and distribution of the Furnells burial alignments can be explained in

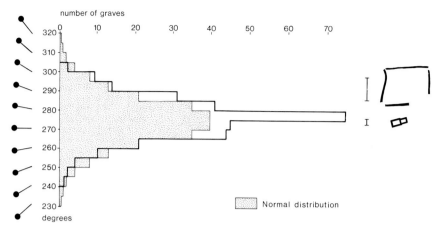

Fig 33   Histogram of burial alignment

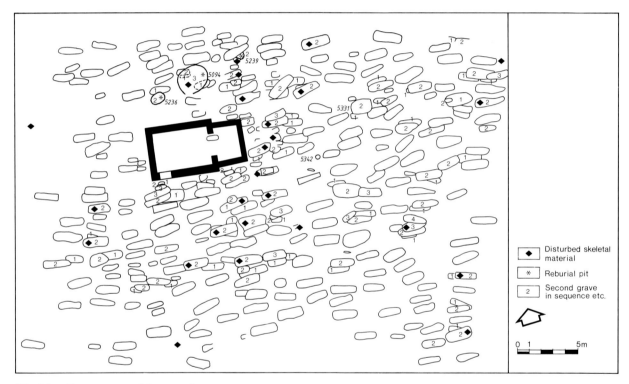

Fig 34   Grave cuts and intercutting graves

terms of a simple statistical model without recourse to more complex hypotheses.

The survival of the skeletal material

The survival of bone within the graveyard was generally good. Although one fifth of graves were cut by a later grave (75/359/21; Fig 34) in many cases no disturbance to the skeleton was caused (Table 11). In only 27 cases were the previous interments more than 50% disturbed (27/359/8). This total excludes the four reburials from stone coffins (p 27). It might be expected that infants were more prone to being disturbed than adults, particularly in view of their concentration around the church within the area of most intense burial, but this was not the case. Disturbance was fairly evenly distributed between age groups overall – around 10% of burials had some disturbance of bone (Table 11).

The survival of bone within the graveyard was generally good though in some graves the bone had become heavily broken, referred to here as *crushed* bone, or had largely decayed and disappeared.

A number of the skeletons suffered from post-depositional crushing of most of the bones of the skeleton (114/274/42, Fig 35; compare with Fig 54). The breakage was presumably caused by the expansion and contraction of the Blisworth clay subsoil and grave fill with changes in moisture and temperature. It was noted that the phenomenon particularly affected infants. For analysis the burials were divided into crushed and noncrushed categories by visual examination of the site record photographs. In the sub-adult category, neonates were crushed in 70% of instances; this proportion steadily decreased with age to only 10% for adolescents. For adults there was an increase in crushing with age, from 20% of those in the 17–25 year age group to 43%

Table 11 Extent of disturbance of burials by intercutting graves

Age group[1]	Total for age group	Total intercut	Total disturbed[2]	% of age group disturbed
Infant	66	15	7	11
Child	89	17	9	10
Adolescent	11	1	1	9
Adult	191	39	19	10
Totals	**357**	**72**	**36**	**10**

Age group	Average depth of graves[3]	Area of skeleton disturbed 0%	1 – 25%	25 – 50%	50 – 75%	75 – 100%
Infant	0.15	8	1	0	4	2
Child	0.21	8	3	3	0	3
Adolescent	0.26	0	0	0	0	1
Adults	0.32	21	2	1	7	8
Totals	**0.26**	**37**	**6**	**4**	**11**	**14**

[1] For definition of age groups, see Table 42. [2] Not all intercutting graves disturbed the earlier skeleton.
[3] These depths may be underestimated as a result of the successive cleanings of the graveyard surface required to locate the graves.

Table 12 Bone crushing, decay and tumble by soil type

Soil type	Crushed	Not crushed	Decayed	Not decayed	Tumbled[1]	Not tumbled
Clay	28 (65%)	15 (35%)	11 (31%)	25 (69%)	5 (19%)	21 (81%)
Clay with occasional limestone	25 (42%)	34 (58%)	4 (7%)	55 (93%)	21 (42%)	29 (58%)
Clay with moderate/frequent limestone	57 (34%)	108 (66%)	11 (7%)	147(93%)	35 (29%)	84 (71%)
Limestone	0	0	0	2	1	1

For an explanation of bone tumble see p 36. [1] For tumbled bone, figures refer only to burials 6 years or over at death.

Table 13 Bone crushing and decay: age and sex distribution

Age	Crushed	Not crushed	Decayed	Not decayed
Neonate	7	3	0	10
0 – 1	22	10	4	18
1 – 2	3	3	0	3
2 – 6	14	15	4	21
6 – 12	9	15	1	23
12 – 17	1	10	1	10
17 – 25	9	36	1	51
25 – 35	9	23	4	29
35 – 45	10	14	3	25
45 +	16	21	6	29
Males	24	25	6	79
Females	23	40	9	57
Sub-adults[1]	63	64	10	96
Adults[1]	51	96	16	136
All	114	160	26	232

[1] Some burials could only be assigned to the general age ranges sub-adult (0–17 years) and adult (17+ years).

Table 14 Estimated percentage bone decay in 26 burials

% Decayed	0–20	20–40	40–60	60–80	80–100
Skull	23	0	3	0	0
Vertebrae	3	2	6	3	12
Ribs	0	0	8	6	12
Pelvis	8	3	6	2	7
Arms	18	4	1	1	2
Legs	18	8	0	0	0

Garland for extensive discussion of the processes of bone decay). Adult bones are more resistant to destruction than those of a child or infant. At birth the mineral content of bone is low but it increases rapidly and is high throughout the middle adult years (Baud 1982; von Endt and Ortner 1984). With increasing old age the mineral content diminishes progressively. While these biological factors may explain the age distribution of crushing, examination of the location of the crushed burials within the graveyard shows that they were more numerous in some areas of the graveyard than others. This spatial variation appears to be related to soil type rather than to differing burial patterns of age groups. To examine the relationship, the Blisworth clay into which the graves were cut was classified according to stone content, again using site record photographs (Table 12). It is apparent that crushing was more frequent where the clay had least stone and that age and soil were the main factors which led to the crushing of the bones of some burials but not of others.

of the 45 years and over age group (Table 13). No significant difference in bone fragmentation was observed between adult males and adult females.

This variable distribution of crushing between age groups can be explained in terms of the changing character of human bone with age (I am grateful to Neil

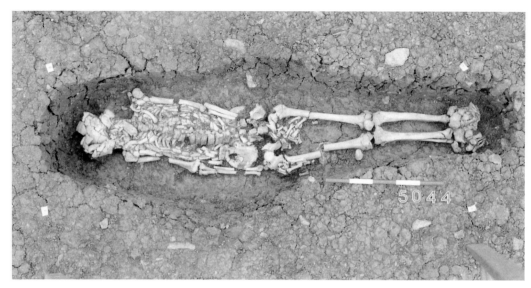

Fig 35   Burial with crushed bones (5044/M/45+)

Fig 36   Skeleton with decayed bones in the lumbar region (5015/M/35–45)

Crushing was not the only form of bone abrasion at Furnells. One in ten skeletons suffered from extensive bone decay (26/258/10). This was usually concentrated in the lumbar region (Figs 36, and 49). Once again there is a correlation with clay soil (Table 12) but not in this instance with age. Twice the proportion of females as males were affected, though this difference is not statistically significant (9/66/14; 6/85/7). A close correlation occurs between those burials which had crushed and those which had decayed bones, as most decayed burials were also crushed (20/26/77). Of interest is the limited area of the skeleton involved – always the ribs and vertebrae, less frequently the pelvic girdle, long bones were only occasionally decayed, the skull very rarely (Table 14). It is also apparent that the process of decay is in some instances more concentrated on the abdominal region than the thorax; in 16 cases both areas are affected but in 9 cases the abdominal region is the more severely decayed.

Besides being related to changes in mineralisation with age, as discussed above, the rate of decay of bone is also related to bone density. The vertebrae are composed primarily of cancellous bone. The strength of cancellous bone is approximately proportional to the square of the apparent bone density (Carter and Spengler 1982). Changes in the material properties of cancellous bone are effected primarily by an increase in bone porosity and a decrease in apparent bone density. Loss of bone mass (osteoporosis) in the elderly is common. The loss of bone mass results in a reduction of the cortical thickness of the long bones and a decrease in the apparent density of cancellous bone. The most obvious changes seen clinically in osteoporotic patients are in the spine. This may be a partial explanation of the dramatic effect that decay had on the vertebrae of the Furnells burials, though it is well spread through the age groups with only a hint of an increase with age (Table 13). It is not, however, entirely clear why the lumbar vertebrae should decay in preference to the thoracic and cervical. It is also possible that females suffer more from the process of mass loss in bone since the osteogenic effect of oestrogens is no longer present after the menopause. Unfortunately, the number of burials exhibiting decay at Furnells is too low to attach significance to the higher number of females with decay.

These statistics reveal that crushed bones are correlated with both age and soil variation while the loss of bone through decay is perhaps related to sex, more certainly to soil type. Few soil samples were taken during the excavation. This prevents further examination of any specific soil factors which might be responsible for enhanced decay.

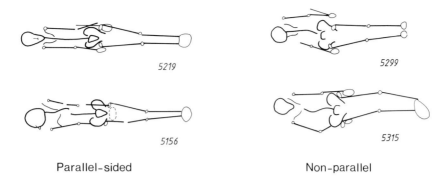

Parallel-sided   Non-parallel

Fig 37   Parallel-sided and non-parallel burials

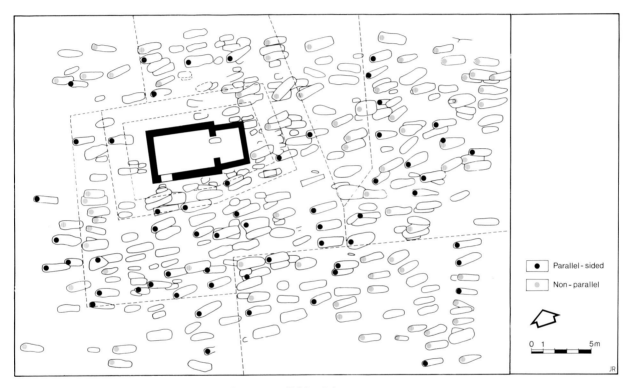

Fig 38   Distribution of parallel-sided and non-parallel burials

Body posture

The posture of the body within the grave was classified according to its parallel or non-parallel state and in more detail according to the posture of the head, hands and feet. In many burials the bones had moved from their original positions and had a 'tumbled' appearance.

The burials were all supine, nearly all with arms at side and legs straight. Most commonly the head faced toward the foot of the grave (67/142/47). Almost as often it faced to either side (50/142/35). The head looked upward least frequently (25/142/18). The majority of burials had their hands placed either side of the pelvis, close to the body (178/226/79); in the balance of cases one or both hands were on the pelvis. Sixteen burials had hands 'clasped' (16/226/7); none had wrists crossed. Normally the feet were together, that is within 0.1m of each other (189/211/90). Rarely, the feet were crossed (6/211/3); only one burial had its ankles crossed as well (5232). These variations of detailed limb posture did not seem to vary by age, sex or graveyard location.

The burials exhibiting the parallel-sided effect have arms close to the thorax, hands tight against or over the pelvis, and feet together (Fig 37). A burial is considered to be parallel-sided if the feet are together (within 0.1m) and if, when straight lines are drawn from the top of the humeri to the base of the tibiae, no bones (other than those clearly disturbed) fall outside the lines. Burials with their legs splayed or arms clearly extending beyond the lines are classified as non-parallel burials. More than a third of burials remain unclassified due to bones being only marginally over the line or due to subsequent disturbance (133/339/39). The parallel-sided effect can be conferred on burials in coffins (for example, Rodwell 1981, pl 71A), while those burials in a non-parallel posture are less likely to have been in coffins. Some 67 burials can be classified as parallel and 77 as non-parallel (67/339/20; 77/339/23). Parallel burials were concentrated in the central zone around the church, where they formed two-thirds of classifiable burials, double the proportion found elsewhere (Fig 38, 33/52/63; 34/91/37).

Tumbled bones

The chaotic, disorderly appearance of the skeleton in one third of the classifiable Furnells burials is quite striking (65/206/32). Most commonly bone 'tumble' affected the vertebrae, the lumbar vertebrae in particular, and the ribs (Table 15). It was also these bones which were primarily affected by decay, though few burials with bone tumble were also decayed (3/62/5, pp 33–4). Tumbling was distributed equally between the sexes (only adults could be sexed) but significantly more young children were affected than adults. Examination of the age distribution of tumbled bone shows that more than 50% of burials of children under six years old were affected (24/41/59). The bones of the infant and child are small and prone to disturbance by soil movement and animals. For this reason, children under 6 years of age at death are excluded from this discussion, leaving 38 burials for consideration.

Bone tumble shares the distributional characteristics of the parallel-sided effect (Fig 39). Thus in the central zone adjacent to the church 45% of classifiable burials have tumbled bone compared to just 14% elsewhere (24/53/45; 14/100/14). Although there were infrequent occasions on which observations of both body posture and bone tumble could be made, the parallel-sided effect is significantly associated with bone tumble. Some 79% of burials with bone tumble have a parallel posture.

Review of the photographic evidence suggested that the burials with tumbled bone could be divided into two groups. For the majority of skeletons the bone tumble was restricted within the frame of the vertebral trunk (28/38/74); for convenience this is referred to as *internal* tumble (Figs 40 and 41). This may be contrasted with a distinct group in which the bones had moved out of the volume of the trunk, either to overlie the skeletal frame or to rest between the legs (Figs 42 and 43). This is de-

Table 15 Skeletal distribution of bone tumble

Skeletal element	Tumble	No tumble	% with tumble
Skull	7	30	19
Humerus	5	33	13
Ulna	9	29	24
Radius	9	29	24
Femur	12	26	32
Tibia	6	32	16
Fibula	5	33	13
Scapula	3	35	8
Clavicle	3	35	8
Ribs	24	14	63
Vertebrae	36	2	95
Lumbar vertebrae	32	6	82
Thoracic vertebrae	30	8	79
Cervical vertebrae	23	15	61
Sacrum	9	29	24
Pelvis	8	29	22
Hands	8	30	21
Feet	3	35	8

NB *Only burials aged 6 and over included. Not all bones could be classified for all 38 burials due to later disturbance of graves.*

noted *external* tumble (10/38/26). A review of the sex of the burials with external tumble reveals with startling clarity that, with the exception of three sub-adults who could not be sexed, they are all male (Table 10). In contrast, the skeletons with internal tumble are equally divided between the sexes (11 male, 13 female, 4 unsexed). Not only do the two types of bone tumble discriminate by sex but also by location. Those adult inhumations with external tumble can be seen to group south and east of the church walls, while the three sub-adults lie to the west (Fig 39). In contrast, the skeletons with internal tumble are more widely spread, though they still tend to cluster to the south of the church. The density of burials immediately south and east of the

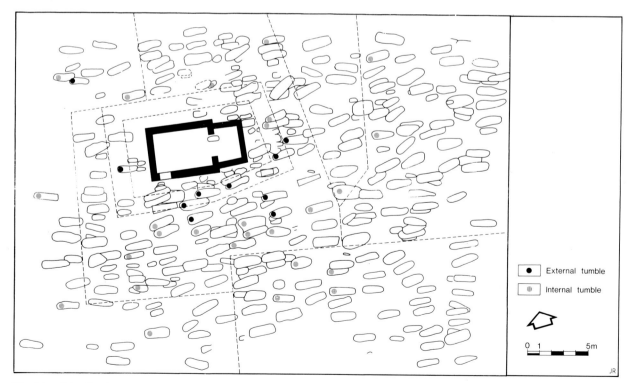

Fig 39   Distribution of burials with tumbled bone

Fig 40   Skeleton with 'internal' bone tumble (5308/?/12–17)

Fig 41   Skeleton with 'internal' bone tumble (5020/M/25–35)

church and the presence of carved grave covers and a stone coffin demonstrate the importance that was attached to burial in that area. From this it might be inferred that the burials with external tumble were significant members of the community.

Table 16 Correlation of bone tumble and parallel-sided burials

	Tumble	No tumble	Totals
Parallel-sided	19[1] (39) (86)[2]	30 (61) (35)	49 (45)
Non-parallel	3 (5) (14)	56 (95) (65)	59 (55)
Totals	22 (20)	86 (80)	108

[1] *Numbers refer only to burials aged six years and over at death.*
[2] *Numbers in brackets are percentages.*

Grave fills, charcoal and artefacts

The grave fills are not of analytical interest as, with the exception of certain clay layers (pp 47–8), the graves were filled with the material through which they were cut.

No 'charcoal burials' as such occurred but charcoal was present in several graves (15/363/4). In four cases burnt pieces of wood occurred alongside the burial or against the grave cut; pieces from one grave were identified as oak. The original nature of these wooden fragments could not be determined; certainly they do not appear to be accidental inclusions. On eight occasions 'charcoal' smears of indeterminate origin occurred on or under the body. The highly degraded material of which the smears were composed might not have been charcoal and it is possible that the smears beneath the heads of two burials (5011, 5132) and beneath the feet of one other (5282) might represent decayed organic pillows, though this could not be verified. Charcoal flecks were scattered around the heads of two burials (5206, 5210) and around the body of another (5253).

A few small artefacts were found in the grave fills (p 92). These included iron nails, and lead and iron strips, but all would appear to be redeposited from pregraveyard contexts. None was in a position that suggested an association with burial rite; no shroud pins or coffin fittings were discovered. Four sherds of Thetford type ware from graves 5285, 5297, and 5204 appear to be contemporary with the use of the graveyard rather than residual (p 80).

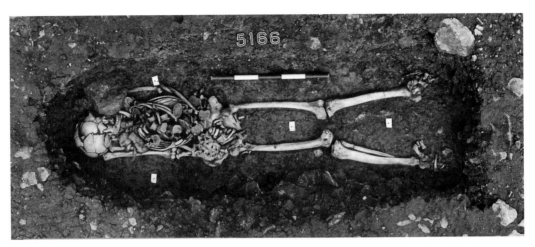

Fig 42   Skeleton with 'external' bone tumble (5166/M/25–35); note the inverted sacrum over the lower right arm

Fig 43   Skeleton with 'external' bone tumble (5288/M/25–35)

Stone arrangements

Stones placed within the graves served one or both of two functions: to support the body, particularly the head, and to protect the body against the earth backfill and later intrusions. As argued below, the stones must be considered in conjunction with wooden covers or coffins, the presence of which can now be inferred only from secondary evidence. Softer organic components may also have been present, in particular cloth or vegetation may have been used as a pillow for the head. Such organic pillows may have been present at the heads of two burials and at the feet of another.

Stone arrangements occurred in more than half the graves (188/339/55) and were distributed quite evenly across the graveyard (Fig 44). The type of stone varied from round, irregular, rough limestone to large, angular, rather smoother fragments (eg Fig 54). These two stone types in practice define the extremes of a fairly continuous scale of variation. Both Blisworth limestone and cornbrash were used, along with occasional glacial pebbles. A rough classification of stone types, utilising the record photographs, demonstrates a concentration of graves with small fragments of rough limestone in the extreme south-east corner of the graveyard (Zone 5), while this stone type is absent from the west and south-west

Table 17 Stone arrangements by age and sex of burial

Age/sex group	All types of stone arrangement		Head pillows	
Infant	25	(37%)	9	(13%)[1]
Child	33	(42%)	17	(22%)
Adolescent	9	(60%)	6	(40%)
Adult	121	(68%)	69	(39%)
Male adults	69	(72%)	46	(48%)
Female adults	52	(67%)	23	(30%)

[1] *Percentage of all graves of the group*

(Zone 3). The stone may have been on occasion derived during the excavation of the grave itself; this was particularly the case in the south-east corner. Most often, though, it must have been collected from quarries external to the graveyard, perhaps from some of those discovered elsewhere in the excavation area (*North Raunds* forthcoming).

Stone arrangements were classified according to whether they overlaid or underlaid the body and whether they extended along the complete length of the burial, part of that length or were just placed at single or

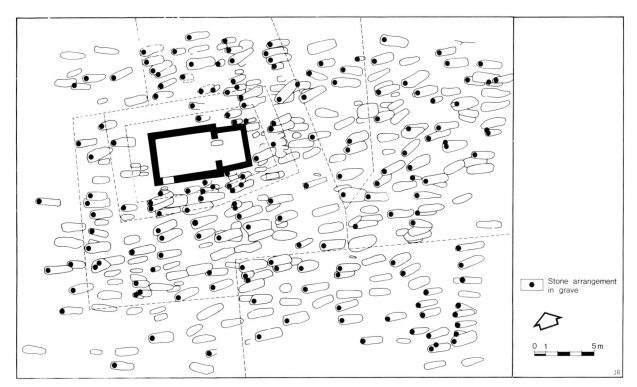

Fig 44 Distribution of stone arrangements

scattered locations. Such was the variety of arrangements that classification was often a difficult task. Here
the function of the various types of arrangement are
discussed; the description of the arrangements is best
conveyed by the plates (Figs 45–50, 52, 54-57, and 64).

With the exception of head pillows there was no
distinctive provision of type, or frequency, of stone
arrangement by age or sex (male: 69/96/72; female:
52/76/68). The frequency of stone provision was,
however, greater for adults than sub-adults, a statistically significant difference (121/178/68; 67/160/42;
chi-squared=23.28, df=1, chi-squared$^{(0.05)}$=3.84).

The most common type of stone arrangement was the
head pillow (101/188/54). Most pillows were single or
small clusters of stone behind and beneath the head supporting it so that it looked along the length of the grave
(63/101/62; Fig 45). In one grave the head was placed on
a ledge of limestone left in the grave side to achieve the
same effect (5209). For a further 29 burials these
arrangements extended either side of the head to prevent
it from rolling to one side (29/101/29); while for just
5 burials stones acted as 'ear-muffs' only, the head not
being propped forward (5/100/5).

Head arrangements were extended to cover completely the faces of 11 burials (eg Figs 46, 47, 48, and
49); in 3 of these burials the head was also propped from
behind to look down the grave. Of the 11 burials, 9 were
non-parallel and 2 unclassified. The phenomenon of
non-parallel posture suggests that complete face covers
were not associated with coffins, indeed most face covers
are so extensive that it is hard to see how they could have
been.

The stone supports propping the head into a more
aesthetic position were also clearly intended to prevent
soil being thrown directly on to the face during the filling
of the grave. The head was further protected in 21

Fig 45 Simple head pillow (5017/F/17–25)

Fig 46   Burial with stones enclosing head and a single stone alongside the right leg (5158/F/17–25)

Fig 47   Burial with head entirely enclosed by stones (5291/M/45+)

burials where the heads were completely covered by some form of stone arrangement. Wood coffins and covers would also have served to protect the faces of many other burials.

Complete cists were provided for five young children (5/67/7, Fig 50). Only one adult was completely covered by flat stones; a vertical stone stood at the foot of this grave either as a marker or as an 'end stop' for the grave mound (5126, Fig 51). More often, adults were covered by stones over the upper chest and head (10/121/8), an arrangement which occurs with only one sub-adult. More frequent still was the occurrence of single or small

groups of stones over the body (33/188/18). These varied from a cluster of stones over the pelvis to single stones in various positions over the body. The feet and the tibiae were the most common locations, followed by chest and hands, then pelvis, femur and knees. In at least three instances these stone arrangements were placed over a wood cover or coffin lid and subsequently settled on to the body (5139, 5219, 5238). In 12 graves the cut was lined on both sides with upright stones, eg 5139, Fig 52. This arrangement was clearly intended to support a wooden cover. Of these 12 graves, only 2 skeletons have bone tumble. In three other cases, the lining was present

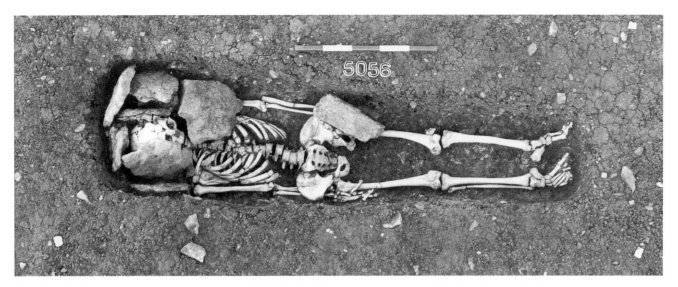

Fig 48   Burial with stones enclosing head (5056/F/17–25); the stone in front of the face has probably slipped

Fig 49   Burial with stones over head and knees (5234/M/35–45); note also the bone decay in the lumbar and pelvic region

along only one side. More frequently, scattered stone occurred alongside the burial (27/188/14; Fig 52).

Deposits of clean clay, clearly not derived from the digging of the grave itself, occurred in 17 graves. In all instances the clay was used in conjunction with stones, often to support stones which covered all or part of the body (11/17/65). In one burial, the clay was apparently laid over stones, which in turn lay over a wooden cover supported by a stone lining. The clay and stones subsided into the grave after the decay of the cover (5139, Fig 52). Less often the clay complemented and extended the coverage of the overlying stones (4/17/24). In the remaining two cases, the grave had been lined before burial; these burials both had scattered stones over the body.

Some spatial patterns can be observed in the distribution of particular types of stone cover; invariably, though, the numbers involved are low and it is not possible to isolate statistically significant trends. Burials with stones placed at scattered or single locations over the body were distributed throughout the graveyard. Those burials with stones, or with only the upper part of the body covered, were largely in Zones 4 and 5 at the east edge of the site, with outlying occurrences at the east edge of Zone 2 and the west edge of Zone 1. This might indicate that stone arrangements became more extensive and complex as the graveyard developed. Graves with linings along both sides had a distinctly northern distribution, only two occurring south of the church.

While there was no significance in the provision of stone types between sexes overall, head pillows were provided for males twice as often as for females. This is a statistically significant difference (46/100/46; chi-squared=6.16, df=1, chi-squared$^{(0.05)}$=3.84). Head pillows were evenly distributed throughout the graveyard, though there were few present in Zone 3 (3/15/20), probably reflecting the high proportion of females in that zone.

Stone occurs with both parallel-sided burials (45/67/67) and in burials with bone tumble (40/65/62) at about the same frequency as it does in the graveyard generally (188/339/55). The range of stone types was, however, more limited, with head pillows predominating for parallel-sided burials, and stone linings and scattered stones along the edges of the grave for those with bone tumble.

There were few obvious associations between stone arrangements and pathology. One adult male, buried north of the church, uniquely had a stone in his mouth (5218/M/17–25; Fig 53). This man had suffered from

Fig 50 (above)   Infant in cist (5038/?/1–2)
*Fig 51 (left)   Stone marker at foot of grave of burial
entirely covered by flat stones (5126/M/35–45)*

poliomyelitis in his youth and subsequently developed
tuberculosis (p 120). The left fibula shaft of a juvenile
had marked periostitis; here both fibulae were covered
with a group of four stones which extended to cover the
right knee (5311/?/12–17). The left knee of an adult
male was supported against the side of the grave by a
group of three stones (5074/M/17–25). The swollen
head of the tibia is apparent from the photographs (Figs
54 and 55); possibly this knee was crippled and could
not be straightened for burial. The head of this crippled
individual was covered by a large flat stone carefully
placed on a layer of clean clay, so as not to crush the skull.

Coffins

As uncarbonised wood did not survive at Furnells and
wood stains were absent, there was little direct evidence
for wood coffins. Neither were there any nails or fittings:
any coffins must have been constructed with wooden
pegs in the manner of those at Barton-on-Humber
(Rodwell and Rodwell 1982). In two graves, a rectangular interface within the grave fill was located; this apparently represented the position of the sides of the coffins
(5041/?/6–12; 5040/F/17–25; Fig 26). In another grave
the bones of an earlier interment had been reburied
alongside the skeleton in a position that suggested

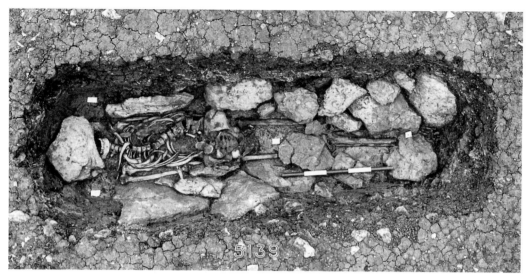

Fig 52   Grave lined with stones (5139/F/25–35); the stones over the skeleton have probably settled from above a wooden cover; note the displacement of the lumbar vertebrae

Fig 53   Skeleton showing effects of tuberculosis and/or poliomyelitis affecting left upper and right lower limbs (5218/M/17–25)

that they had been packed alongside a wood coffin (5118/M/45+; Fig 25).

Evidence for a maximum of six stone coffins has been recovered; one complete, five fragmentary. Rosemary Cramp's report indicates that two fragments are so similar that they are probably from the same coffin (pp 102–3), therefore about five coffins may be represented. All were of 'Barnack' stone. Four reburials in the north graveyard were clearly from stone coffins (Table 18); it is also assumed that 5282 was at least the second occupant of its coffin. The contexts of the reburials and the coffins suggest that they were all contemporary with the chancel phase of the first church (SP4).

The one coffin to survive *in situ* lay about 2m south of the church, just west of its doorway (G5282, [1117]; Figs 11, and 56). It was a tapered coffin with a rounded head recess. As the area around the coffin was eroded

subsequent to the 1975 trial trench, the coffin was stratigraphically isolated. Nevertheless the level of its cover was equivalent to the level of the nearby first church surfaces, indicating that it was associated with the first church. As found, the original coffin cover was broken and inverted, with its rough side uppermost ([304/306]). This suggests that the occupant (5282) was not necessarily the original occupant. The broken head of the coffin was replaced with a fragment of cross-shaft ([302]) and rough stones. This placing of the shaft, repairing the broken lid, is assumed to post-date the second church and perhaps dates to the conversion phase (SP6). The occupant was, however, presumably inhumed before the conversion phase, presumably during the life of the second church (SP5).

It is quite possible that there were more coffins at Furnells which were subsequently removed from the site.

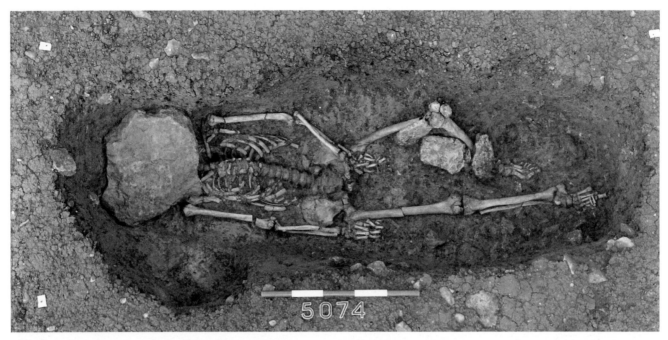

Fig 54   Adult with head cover and left knee supported by stones (5074/M/17–25)

Fig 55   Detail of left knee with supporting stones (5074/M/17–25)

Fig 56   Stone coffin [1117] and slot 'marker' for adjacent grave (5282/M/45+; 5207/F/25–35)

Table 18 Burials below stone covers and in stone coffins

Burial	Sex	Age	Coffin/ cover	Find number
5094A	M	45+	Coffin?	
5094A	F	45+	Coffin?	Possibly from the coffins
5236	F	17–25	Coffin?	represented by fragments
5239	F	25–35	Coffin?	[137] [139] [178] [182] [189]
5280	?	0–6	Cover	[300]
5282	M	45+	Coffin	[1117]
5283	M	35–45	Cover	[305]

In a letter of 1956 C.R. Berwick of 'Wildacre', Hargrave, writes:

'A baby or child's coffin stands in the garage yard of Mr. W. Gell of Raunds, and is now used as a receptacle for plants . . . I examined the little one at Raunds unearthed in Rotton Row. I was accompanied by the late Mr. L.G.H. Lee, who declared it to be Saxon-Roman.'

(I am grateful to Brian Dix for drawing my attention to this information from the Weldon Villa Archive in the Northamptonshire County Archaeological Archive.) Regrettably this little coffin is not extant but it does seem to indicate that at least one child's coffin was present at the site alongside the adult coffins.

Grave covers

Two decorated limestone covers were found, both during the 1975 trial trenching. One was decorated with interlace ([300]) and was laid over a middle-aged man in an earth-cut grave set within an exclusive plot (5283/M/35–45; Figs 11 and 25). The other was decorated with a wheel-cross on one face and a crude cross on the other ([305]). This overlay a child whose grave was lined with stones (5280/?/0–6). The grave cut the grave of an adult (5000), disturbing most of the adult above the knees. While, in its final position, the cover clearly marked the infant grave, the crosses carved on two faces of this stone hint at reuse and the stone may have originally marked the adult or may have been moved from elsewhere in the graveyard. Details of covers are given in Rosemary Cramp's report on pp 105–7. All were of 'Barnack' limestone.

Grave markers

Undoubtedly most or all graves were marked by at least a humble mound but such features have been lost to later erosion. Evidence does, however, survive for the marking of about 36 graves at surface level (36/339/11; Table 19). Included in this total are the five stone coffins, which are presumed to have been marked at ground level by plain slabs in the manner of that for the coffin of burial 5282 (p105).

Table 19 Types of grave markers

Marker type	Number
Covers	
Coffins covered by plain slabs	1 confirmed, 5 possible
Decorated slabs	2 in situ, 1 in fragment in foundation of second church
Single rough stone	1
Several rough stones	5
Crosses	3 crosses, 1 possibly marking founder's plot; others may or may not have been markers.
Slots	
Slot to north	1 for group of 4 or 5 graves.
Slot above	1
Rough stones	
At foot end	5
At head end	2
Posts	
At foot end	2
At head end	5
Other	
Pitched stone in top of grave fill	1

The area to the north of the early church chancel has been well protected from later disturbance by the demolition deposits from the first church and by the surfaces laid for the second church. This area gives just an impression of the types and arrangements of grave markers that have been associated with graves elsewhere in the graveyard where the surface is more eroded. The demolition deposits protected a complex sequence of markers (Fig 11). The sequence would appear to have originated with a large post (G766) which stood originally northeast of the single-celled first church before the introduction of burial. This post, which eventually stood between two rows of graves, was recut twice (G2328, G3031) and finally uprooted, and its posthole sealed by mortar spreads, during the demolition of the first church. In diameter this sequence of postholes varied from 0.4–0.8m and in depth from 0.2–0.5m. Presumably it was the foundation for a substantial post or wooden cross. To its west a single large post, presumably a grave marker, was set into the head of the grave of a woman (5237/F/17–25). Set in alignment between the two posts were the head and foot markers of a child's grave (5258/?/c 6; G1668, G1256). These were neatly rectangular and may have held small dressed stones or blocks of wood. To the north, another child's grave was also marked by a post at its head (5274/?/2–6; G1756).

One group of four or five graves, at the south end of Row 13 in Zone 4, was marked by a slot to the north of the group (G735; Fig 60). The slot (4.2m by 0.4m by 0.2m deep) apparently held two posts, 3.5m apart, set at each end. Perhaps some sort of fencing or screen was supported by the slot between the posts. Alternatively it may have held a board to identify the occupants; such boards were common in the south of England in the eighteenth century (Weaver 1915) but there is no evidence for their use at an earlier date.

One other 'slot' marker occurred immediately outside the church door above the grave of a woman (5207/F/25–35). It comprised a narrow slot 2.5m long, 0.3m wide, with an upright stone at either end and an intervening fill of close-packed limestone rubble (Figs 11 and 26). There were no indications of post-positions along its length and the precise nature of this feature remains obscure. To its south the grave for 5178 was marked by a stone at its south end; this roughly shaped fragment was supported by a stone pushed into the side of the grave to ensure that it protruded above ground level (Fig 57).

Stones occurred at the foot end of the grave in another four instances, including the stone covering arrangement for 5126 (Fig 51); two examples at the head of the grave were also noted. These stones were all rough and uncarved and must have protruded only a small distance. Functionally, they not only marked the grave but must also have supported the end of the grave mound. Five burials were marked with posts at the head and two with posts at the foot. These postholes ranged in size from 0.3–0.8m in diameter and held upright posts or crosses marking the position of the grave. Alongside the major cross at the head of 5283 (the 'founder's' grave), one cross fragment recovered from the medieval manor foundation might possibly have been a grave marker ([301], p 105).

Not all graves would have been marked with upright markers. At least 11 graves were marked with horizontal covers of some form. Of these, one was a cover of a stone coffin (there may have been five others) and two were

Fig 57 Stone marker at foot of grave (5178/M/45+)

Fig 58   Cover stones over the grave of an infant; these may originally have marked the grave at ground level

decorated grave covers over earth graves. One further grave was covered by a single stone, in this case a large block of rough unshaped limestone (5002; 1.5m by 0.6m by 0.2m thick). Other grave covers, apparently originally at ground level, comprised rough limestone fragments of varying size (5086, 5155, 5209, 5276, 5300; Fig 58). In one instance the top of the grave was packed with limestone pitched vertically (5321).

Discussion of burials and graves

Where does this description of the various features of the Furnells burials lead and what explanations can be advanced for the phenomena observed? Firstly, there is a need to characterise the main points of the evidence. The predominant characteristic of the graves was burial with some form of stone arrangement. The posture of the skeleton within the grave is also of importance; two characteristics were dominant, tumbled bone and parallel-sided burials. Most burials with tumbled bones were also parallel. Most tumbled burials occurred in the central zone (p 48). Within that central zone most parallel burials were also tumbled. Burials with external tumble were probably all male, and they were clustered to the south of the church walls. Tumbled bone was commonly associated with scattered stone along the grave sides.

The phenomenon of bone movement independent of intrusive disturbance was first reported by Reynolds for the pagan Anglo-Saxon cemetery at Empingham, Rutland (Reynolds 1976). For the most part Reynolds' examples relate to displacement of the skull and long bones and hence they differ quite considerably from those at Furnells and Jewbury, York (Brothwell 1987), where it is the small bones of the vertebral trunk and pelvis that are most involved. For some cases, those classified here as external tumble, the degree of bone tumble is such that a void must have existed around the skeleton for the process to occur. Reynolds conjectured a wooden cover above the burial, the subsequent collapse of which

dislodged the bones. Such an explanation is unlikely to result in the complexity of tumble observed at Furnells, though on some occasions the collapse of a cover might have been a contributing factor to bone movement. Neither does the pattern and degree of tumble suggest animal disturbance.

How then should bone tumble be interpreted? Why is this feature so evident at this cemetery? To answer these questions it is necessary to consider the factors that influence the rate of body decay. The consideration of decay rates below owes much to discussions with Neil Garland and Rob Janaway.

The processes of decay and putrefaction are complex and depend upon a series of correlated factors. Chief among them are:

- The ground temperature at the time of burial, variable with location and season
- The delay between death and burial
- The depth of the inhumation
- The soil condition, whether acid or alkaline, waterlogged or desiccated
- How the burial was wrapped or enclosed
- The presence or absence of clothing
- The level of body fat possessed by the individual

Of all these influences, four may be pertinent at Furnells: the soil type, use of shrouds, the presence of a coffin and the delay before burial.

The Furnells burials were cut into Blisworth clay, which provided a moist environment encouraging bacterial activity. Had the site been on sand it is possible that bone tumble would have been absent altogether, as the desiccated environment would not have sustained the bacteriological agents of decay.

A second contributing factor might be the use of shrouds. It has been suggested that bone tumble is absent from pagan Anglo-Saxon cemeteries and is restricted in occurrence to the Christian period (Boddington 1987a). Pagan burials were normally clothed, and often provided with a variety of artefacts. Most pagan inhumations thus have a distinctly non-parallel appearance, as burial in clothing allows greater variation in limb posture. This might be contrasted with burial in shrouds. If the shroud was a single sheet tied at head and foot, as in some medieval illustrations, it is probable that the body would take on a more parallel-sided appearance. Unfortunately, there is a notable lack of information concerning the introduction of burial in shrouds. Conventionally it has been assumed that most Christian Anglo-Saxon burials were in shrouds, an assumption based on the absence of artefacts rather than any positive evidence for the shrouds. Such positive evidence, in the form of shroud pins, is not available until the post-Conquest period. At Furnells there were no shroud pins; neither were there any artefacts that might be associated with burial in clothing. One skeleton, however, was so tightly positioned that there seems little doubt that it was buried in a shroud (5156, Fig 31). If burial in shrouds is assumed, then we might expect faster decay rates than would have been the case if burial in clothing had occurred. As Mant has noted, 'clothing had a profound affect upon the subsequent post-mortem changes. Those parts of the body covered by clothing frequently showed remarkable preservation' (Mant 1987). Thus it might be argued, if tenuously, that bone tumble occurs for the first time in Christian-period cemeteries as a result of the introduction of shrouds and an associated increase in the rate of putrefaction.

Another factor might be the provision of coffins. Here the partial correlation between bone tumble and the parallel-sided effect might be noted. It has been argued that for 'external' tumble to occur, a coffin was probably present. But it is quite clear that the presence of a coffin or shroud did not on all occasions lead to bone movement – there is no shortage of evidence for wooden coffins without bone tumble in the Christian graveyards of England. With the complexity of factors affecting putrefaction and skeletal decay it is not surprising that there can be no simple equation – coffin equals bone tumble or tumble equals coffin. Nevertheless it is clear that the presence of a coffin increases the rate of putrefaction (Mant 1987), hence the presence of a coffin can be seen as a contributing but not decisive factor.

There can be no doubt that the burials with external tumble at Furnells are in coffins. Only one is non-parallel, this having a rather peculiar splay of the legs (5166, Fig 42), while another has a stone pillow which surely must have been set within the frame of a wooden box (Fig 43). There can also be little doubt that these burials were in an advanced state of decay before they were laid to rest, hence it may be postulated that there was some delay before burial. At Furnells it is clear that the burials with external tumble were of people of some relative social distinction, as they were buried within the prime area of the churchyard in coffins. Why they were in such an advanced state of decay is a matter for speculation. While we must keep in mind the complexities of the factors affecting decay rates and the consequent difficulties of interpretation, two hypotheses might be suggested. The delay in burial might be due to death occurring at a distance from Furnells and the corpse being returned to its manor or birthplace. Jewbury, York, is the closest parallel to Furnells in respect of bone

tumble and for this cemetery Don Brothwell has outlined a hypothesis in which the Jewish occupants of coffins were carted around the countryside with all that that implies for advanced decay before burial (Brothwell 1987). Alternatively the funeral might have been delayed to allow a social gathering of a scale commensurate with the individual's importance. Here the time lapse between death and burial is of critical importance. Could, for example, the corpses have been interred initially in tombs within the church and subsequently buried in the graveyard? There would, however, have been little room for tombs within the tiny first church.

For those burials with internal tumble the interpretation is less clear; as most were parallel, perhaps here also we have coffins but with less advanced decay before burial, or perhaps these bodies were buried only in shrouds.

The majority of graves throughout the graveyard were not provided with either wooden covers or coffins but with stone arrangements. The form of arrangement varied considerably but it is clear that the stones acted either to support the head, so that it looked down the length of the grave, or to protect part or all of the body from the process of backfilling and from later disturbance. Stones were used extensively to support covers, and the association of head pillows with parallel-sided burials with bone tumble strongly suggests that pillows were used within coffins, as has been demonstrated at Barton-on-Humber (Rodwell and Rodwell 1982).

The correlation of stone arrangements with pathology was not strong. This is not surprising given that most medical conditions affect only the soft tissue and that in many other cases the person must have died before the bone could be transformed. The few cases that do occur reveal some degree of compassion and care for the individual. In particular, 5074 had his head carefully covered with clay and sealed with a stone, while his apparently crippled knee was propped up against the grave side (Figs 54 and 55, p 42). Indeed, throughout the graveyard stone arrangements can be seen contributing to a general theme of body protection, in which we can also include the coffins, covers and clay layers. The Raunds evidence does not suggest that the stones were used to weigh down the corpse for any superstitious reasons. Neither is there any question of any corpse having been stoned, as has been suggested for pagan cemeteries such as Winnall (Meaney and Hawkes 1970, 31).

The graveyard surface

The graveyard surface sloped from west to east and more steeply from the church to the south boundary (Fig 59). The surface was not severely eroded except in the south-east corner and here only by an estimated 0.14m (p 46). Its original surface survived only adjacent to the church. For the first church, a small area of pitched limestone rubble abutted the east chancel wall. For the second church, limestone rubble was found in most of the graves adjacent to the church. The rubble sealed an extensive spread of mortar which derived from the demolition of the first church and filled several hollows created where the backfill of graves had subsided. At least three grave markers had been uprooted and the postholes left empty, to be filled by demolition material.

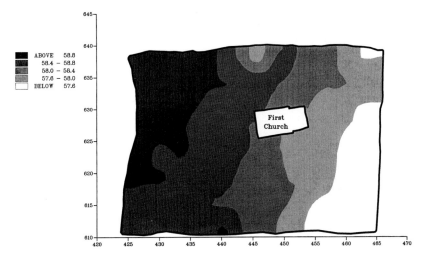

Fig 59   The contours of the churchyard

It is surprising that no evidence for paths to and from the church was recovered, neither was any entrance to the graveyard apparent. The arrangement of the graves and the markers south of the first church door reveals the position of the path at that point but it is impossible to trace this through the graveyard to any boundary.

Graveyard boundaries

The boundaries of the graveyard were composed of a series of independent ditches. Although not necessarily planned together, the ditches form a contemporary unit partitioning the activities outside the graveyard from those within. The ditches were set back from the outer limits of the graves by 1.5–2.5m on the west and north sides, strongly suggesting the presence of an internal bank (Fig 5). Additional evidence for a bank on the west side is provided by an exceptionally shallow grave which is adjacent to the ditch and may be shallower because of being cut through a bank (G5293, Fig 25). On the east side the gap is rather less, only reaching a maximum of about 1m. While a bank may have been present here it seems less likely. For the north, east and west boundaries there appear to be no natural topographical constraints on the boundary locations. The south boundary, however, followed a natural, shallow valley leading east to the village brook; the north side of this small valley became more pronounced after the cutting of the quarry ditch for the second church.

The west side of the graveyard enclosure entailed infilling of the manorial enclosure ditch (SP109, G1293) and cutting a new ditch 5m further west (SP25, G2365; Fig 5). This boundary was recut once during the lifetime of the graveyard (SP25, G2361) and twice to a considerably reduced size in the post-graveyard period. Ditches were also cut to delimit the north and south edges of the graveyard (SP24, SP27). Stratigraphic links did not survive between the west and east ditches and the north ditch. For the north ditch, however, it is apparent that it is cut up to the north-west corner of the western ditch and consequently must either be contemporary with it or post-date it. About four recuts of the north ditch were located. It is not clear whether the east ditch was cut specifically as a boundary for the graveyard or whether it was dug to delineate the rear of plots along

Rotton Row. In either case, it eventually constrained the easterly spread of graves.

Excavations of the south ditch revealed two phases: the first (SP27, G69) was contemporary with the first church chancel (SP4). This boundary was a small ditch about 1.2m across extending from the west ditch, where the interrelationship was not discerned, to a point *c* 16m from the east limit of the graveyard. After construction of the second church, this partial or eroded boundary was replaced by a large ditch, 2.5m across and 1.5m deep (SP29). The new ditch extended along the entire south edge of the graveyard. It was cut into the top of a large linear quarry ditch 2.0–3.5m wide and 1.5–2.0m deep. The quarry had extracted Blisworth limestone, in all probability destined for the walls and foundations of the second church (SP28, p 22). As very little human bone was recovered from this quarry, it might be inferred that it destroyed few burials, though the area excavated was limited.

Grave plots

A characteristic of the majority of pagan and 'final phase' Anglo-Saxon cemeteries is that very few graves cut earlier interments. Where 'multiple' burial does occur in these cemeteries it is isolated groups of two or more individuals buried successively, on rare occasions simultaneously, above or closely adjacent to each other in parallel grave cuts. A few cemeteries do not conform to this pattern but by far the majority show a distinctive non-intercutting pattern with occasional clusters of intercutting graves. In contrast, the cemeteries of medieval churches, and at an earlier period the cemeteries of the minsters, exhibit a complex pattern of intercutting which reflects repeated clearances of areas of the graveyard and the reuse of the limited consecrated burial space by successive 'generations'. Furnells has a pattern of burial lying between these two extremes. Intercutting occurs: 21% of all graves cut an earlier grave, but there has not been an overall reuse of the graveyard for successive generations. It is clear that the graveyard was 'frozen' just at the beginning of the second generation of burial associated with the second church.

Some of the intercutting was no doubt accidental, resulting from inadequate knowledge of previous burial

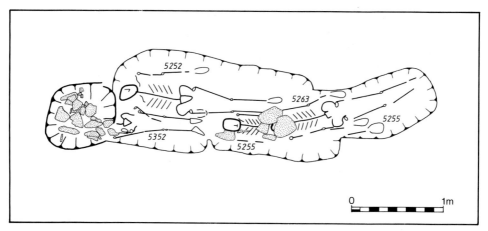

Fig 60   Burial 'plot' in south-east churchyard

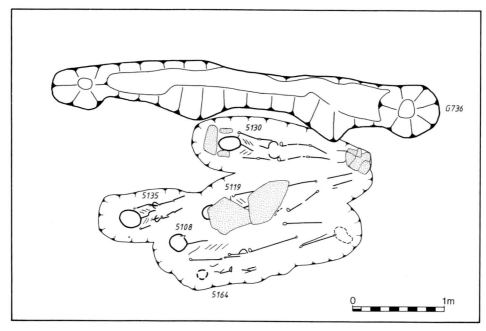

Fig 61   Burial 'plot' at east edge of churchyard with 'slot marker' to north

positions. On other occasions it may have been due simply to a careless disregard for the previous interments, though the examples of careful reburial of disturbed bones indicate that this was not generally the case (p 28). Additionally, the level of disturbance of the skeleton is low in relation to the number of actual intercutting graves. This suggests that intercutting derived from the need to squeeze a maximum number of burials into the available space without disturbing prior interments. The position of existing graves would have been known from the mounds or grave markers present, since clear evidence for the surface marking of 36 graves has been obtained from the graveyard (p 45).

Little variation in density of intercutting occurred across the graveyard, with the exception of the low level of Zone 3 where there was only 1 intercutting grave out of 37. Within this generally uniform pattern of graves specific clusters occurred, particularly in the east graveyard. In the north-east corner of the graveyard (Zone 4) four graves were intercut in a line (Fig 60) and occupy an area just 1m wide north-south and 3.8m long east-west. The close positioning of these four adults, combined

with the small variation of alignment between their graves (22°), suggests that they were deliberately inserted into a single narrow plot. This would appear to be a burial plot of three adults and one adolescent, secondary to the original row of interments along the east boundary (Row 16; 5252/M/35–45; 5255/F/25–35; 5263/F/25–35; 5352/?/12–17). Only one burial was extensively disturbed (5255). The head of burial 5352 was marked by a post, and burials 5263 and 5252 were interred east of this post.

A similar cluster of five graves occurred at the south limit of Zone 4 (Fig 61). This cluster was the only occurrence within the churchyard of a sequence of four successive intercutting graves (5164, 5108, 5119, 5130). The fifth grave (5135) could not be related stratigraphically to the other burials. Each of the four successive grave cuts was progressively north of its predecessor, the latest (5130) being against an east-west linear slot which might be suspected of supporting a marker or fence. Once again this would appear to be a marked plot, with two female adults, one male adult and one or two children. No features survived to mark the

Fig 62   Grave cover [300] in situ showing setting of stones at the head

south edge of such a plot but it may have been unnecessary to do so. It is notable that the cluster of graves was at the south end of an irregular curving row of graves. To the south there was a discontinuity in the grave pattern and the rows were laid out without regard to the pattern lying to the north of the cluster. This (and other considerations described on pp 53–4) suggests that this plot lay at the south edge of the graveyard at one point during its development; hence there was no specific need to delineate the south edge of the plot.

Elsewhere in the graveyard there was only one other clear example of a defined plot – this was the area almost empty of graves surrounding the covered grave 5283. Here the grave of a 35–45 year old man was sealed by a fine, but worn, stone cover decorated with interlace

([300], Fig 62, p 106). It was set in the centre of an area measuring 1.6m north-south by 1.5m east-west, empty of other graves except for one infant (5171) and one infant or child (5342/?/0–6). These youngsters need not have been related to the adult. Rather, these insertions into this otherwise vacant plot reflect the special treatment of infants in the same way as the concentration of infant burials against the church walls. No photographs survive of the burial, which was excavated during the 1975 trial season. The site notes, however, show that it was in an earth grave without stone arrangements. Possibly it was in a wood coffin, or at least had a wood cover, as the site notes record what seems to have been bone tumble – 'some disturbance to the pelvic area and feet; one heel bone at the patella, the other at the pelvis'.

Fig 63   *Reconstruction of cross ([164], [302/7])*

Site photographs reveal an arrangement of stones on the graveyard surface at the head of the cover (Fig 62). No other record is available for this arrangement but it might be speculated that it was associated with the burial and that it formed the base for a cross standing at the head of the grave. The fragments of shaft recovered from elsewhere on the site ([302/7]; p 105) are of similar workmanship to the interlaced cover and might well have stood in this position – certainly there is no other obvious location for this sculpture. Unfortunately little information about the structure of the stone arrangement is available and its role as support for a cross-base must remain speculative.

There is evidence for four 'multiple' graves – three graves with secondary interments and one double burial. In the south-east corner of the graveyard (Zone 5) a child had been inserted into the north side of the grave of a man (5121/?/6–12; 5120/M/25–35). Both have an identical arrangement of stones around the head (Fig 64), that for the child completely surrounding its head, while that for the adult has been disturbed by surface erosion. It would seem that the second burial followed shortly after the first as no bones were disturbed, indicating that decay of the adult was not advanced. An almost identical burial arrangement occurs in Zone 4, where the stones covering a woman were rearranged to accommodate the insertion of a child (5226/F/17–25; 5227/?/6). Again no bones were disturbed. In contrast, immediately to the north the grave for a child was cut through the grave of a male

Fig 64   *Man and child in 'double' grave; (5120/?/6–12; 5121/M/25–35)*

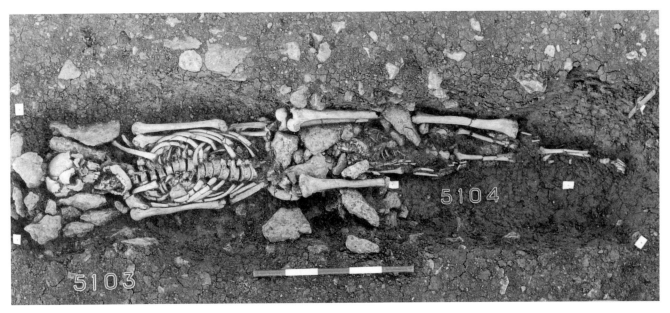

Fig 65   Child burial cut through adult male burial (5103/M/Adult; 5104/?/c 6)

adult disturbing the right leg which was replaced along-side the child (Fig 65; 5103/M/adult; 5104/?/c 6). Only in one further instance does the position of burials suggest a specific relationship. Two infants, both aged less than six months, were buried in the same small grave in Zone 1 south of the church, apparently at the same time (5189, 5196). This double inhumation may have been of twins who died shortly after birth.

Elsewhere in the graveyard there were numerous examples of two, occasionally three, graves intercut or adjacent to each other which may be specifically related or may simply be fortuitous clusters. For these their relative position does not suggest that they were within a defined plot, or a reused grave, similar to the examples above. It is notable that the four multiple graves lie in the east graveyard; they may, therefore, reflect a later burial practice.

Rows and zones

Visual examination of the graveyard plan reveals certain key characteristics. First and foremost is the common alignment of the graves, orientated to the church rather than the graveyard boundaries (above). A second char-acteristic is the intercutting that occurs between graves in some areas (p 49). The third visual characteristic, which is discussed here, is that most of the graves were laid out in rows. Some of these rows were straight, others curved; some well defined, others nebulous; some evenly spaced, others erratically spaced. In all, 23 rows have been identified (Fig 66). These have been defined on visual criteria by linking adjacent graves whose head positions form a slightly curved or straight line, and which show a narrow range of alignment values. Some infants were included in the rows even though their heads were not aligned at the west edge in the same manner as the adults. Thus the definition of rows is based upon visual and not statistical criteria. The number of graves in each row ranged from 4 to 18. A glance at the plan will reveal how difficult it has been on occasion to decide whether to include a particular grave in a row. While some of the

inclusions or exclusions from rows might be questioned, the overall scheme of rows merits confidence.

Continuing a visual examination of the graveyard plan, it is apparent that certain areas of the graveyard do not have any row structure. One such disordered area lies to the east of Row 10 and to the west of Rows 12 and 13; the other links the north-west and south-east corners of the graveyard. The disordered area east of Row 10 might be argued to represent an informal addition to a formally defined area. Further, Row 12 is curved in such a manner as to suggest that it was laid out around the east edge of this informal addition. Such patterning suggests three zones in the central and east graveyard; a formal core with straight rows to the north, south and immediately to the east of the church (Zone 1); an unplanned area of graves to its west (Zone 3) and east (Zone 2); and a planned area to the east of this arranged its row structure to flow around the edges of the disordered area and fit within the north and east bound-aries of the graveyard (Zone 4, Fig 66).

About 9m south of the church, there was a disconti-nuity in the row structure. At the same position the more intense area of intercutting south of the church appears to end. This discontinuity continues as far as the east edge of the graveyard where there was a discontinuity between Rows 13 and 22 and a notable gap between Rows 14 and 23. The dense cluster of five graves seems to mark the end of Row 13 (see pp 50–1). These consider-ations define a zone of graves in the south-east graveyard separated from those to the north (Zone 5). This zone is distinguished from those to the south-west which are more dispersed, lack any row structure and are part of the disordered Zone 3 to the west of the central Zone 1.

Internal development can be observed within Zone 1. Row 11 would appear to be an insertion of an extra row behind the 'primary' Row 10 to the east of the church and the chancel. Additionally the position of the graves south of the church suggests that originally the rows ended 2.5m away from the church walls. The situation is less clear to the north but, nevertheless, it would appear that the first burials were no closer than 2.3m to the

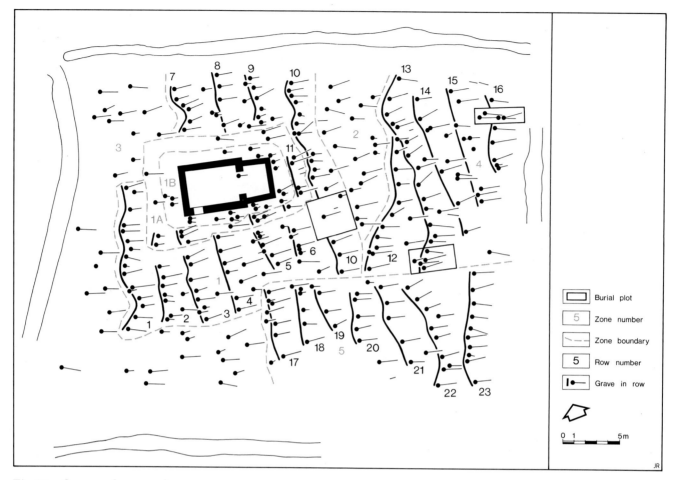

Fig 66   Graveyard rows and zones

church walls. The gap between church and graves was subsequently narrowed to 1.0–1.5m (Zone 1A). Finally, graves were dug right up to the church walls (Zone 1B). Infant burials predominated in this last stage of infilling of the central zone.

From this topographical analysis emerges a coherent graveyard structure which appears to reflect chronological development (Figs 7 and 9):

– **Zone 1** Initially the burials were confined to an area extending 9m to the north and south of the church, 6.5m to the west and 5m to the east (the primary zone). No burials were allowed within a distance of 2.5 to 3m from the church walls. It is notable that the church is central within this early core of graves whereas it is not within the final graveyard boundaries.
– **Zones 1A and 1B** Subsequently, graves encroached on the exclusion zone around the church (Zone 1A). This may have occurred in two phases or it may be that only infant burials were allowed within 1.5m of the church walls (Zone 1B).
– **Zones 2 and 3** Around this core a pattern of informal overspill occurred to the east, Zone 2, and west, Zone 3.
– **Zone 4** To the east of the Zone 2 overspill the north-east corner of the graveyard was subsequently infilled with rows of graves.
– **Zone 5** Finally the south-east corner of the graveyard was utilised for further rows of burials.

Table 20   Graveyard zones

Zone	Graves	Description
Central zone	**171**	
Zone 1	116	Primary zone centred on church
Zone 1A	25	Graves within 1.5 – 2.5m of church walls
Zone 1B	30	Graves within 1.5m of church walls
Overspill zones	**59**	
Zone 2	22	Irregular graves east of Zone 1
Zone 3	37	Irregular graves west of Zone 1
Eastern zones	**130**	
Zone 4	76	North-east area of graveyard
Zone 5	54	South-east area of graveyard
Outer zones	**189**	Zones 2-5

Zones 1, 1A and 1B are collectively known as the *central zone*, Zones 2 and 3 as the *overspill zones*, Zones 4 and 5 as the *eastern zones* and Zones 2–5 as the *outer zones*.

Although the graveyard would appear to have been divided into distinct successive zones, no internal boundaries, such as ditches or fences, were evident. Burial density was most intense near the church (Zones 1, 1A and 1B, 0.6 burials per square metre) where it was twice that elsewhere (Zones 2, 4, 5; 0.33, 0.36, 0.27) and four times that in Zone 3 (0.13) which includes the barely used north-west corner of the graveyard.

This sketch of development can now be supported and refined by analysis of the demographic structure of the zones (Tables 21 and 22). Two features are of interest. Firstly, that females were evenly distributed within Zone 1 while males were concentrated south of the church (Fig 67). Secondly, that infants were almost absent from Zone 4 and Zone 5. In contrast there was an undue proportion of infants in Zone 1B (Fig 68). Males predominated in all zones except the 'overspill' Zone 3, as they did in the population overall. Apparently, as Zone 1 became crowded, burials were increasingly displaced beyond its periphery; this displacement affected females more often than men. Displacement of females to the peripheral, presumably less popular, areas of the burial ground can also be seen within Zone 1. While there was an equal number of females buried to the north and west of the church as to the south and east, just 23% of Zone 1 males were buried north and west of the church.

Children (aged 2–12) form 25% of the population overall and were reasonably well represented in all zones except for Zone 5 where they comprise just 12% of burials (Table 22). Infants, comprising 18% of the overall population, were under-represented in Zones 4 and 5 and over-represented in Zone 1B, this sub-zone being defined primarily by its concentration of 25 infants and 10 children.

It remains to be considered how this zonal pattern relates to the development of the church. It is argued here that stratigraphic and demographic evidence suggests that the graveyard expanded to its full area during the life of the first church and that very few burials are associated with the second church. Stratigraphic evidence shows that most graves within 2.5m of

the second church walls predate that church; none could be demonstrated to be contemporary with it. It is possible that the overspill and eastern zones were largely contemporary with the second church but the distribution of infants within the graveyard suggests otherwise. The outer zones have few infants while Zone 1B, the zone closest to the church, is dominated by infant burials. If the outer zones are contemporary with the second church then it would be necessary to argue that, during the period of the second church, most infant corpses were being disposed of outside the churchyard, reversing the special attention given to infants by burial in the 'eaves-drip' location of Zone 1B. It would be necessary to argue that the area closest to the south and east walls of the church, generally considered to be most favoured for burial (as indicated by the higher concentration of burials in the central zone), was not used during the life of the second church. These arguments cut across the grain of the archaelogical evidence from this site. A more probable scenario is that the graveyard expanded to its full area during the life of the first church, that later in the use of the first church infants were preferentially buried in the 'eaves-drip' location, and that few burials took place during the use of the second church. Just two burials might reasonably be argued to be associated with the second church, though there must have been others for which the stratigraphic or circumstantial evidence for a link with the second church is absent. One candidate burial lies east of the second church with its head adjacent to the east chancel wall and aligned about 30° askew to the underlying burials (G5222, Fig 21). This position suggests that the grave is of second church date rather than earlier though there is no stratigraphic evidence to confirm this. It is evident that the burial in

Table 21 Demographic structure of graveyard zones: sex

Zone	1	1A	1B	2	3	4	5	Total	Central	Outer
Male	28	10	1	9	7	22	23	100	52	46
%	59.6	66.7	100.0	60.0	35.0	47.8	82.1	58.1	54.7	61.3
Female	19	5	0	6	13	24	5	72	43	29
%	40.4	33.3	0	40.0	65.0	52.2	17.9	41.9	45.3	38.7
Totals	47	15	1	15	20	46	28	172	95	75

Table 22 Demographic structure of graveyard zones: age

Zone	1[1]	1A	1B	2	3	4	5	Total
Infant	25	3	23	3	6	3	2	65
%[2]	21.9	12.0	76.7	13.6	16.2	4.0	3.8	18.3
Child	34	6	6	3	8	22	10	88
%	29.8	24.0	20.0	13.6	21.6	29.3	12.0	24.8
Adolescent	4	1	0	1	2	3	1	11
%	3.5	1.0	0	4.5	5.4	2.7	13.3	0.3
Adult	51	15	1	15	21	48	39	191
%	44.7	60.0	3.3	68.2	56.8	64.0	53.3	54.8
Totals	114	25	30	22	37	75	52	355

[1] Excluding 1A & 1B [2] % of burial zones

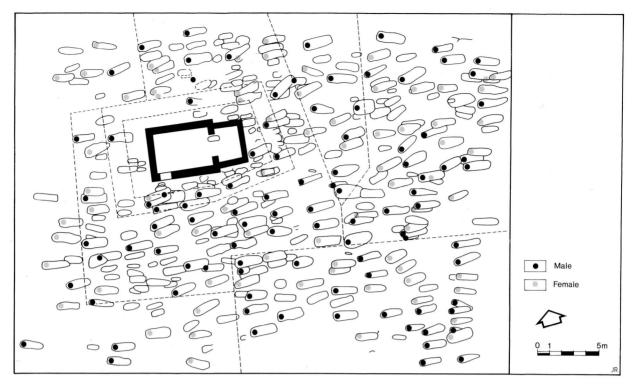

Fig 67   Distribution of males and females

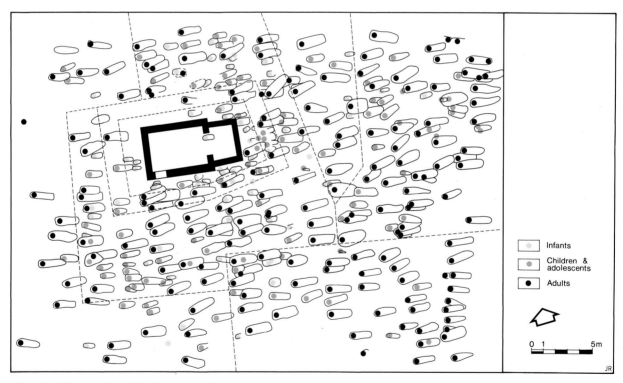

Fig 68   Distribution of burial age at death

Table 23 Summary of burial characteristics by zone

Rows and plots	Age	Sex	Grave provision	Posture and tumble
Central zone (1, 1A, 1B)				
Straight rows	Infants concentrated	Male concentration	Stone coffins	Concentrations of parallel-
Founder's plot	close to church (1B)	south of church	Stone covers	sided and tumbled skeletons
Double burial			Markers	
Burial most dense			Stone arrangements	External tumble
Overspill (2,3)				
No rows		Female concentration	Stone arrangements	
		in zone 3		
Eastern (4,5)				
Curving rows	Few infants		Stone arrangements	
Plots to east			(some more complex)	

the surviving stone coffin south of the church is secondary (G5282, p 43); this may also be put forward as a burial of second church date.

The proportion of the burials in Zone 1 that are earlier than the burials in, say, Zone 5 cannot be resolved from the data recovered. Thus it is not possible to separate fully the two influences of chronology and spatial location

(ie distance from the favoured areas immediately south and east of the church). It would seem likely that the increase of stone provision in graves is chronological, as is the special treatment of infants and the use of family plots. But what of the parallel-sided effect and bone tumble? These appear to be primarily spatial effects but some interaction with chronology cannot be ruled out.

5 Liturgical and social aspects

by David Parsons

Introduction

The pottery vessel buried in the church floor at Furnells is an unusual feature, at least in the context of British church archaeology. Its interpretation is of some significance for both practical and liturgical aspects of the early medieval church. In archaeological terms it is a fairly complex feature and its interpretation hinges on the recognition that there were two major phases in the life of the pot (Fig 69). In the first, it was subject to heavy burning and fracturing at the base, and acquired internal deposits of calcium carbonate and a wax–honey–tartaric acid mixture. In the second phase, the badly damaged pot was buried in the floor, where it was subject to pressure from above, which further broke the upper parts of the vessel; it was partly filled with ashy soil, and fine silt was subsequently deposited in it.

The primary use of the pottery vessel

Judging by the amount of calcium carbonate deposited on its inner surface, limestone-rich water must have been heated in the pot on numerous occasions before its burial in the church floor (p 96). On the final occasion the base of the pot cracked, and the contents, which – apart from any water present, consisted mainly of wax – melted, ran into the fissures in the pot and there burnt on. The obvious interpretation of this evidence for both heat and wax is that the pot was used for some part of the wax-making process itself, either the initial refinement of the honeycomb or the remelting of finished wax for candle-dipping or for casting statuettes.

It is surprising that more evidence for wax-making in the Middle Ages has not come to light, since the demand by the medieval church for wax was prodigious. Not only was there a multiplicity of altars in every church, at which lights were kept burning, but the Paschal candle alone, made or remade annually, required several pounds of wax. At the end of the Middle Ages, when evidence becomes readily available from churchwardens' accounts and wills, the weight of the Paschal candle varied from a modest 2lb at Thame to a massive 30lb in the London church of St Mary at Hill in 1478 (Feasey 1906, 362). Surviving candlesticks, such as that from Gloucester, suggest equally huge Paschal candles earlier in the Middle Ages, at least in the more important churches. Even after the breach with Rome, a very large proportion of parish expenditure was often devoted to buying wax for candle-making, as frequent references in the Cossington, Leicestershire, churchwardens' accounts for 1534–1601 make clear (LRO 44' 28/1318). At the same period bequests to Northamptonshire churches also show that considerable quantities of wax were used for making candles for the Easter sepulchre, torches for funerals and other purposes. At Church Brampton in 1528 Richard Cosby left 'ij torchis of waxe in wayght xiiij powndes' (Serjeantson and Longden 1913, 284).

More modest was the quantity of wax frequently bequeathed for the sepulchre light, in most cases one or two pounds: at East Carlton and Easton Maudit a mere $^1/_2$ lb was left, though at East Carlton the same testator gave 1lb to the 'image of Seynt Katryn'; while in more prosperous parishes amounts of 6lb and 10lb are recorded at Daventry and Higham Ferrers respectively. At both Brackley and Irthlingborough there were two bequests totalling 6lb, and at Bradden two testators gave amounts totalling respectively 2lb and 6lb. T Kenersley's bequest to the small church at Syresham of 13lb of wax in 1528 must be regarded as atypical, however. Gifts of wax for other purposes are also known, for example at Welford: 2lb to Our Lady's light and 3lb to the rood light. The evidence for all these examples is recorded in the gazetteer to Serjeantson and Longden (1913) under the appropriate parish name.

In spite of these examples, which give an impression of the demand for wax, it is impossible to make any objective assessment of the quantities involved. In the first place, the majority of bequests are of cash or chattels; typical donations for the maintenance of the sepulchre light were one or two sheep or a strike of barley – a strike being a level measure of volume, usually a bushel. Secondly, legacies in favour of saints' images may have been used to buy wax with which to repair the statues themselves: not all images in the round were of wood or stone. Though Richard Cosby's will mentions two torches, most of the bequests refer to raw wax, which is emphasised by the rector's donation to Broughton church in 1500 of 'ij lib. waxe *unmade*' (Serjeantson and Longden 1913, 289; my emphasis). The candles or images then had to be made, and this is recorded in some churchwardens' accounts. The account for 1553 at Melton Mowbray notes tersely 'payed . . . for a li of waxe and the making of it . . . ix^d' (LRO DG 36/140/6).

At Hythe in Kent an unknown number of men received payment in 1412–13 for making the Paschal candle and two others: 'Item in lymeum ligno et victualibus datis hominibus operantibus circa cereum paschale cum aliis duobus cereis . . . xiiij^d' (Feasey 1906, 362). In 1511–12 the London parish of St Andrew Hubbard, East Cheap, provides evidence for the employment of specialists to make the candles: 'Item, paid to the wax chaunler for makyng of the pascall and the beme lighth the Judas tenebre candles and the taper hallowing at the font . . . vij^s' (Feasey 1906, 362).

In some instances not even the wax was provided; it had to be refined from the honeycomb. Once again, the researches of Serjeantson and Longden (1913) have uncovered evidence from parishes in Northamptonshire for bequests of hives (figures in brackets refer to page numbers in the gazetteer). More often than not benefactors left a single hive to the sepulchre or its guild: Byfield (294), Weekley (427); or to the rood: Syresham (412). Robert Henson of Polebrook (393) specified 'to Seynt Jams awlter a hewe and a lambe and a bee hive wythe the been', and the bees are also mentioned specifically at Walgrave (422). The sepulchre at Stoke Bruerne (410) had the benefit of two hives, while in a curious bequest at Brixworth (287) the Lady Chapel acquired an interest in three hives. In an access of generosity – or ostentation? – Myles Roos left all his hives to the rood and sepulchre in Naseby church (368), and Sir John Pollard, the parson of Luddington (360), gave ten to the sepulchre of his church, 'which x bee hyves shall be in custody of ye chyrch wardens'. The parson of Old (435), Humphrey Garrad, a mite less generous, spread his favours a little more widely: Our Lady acquired two hives, as did the light before the Blessed Sacrament, while the rood and the sepulchre inherited one each.

Whether or not obscure rural parishes could call upon the services of a specialist wax chandler, as the town parishes obviously did, the honeycomb would have to be processed to make the wax available. The number of references to hives implies that the expertise was available locally, especially in the case of Aldwinkle, where in 1527 Richard Wolaston left all his hives to a private individual with the stipulation 'I will that half of the wax of those behyves shalbe brent in the church . . . aslonge as they will endure' (Serjeantson and Longden 1913, 270). Wax refining is a fairly simple operation, though the level of skill required increases with the degree of refinement desired. These instructions, written down in the seventeenth century, probably represent fairly accurately what was done in the Middle Ages:

'When the honey is all gotten out, put all your combes . . . into a good quantity of faire water . . . and boyle them a little while, till the Combes are well melted, then put the Combes and water together into a canvas bagge . . . and straine as much as you can thorow the same, letting it run into a vessell of cold water . . . After this, gather the wax well together and melt it in a posnet or such like at a soft fire . . . but if it be not purified at the first trying well enough . . . then try or melt it againe.' (Levett 1634, 51)

The presence of the wax deposit in the pot from the Furnells church floor makes it likely that it had first been used for part of such a wax-making process. Either it was the container in which the honeycomb was first boiled up in water, or the earthenware 'posnet', in which the various bits of wax were melted together. Since the successive refining processes would progressively remove from the beeswax the honey originally in the comb, the traces of honey in the deposit inside the Furnells pot suggest that it was most probably used for the initial boiling up of the honeycomb. This suggestion is not accepted by Dr Eva Crane, who thinks that the pot is not large enough for this purpose. In her experience the vessels used in most societies for processing the honeycomb are much larger (pers comm). The capacity of the Furnells pot is about 2.7 litres (4.75 pints), which would certainly limit the amount of wax that could be refined at any one time, but in the period in question there were no pottery vessels of larger size that could have been used. The interpretation of the Furnells pot for the initial processing of wax is reinforced by the further presence in the surface deposit of traces of tartaric acid (p 96). These are most easily explained as a part of the first process of wax extraction. One of the problems attaching to the method described by Levett (1634) is that if the water used is hard, ie containing dissolved calcium bicarbonate, the refined wax tends to be grey and spongy, an effect known as saponification; vinegar or sulphuric acid should be added to the water to neutralise the lime (Cowan 1908, 56). Furnells is certainly in a hard water area, and if groundwater rather than rainwater was used for wax rendering, some such additive would have been required. My former colleague Professor J S Wacher has suggested to me in discussion that the lees of wine would serve the same purpose as vinegar and would explain the presence of tartaric acid in the deposit on the inside of the pot. In this connection it is interesting to note that earlier in this century some factories added tartar to the water used for wax refining (Cowan 1908, 84).

The following interpretation of the primary use of the pottery vessel is therefore consistent with the observed facts and the assumed method of wax refining in the early medieval period (Fig 69). The pot was used for the rendering down of honeycomb in the hard water of the locality. Before or during this use the primary deposit of calcium carbonate accumulated on the interior. The pot continued in use for this purpose for an indeterminate period, until on the final occasion it was inadvertently allowed to boil dry, the evaporation of the water leaving traces of tartaric acid deriving from the addition of wine dregs, and the remains of honey, which had dissolved out of the honeycomb. These substances mingled with the melting wax in the now overheating pot, until the base of the vessel fractured in the heat of the fire, and molten wax with its impurities was able to run into the cracks, where it burnt on to the earthenware fabric, forming the secondary deposit. The pot, heavily burnt and cracked, was now unsuitable for its original industrial use (which may have had a religious purpose), but was pressed into further ecclesiastical service as a liturgical adjunct, as will be described below.

If the postulated overheating of the pot, attended no doubt by a conflagration of the molten wax, sounds over-dramatic and akin to the legend of King Alfred and the cakes, it must be remembered that the heating of wax over an open fire is an essentially hazardous proceeding, as the inhabitants of Llanthony discovered in 1301, when the remaking of the Paschal candle led to a disastrous fire in which not only the church but four bell turrets were destroyed:

'gaudium Paschale . . . turbabatur, quando Paschalem cereum reformando, ecclesiam et quatuor campanaria cum campanis incendium devoravit.' (*Annales prioratus Wigornia* in Luard 1869, 549; Lehmann-Brockhaus 1955–60, no. 2478)

In general terms it is quite clear that the pot was originally used for some part of the wax-making process. It will be suggested more specifically below (p 62) that the occasion for this activity was the consecration of the church itself.

The secondary use of the pottery vessel

The damaged pot was now buried in the floor of the first-phase church (SP3). The purpose of this burial was, for a number of reasons, considerably more than the simple consignment of rubbish:

– The pot was buried in the church in its own pit, rather than put into a secular rubbish pit with other detritus.

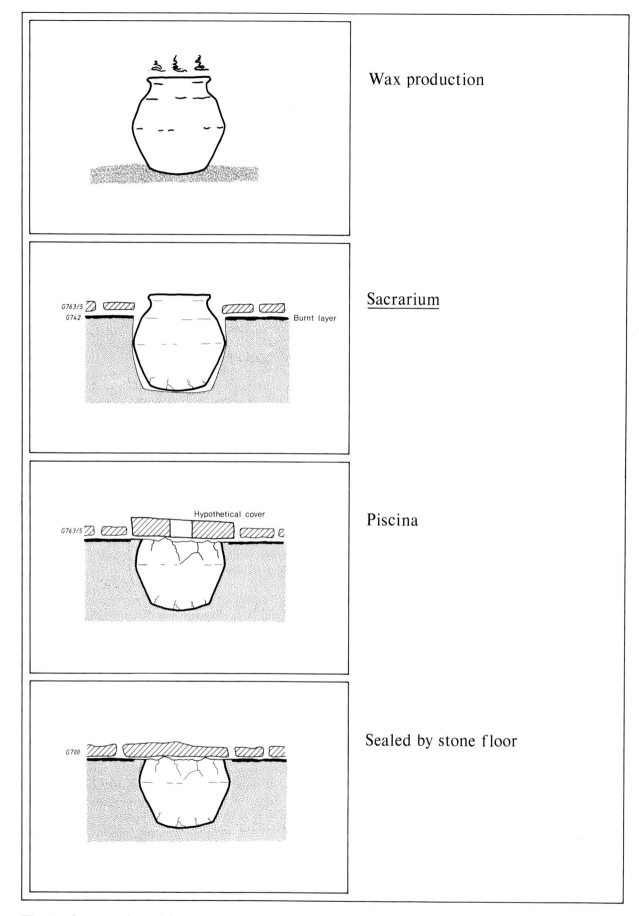

Fig 69   Sequence of use of the pottery vessel

- It was buried whole and in an upright position.
- Its position within the church was significant: on the east-west axis and one-third of the way along from the east end.

Before the addition of the chancel to the first church, the altar must have stood in approximately this position. This is not the place to discuss the niceties of the altar position in the Anglo-Saxon church; the subject is treated in Parsons 1986. In a single-cell building, such as the church under consideration here, there is not a lot of choice in the placing of the altar. The burial place of the pot would have been just in front of the altar, if the latter were placed against or near the east wall; or directly beneath it, if it had a more forward position, allowing the priest to celebrate behind it and facing the congregation.

This is clearly not an appropriate place for depositing domestic rubbish. It is, however, a well-attested area for the deposition of what might be termed 'holy rubbish'; that is to say, sacred objects and materials no longer required or suitable for ritual use. There is literary evidence for this practice going back, as far as England is concerned, to the late seventh/early eighth centuries. In the Penitential of Theodore (Archbishop of Canterbury, 668–90) there is this injunction:

Omne sacrificium sordida vetustate corruptum, igni comburendum est. (Wasserschleben 1851, 196; Haddan and Stubbs 1871, 187)

Every [sacramental wafer] which has become corrupt through the foulness of age must be burned in the fire. (Adapted from Lockton 1920, 43)

This is repeated word for word in Bede's Penitential. By the time that the Penitential of Egbert (Archbishop of York, 735–66) was written, there was an explicit instruction about what was to happen to the cremated remains:

Qui neglexerit sacrificium, ut vermes in eo sint vel colorem non habet saporemque . . . in igne accendatur, cinis eius sub altare abscondatur. (Wasserschleben 1851, 243; Haddan and Stubbs, 1871, 427)

Let him who has neglected the [sacramental wafer] so that there are [maggots] in it, and it has lost its colour and taste . . . let it be burned in the fire and its ashes put away under the altar. (adapted from Lockton 1920, 43)

Not only were the spoiled elements of the Eucharist disposed of in this way, but also items of liturgical equipment, such as altar cloths, which had simply become worn out with age (Lockton 1920, 118).

It is not immediately apparent how the ashes could be deposited beneath the altar, especially in the case of the cube-shaped altar, which were popular, at least in manuscript illustrations, until the twelfth century, or in the case of altars so obviously solid as that at the east end of Eadmer's Canterbury Cathedral in AD 1067 (Taylor 1969, 105 and 128). It may be that in practice many altar slabs were supported on legs at the corners (Pocknee 1963, 38), as shown in some manuscripts as late as the twelfth century (Hope 1899, pl II, fig 2 and pl III, figs 1 and 2) or on two blocks of masonry, one near either end of the altar, with clear space between them, as seems to have been the case in the Anglo-Saxon church at Barton-on-Humber (Rodwell and Rodwell 1982, 299 and fig 6). An alternative explanation is that the Latin expression *sub altare* is not to be taken literally; it may have exactly the same force as the English 'beneath' in later documents, such as the well-known Fotheringhay building contract of 1434, in which 'beneath' clearly means 'to the west', and 'above' means 'to the east' (Salzman 1967, 506–7). Whether the place for deposition of sacred refuse was immediately in front of the altar or directly underneath it, the pit in the first church at Furnells is clearly in a significant position.

There are many comparable features in excavated churches on the continent, conveniently summarised by Binding (1975), though I understand from Professor Binding that many more examples could now be added to those which he published in 1975.

Among various underfloor features in churches, he explores the so-called 'relic grave' or *piscina sacra*, which is a repository not only for relics as such but also for remains of sacred articles. In some cases these underfloor features are elaborate channels, as at Walbeck, with pottery vessels covered by pierced slabs (Binding 1975, 45); at Ilsenburg the underfloor chamber is smaller and simpler, again covered by a pierced stone slab, but with lead vessels in place of the pots (Binding 1975, 45); at Unterregenbach and Prague the chambers are cruciform, but without any vessels (Binding 1975, 45–6). The size of the church and the position of the feature at Höllstein are more closely comparable with Furnells, though the pierced circular slab seems to belong to the larger eleventh-century church (Binding 1975, 48). However, the closest parallel is the church at Oosterbeek (Netherlands), where a pottery vessel larger than, but in many respects similar to, the Furnells one was found in the centre of the building (Binding 1975, 43). The pot has been variously dated. The original excavation report implied a tenth-century date (Glazema 1949, 46–8), but this was amended by Glazema himself to *c* 1050 (ter Kuile 1964, 25); Dr H Halbertsma accepts the earlier date (pers comm, 16 August 1983). The pot was embedded in the thick layer of mortar containing sherds of pottery of a type in use 'depuis l'âge carolingien' (ter Kuile 1964, 27), originally diagnosed as ninth century (Glazema 1949, 47). The pot and its mortar cladding were placed directly over a pit filled with sand, but Glazema thought there was no connection between the vessel and what appeared to be a soakaway, since although the bottom of the pot was pierced, the mortar layer around it was unbroken (1949, 47).

Whatever the interpretation of the Oosterbeek pot, the elaborate mortar covering makes it unlikely that the vessel itself was the 'holy rubbish' for which a sacred resting place was found. At a pinch, however, one might argue that the Furnells pot was. It had been used for processing wax, from which such articles as liturgical candles may have been made, and it may never have had any secular use. However, it is difficult to regard it as 'sacred' in the way that a spoilt Eucharistic wafer or old altar linen is, or even waxen objects such as saints' images, which if damaged had to be consigned to the ground according to Eastern practice (Rohault de Fleury 1883, 141). It seems better to regard the Furnells pot as the container intended to receive other items and materials, as the Oosterbeek pot must also have been.

The question is, what items and materials? A factor common to the directions in the penitentials and many of the relic pits discussed by Binding (1975) is the act of burning: several of the covering slabs were fire-blackened and the underground chambers or the vessels within them contained burnt material. It is tempting to see the layer of burning (G742) at Furnells and the contents of the pot (G754, 741) as representing an almost identical complex with *in situ* burning, but the layer is not contiguous with the pot and there is no evidence on the upper part of the pot that it had been subject to fire at any time after being buried in the ground.

The sequence of events seems to have been as follows: after the construction of the church, but before its first use, a fire was lit on the last pre-church surface, producing the ashy layer (G742); the pot was buried in a pit cutting that surface; and some of the ash was scraped up and put into the pot. The church then appears to have gone into use. In view of what follows it would have been entirely appropriate if the processing of wax in the pot had taken place over this very fire. The association of ash with the immediately pre-church phase is very suggestive, since ashes played a large part in medieval church consecration ceremonies. In the thirteenth century Durandus describes the use of ashes to form a St Andrew's cross on the church floor, from corner to corner of the building; in this the bishop writes the alphabet in the course of the dedication ceremony (Neale and Webb 1843, 122). More recent commentators regard this as a ritual of great antiquity (Frere 1901, 48; Muncey 1930, esp. 48), though the rubrics of the early *ordines* published by Frere, or indeed by Martène (1736–38, 2, cols 668–768), do not seem to specify ashes in connection with the writing of the alphabet. By the end of the Middle Ages the York Pontifical shows that the use of ashes was specified in cases where sand was not available (Henderson 1873, 59). Assuming that this was already part of the ritual in the pre-Conquest period, it seems reasonable to assume that the fire represented by the burnt layer at Furnells (G742) provided the ashes required for the dedication ceremony. Although there is no statement in any of the pontificals about what to do with the ashes after the consecration, it would be entirely consistent with the evidence of the penitentials for them to be collected up and placed *sub altare* or in a *sacrarium* (below, and see Parsons 1986, 112–13): hence the scraping up of the ashy layer G742 partly to fill the pot (above). Ashes were further used in the dedication ritual to mix with holy water, together with salt and wine, for the aspersion of the altar and the building itself. As early as the Egbert Pontifical there is an instruction to empty the remains of this mixture at the base of the altar (Greenwell 1853, 39). This indicates another possible reason for the deposition of ashes in the Furnells pot and, incidentally, another possible source for the tartaric acid identified in the analysis of the residues. The fourteenth-century order in BL Lansdowne MS 451 for including relics in the altar further specifies that ashes from the censing of the altar should be deposited in the piscina (Frere 1901, 90–91).

It seems likely, therefore, that the pot and its contents and the surrounding ashy layer were closely associated with the church dedication ceremony. This suggests a further refinement in the interpretation of the primary function of the pot. The consecration service demands the use of twelve candles, and it may have been these that were being prepared when the conflagration occurred.

It is possible that the pot continued to be used in the first phase of the church, but there is no further evidence for burning, which invites comparison with certain of the continental examples. There was no mention in Glazema (1949) of any burning associated with the Oosterbeek pot, nor was there in the case of Höllstein. The excavator of the latter regarded the feature as a drainage pipe for holy water from the font (List 1967, 33) while the Oosterbeek pot was interpreted in the same way, and labelled *sacrarium* (Glazema 1949, 46–8, esp 47). The meaning of *sacrarium* is not straightforward, and is discussed in detail in Parsons (1986); it is, however, possible to say that in many English medieval texts the word is the equivalent of 'piscina' in its modern use. That is to say, it indicates some sort of drain for the ablution water. Ablutions and piscinas have been discussed in great detail by Lockton (1920, chapters VIII and IX) and in the anonymous article in the *Ecclesiologist* for 1848, and it is inappropriate to rehearse all the arguments here. Suffice it to say that at various stages in the Middle Ages, celebrants at the Mass ritually washed their hands before, during and after the service, and in some rites the chalice was also washed with water. The product of these ablutions, water with traces of consecrated wafer or wine, had to be disposed of within the church itself, and usually near to the altar. Early texts do not envisage what we understand by the word 'piscina' – the Frankish Missal specifies that ablutions should be poured into the baptistery (Lockton 1920, 121), but by the time of the Constitutions of Cluny in the late eleventh century there had developed a special 'hollow place made of brick tiles' near the altar (Lockton 1920, 123; Anon 1848, 338); elsewhere in the text this is called *piscina*.

The interpretation of the Höllstein, Oosterbeek and Furnells features as ablution drains is entirely consistent with the lack of burning directly associated with them, though the texts make it plain that burnt sacred objects and ablutions were dealt with in the same way: some texts indicate that ashes should be put into the baptistery, the point being, presumably, that they could be rinsed down into the soakaway of a font exactly as they would be in a piscina mounted above floor level. In the case of Furnells, the excavation record bears this out. The upper parts of the pot were fractured after it had been put into the ground, but not apparently because of pressure from the laid floor overlying it (G700), which was not laid until after the feature went out of use. For the phase preceding the laying of this floor, it is necessary to postulate a perforated cover-slab of the Oosterbeek type (see Fig 69). After the breakage, fine, water-borne silt accumulated in the pot, which would be consistent with the constant pouring of ablution water into it. This water would find its way into the ground by seepage through the fractured base. There is one further English example, albeit of later date, of a more complete pot buried in a church floor. In phase K of St Mary's, Tanner Street, Winchester, a cooking pot of not later than *c* 1150 was found, broken but complete. It was in an irregular pit against the south wall of the sanctuary, close to the position now regarded as normal for a piscina. It is provisionally interpreted as the soakaway of a piscina (Biddle 1970, 303). In the Saxon period itself the only comparandum so far is the mysterious tank observed in the chancel of St Nicholas, Colchester, during demolition (Rodwell and Rodwell 1977, 31). Further examples of features which may be relevant are the 'rectangular cist-like structure sunk beneath the floor in front of the chancel arch', probably of thirteenth-century date, on Barry Island, Glamorgan (Knight 1976–8, 44) and the channel running north-south in front of the chancel arch at Ormesby, Cleveland (Brown and Gallagher 1984, 51–63).

The chancel of the early church

The noteworthy characteristics of the chancel added to the first-phase church are its extreme shortness, the internal east-west dimension being no more than 1.95m, and the feature built of limestone slabs against the east wall (G123, Fig 19), taking up almost one-third of the available floor space. Another example may be the trench found in a similar position in the twelfth-century chancel of St Wilfrid, Hickleton (South Yorkshire), which probably represents a robbed-out foundation of the same sort (R E Sydes, pers comm, August 1983). The initial suggestion, that the feature at Furnells was an altar base, with its implication of an eastern altar position of a relatively early date, now needs reexamination (Boddington and Cadman 1981, 107). There was a small amount of evidence for a second course of masonry, so that the feature may be assumed to have been at least slightly raised above the level of the chancel floor. It can hardly have been a conventional altar base, however, since an altar of normal dimensions would have appeared to be perched on the edge of the platform, which measured only 0.6m from west to east. Not only would it have been impossible for the celebrant to stand or kneel on the step in front of the altar, but the altar would have been at an inconvenient height for a priest celebrating at floor level. The altar itself could have been less high, but this would have defeated the object of the raised platform. Disregarding the evidence for a second course of stones, which was admittedly slight, the feature could be regarded as a simple altar foundation at floor level, but in this case what was the purpose in extending it beyond the altar area to meet the north (and presumably the south) chancel wall?

A more general objection to an altar in this position, whether on a raised platform or at floor level, is the small amount of floor space remaining in the chancel. The distance between its edge and the chancel arch was only about 1.3m, and although the chancel seems to have had ample width at c 2.7m, one or two items of movable furniture (eg priest's stall) would have so restricted the area that it is hard to see how the celebrant and the necessary assistants at Mass could have conducted the service with any dignity.

Bearing in mind the example of Reculver (Taylor 1973, 53), an alternative explanation of G123 could be that it was the base of a bench against the east wall. This could have accommodated with some degree of comfort the clergy serving an altar placed further to the west. The exact position of the altar is possibly indicated by grave G5233 (Figs 25, 26). If this burial is comparable with

those in the Anglo-Saxon chancel at Barton-on-Humber (Rodwell and Rodwell 1982, 299 and fig 6) the most likely altar position would have been the exact centre of the free area of the chancel, but there is no trace of a foundation here and the occupation layers are unbroken; moreover, an altar in this position would have been impossibly close to the postulated clergy bench to the east. The alternative position, at the head rather than at the foot of the grave, would have been directly to the west of the chancel arch. Unfortunately the evidence in this area was destroyed by the foundation of the nave/chancel cross wall of the second church, so this interpretation is incapable of proof. However, this altar position is one of the two implied by the pit containing the pottery vessel in the single-celled church of the first phase. It is therefore possible that the original altar position was maintained throughout the life of the first church, even after the addition of the chancel. The further implication of the new arrangements in the second phase (SP4) is that the officiant celebrated the Mass westward from a position under the chancel arch. This is at variance with the continental evidence. Especially in the Frankish church, the habit was to place important burials directly to the east of the altar on the axial line, which clearly would not have been possible unless eastward celebration from a position west of the altar had already been introduced. The arguments against eastward celebration in the chancel at Furnells have already been stated. Eastward celebration in the nave at this phase would have made the addition of the chancel unnecessary. Westward celebration at a nave altar makes perfect sense in the context of the infant burial, which was displaced to the north of the axis, thus leaving room for the priest to celebrate from a position directly beneath the chancel arch. In support of the notion of celebration *versus populum* in the Anglo-Saxon church there is the evidence of Eadmer's description of Canterbury Cathedral in 1067. In the chapel of St Mary at the west end of the church the normal orientation was reversed, and the priest, though celebrating eastward, faced the congregation across the altar (Taylor 1969, 106, §15(j)).

An assumed altar position at the east end of the nave may provide an explanation for another puzzling feature, the posthole G1522 (Fig 11). This posthole appears to have been respected in the laying of the stone floor G700 and thus seems to have been in use during the final phase of the first church. It would have held a post of no more than 160mm diameter, which would be consistent with a fairly light structure. It is possible that this post was one of the four corner supports for an altar canopy of the sort identified in the excavation of the Old Minster in Winchester (Biddle 1968, 270; Taylor 1973, 53 and fig 2). The Old Minster altar base was square in plan and the corner posts also formed an approximate square, but the canopy at Furnells – if it existed – must have been rectangular, implying an altar of that shape. Once again, the construction of the second church would have destroyed any evidence which might have existed for posts at the north-east and south-east corners of the postulated canopy. There is no posthole opposite G1522 to serve as the north-west corner, which tells against the hypothesis, though only a small error in setting out could have led to the digging of the posthole in the area later disturbed by the building of the second church. The hypothetical liturgical arrangements at the east end of the first church in its final phase are shown in Figure 24.

When the chancel was added, or soon thereafter, the *sacrarium* must have gone out of use. It was covered by the stone floor (G700), which was apparently contemporary with the chancel; the flooring slab over the pot was not perforated, so that the *sacrarium* could not have functioned regularly as a drain for ablutions. Once the floor had been laid there must have been a new arrangement but this was not discovered by excavation. The most likely position for the new ablution drain/piscina would have been to the south of the altar but the disturbance caused by the building of the second church would have destroyed any evidence there might have been.

The change in liturgical arrangements would have had the effect of increasing – however slightly – the congregational space in the nave. The space available in the single-celled building was very restricted. Whether the altar was placed over the *sacrarium* with the priest celebrating from the east side of it, or in the easterly position shown in Figure 24, with the priest celebrating from the west side, the length of space available to the congregation would have been only about 2.5m. If the bellcote had already been added, then this would have been reduced to about 2.1m. Given a nave width of 3.1m, the respective areas would have been approximately 7.8sq m and 6.5sq m. It is difficult to judge how many people the church would have held, but if three adults can stand fairly close together on one square metre the maximum capacity of the first church would have been 23 people (19 with the bellcote). This calculation disregards space required for opening the door, movement to the altar to receive communion, and so on. The actual number attending service would probably have been rather smaller. With the withdrawal of the celebrant into the chancel and the abandonment of the *sacrarium*, the congregational space could have expanded as far as the postulated canopy, giving an area of 8.6sq m. This modest increase of just over 2sq m could have accommodated a further six people. The spaces flanking the canopy have not been included. It is doubtful if they would have been used by the congregation, especially that on the south side, since it can be argued that the *sacrarium* would now be located there. The space on the north side, however, might have offered standing room to a further two people.

The west end of the nave

Against the west wall of the nave and parallel to it there was a relatively deep trench with two areas of heavy stone packing at the bottom (G2194, Fig 11). These are interpreted as post bases. The more northerly of the two areas included three upright stones which might originally have formed a socket for the bottom end of a post; they suggest a squared timber some 300mm by 400mm in size. Posts of such dimensions were clearly intended to support a substantial structure. This cannot have been a gallery, since the post foundations are very close to the wall. Although the posts were not quite symmetrically placed about the longitudinal axis of the church, the extent of offset to the south might have been as little as 150mm, so that a feature connected with the west gable

of the nave seems a reasonable assumption. The most likely gable-mounted feature in the context of a church building is a bellcote. There is virtually no evidence for bellcote structures in the pre-Conquest period, although one possible example has been identified at Corhampton (Taylor and Taylor 1965, 177 and fig 440), and one is forced to rely on post-Conquest examples as a guide to the form that the Furnells bellcote might have taken. In the twelfth and thirteenth centuries two main types can be identified. The first consists simply of an upward extension of the masonry of the gable, which may be supported by a single buttress in the middle of the elevation or by two buttresses, one on either side of the centre line. The second type takes the form of a small square or sub-square turret made of timber; in some cases the turret protrudes through the roof just inside the line of the west gable and is entirely supported by four, six or even eight posts inside the nave, but in others the west half of the turret is carried by the gable itself, leaving only the north-east and south-east corners to be supported on posts inside the building. The hypothetical bellcote at Furnells seems to be something of a hybrid. The two posts close to the west wall imply a structure only partly supported on the gable, but the overall dimensions of the bellcote postulated in Figs 11 and 24 (1.8m by 0.9m) do not suggest the second or turret type. Perhaps the posts may be regarded as performing a similar function to the flanking buttresses of the first type. It is unlikely that a bellcote could have been entirely supported by the gable of a wall whose thickness was only 0.5m, and a bellcote of this thickness would itself have been somewhat unstable. There must have been some thickening of the wall at about roof level, with the posts introduced to support the overhang and to lend rigidity to the whole structure. The church at Bisbrooke (Leicestershire, formerly Rutland), which was totally replaced in the nineteenth century, is shown by pictorial evidence to have had an internal buttress supporting its bellcote (Dickinson *et al* 1983, 28), and thus provides a parallel for the arrangement suggested here.

While this seems an acceptable explanation of G2194 from the mechanical point of view, how likely is it in the context of east Northamptonshire in the pre-Conquest period? In the absence of evidence for Anglo-Saxon bellcotes one can only argue from the distribution of post-Conquest examples. It must be admitted that Northamptonshire is not well endowed with bellcotes, considering the size of the county. There are five Victorian examples, some of which may represent earlier structures of the same sort, but only three genuine medieval specimens. These are widely separated from each other within the county, with Slipton, just west of Kettering, the nearest to Furnells. Of the immediately adjacent areas, Bedfordshire has only three or four examples, all Victorian; in the former county of Huntingdonshire there are six nineteenth-century examples, and three surviving or attested from the Middle Ages. Further north, the concentration increases. In the fairly restricted area of the Soke of Peterborough there are five bellcotes dating from the earlier part of the post-Conquest period, one of which (Peakirk) may be of eleventh-century date. Of the nearly fifty churches in the former county of Rutland, six have surviving bellcotes assumed to be of thirteenth century date, and there is pictorial evidence for at least one more before the period of Victorian restoration, which amounts to almost 15% of all the churches in the area. In Leicestershire the percentage is lower (about 5%), but this represents eighteen examples. These are attested by the mainly eighteenth-century engravings published by Nichols in his monumental county history (1795–1815). The fabric of many of them is now entirely nineteenth century, and only a few are still substantially in their medieval form, which suggests that the Victorian examples in other areas may be more significant than appears at first sight.

In summary, then, the areas south and west of Furnells are almost devoid of medieval bellcotes, the area to the east has only a few, while to the north they occurred with relative frequency. On this showing a bellcote at Furnells would have been slightly unusual in the context of the immediate area but not entirely out of place as a southern outlier of the Leicestershire–Rutland–Soke concentration. It has to be admitted, however, that there is no firm evidence for a tradition of bellcote building surviving from the Anglo-Saxon period, even in this area. Of the thirty examples referred to above, only three or four are assigned in the literature, either explicitly or implicitly, to the 'Norman' period. Only one has any claim to date from the eleventh century, though this is a potentially significant example. The west wall of Peakirk church, which supports the bellcote in question, apparently replaced the end wall of an Anglo-Saxon church identified by Taylor and Taylor (1965, 488–9), and attested as a possible early church site by its unique dedication. Here one might argue for the continuity of a putative pre-Conquest tradition, but, apart from this, historical probability lends no support to the interpretation of feature G2194 as the base of a bellcote structure.

The significance of the bellcote

The exact position of G2194 in the chronology of the church is not clear. Its trench was dug deeper into the ground than the nave walls and the stone packing was of a different character from the wall foundations, though this may simply reflect a difference in function. There are subjective reasons for assigning the feature to the second phase of the church (SP4). Space would be at a premium in the single-celled first phase of the church, which necessarily had a nave altar; this may have stood over the *sacrarium*, leaving little more than 2m of floor space between the altar and the bellcote posts. However, now that a forward altar position is also postulated for the second phase this argument can no longer be sustained. The chronological position of the proposed bellcote is important only in terms of the status which it implies: should this be assigned to the church right from the beginning or only in the second phase of its development?

The status of the church may be inferred from the so-called Promotion Laws, which may be contemporary with it (Liebermann 1903, 4): 'If a ceorl throve so that he had a full five hides of his own land, a church, a kitchen, a bell-house, a *burhgeat*, a *setl* and special office in the king's hall, then was he thenceforth worthy of the rights of a thegn' (Loyn 1971, 119).

Professor Loyn's article emphasised other items in the list of qualifications for elevation to the thegnhood, but it

may be noted here that the possession of both a church and a bell-house was essential to obtain promotion. The suggested bellcote on the Furnells church may thus imply that the owner was a man of substance with aspirations to becoming a thegn. In view of the manorial context of the church and its actual incorporation into the structure of the later manor house, it would hardly be surprising to find evidence as early as the Anglo-Saxon period for the seigneurial status of the owner. A similar argument has been put forward in connection with the eleventh-century tower at Portchester (Cunliffe 1976, 303).

If the bellcote may be accepted as a secondary structure, though there is no archaeological evidence to confirm this, then the church would appear to reflect the social progress of its owner. From being initially a simple rectangular single-celled building (SP3), no more than a private chapel, it becomes, with the addition of a bellcote and a chancel with clergy seats, a fully fledged – though small – proprietary church (SP4). Apparently the owner (now a thegn?) continued to thrive, or he was supplanted by someone of at least equal status, with the result that the church was totally rebuilt on a rather grander scale in the final phase.

Church and cemetery

In the late Anglo-Saxon period there were four legally recognised categories of church: chief minsters, lesser minsters, small churches with cemeteries, and field churches (Barlow 1979, 187). The chief minsters were the bishops' churches from which traditionally the pastoral care of the people had been exercised. In practice the diocese was too large a unit for effective care and in most cases the responsibility devolved upon the lesser minsters. There were, of course, many more of these but they might nevertheless be at some distance from a fair number of their 'parishioners', since they were usually associated with the centres of what had originally been large estates, and they often served very extensive territories. For convenience smaller landowners began at a later date to build private churches on their own property, but apart from the celebration of the Mass these proprietary churches could initially provide none of the major sacraments and had no claim on church revenues: both the services and the income were the prerogative of the minsters. Gradually the private churches managed to acquire the right to hold certain services and to receive the appropriate revenue for doing so. Commonest, probably because it was the greatest convenience to the bulk of the population, was the acquisition of burial rights along with the attendant 'soul scot' (Blair 1988, 8); hence the distinction in the laws between 'small churches with cemeteries' and 'field churches'.

The first church at Furnells appears to have started life in the latter category. Not only was it just outside the actual settlement area but it seems not to have attracted burials in the early phase. Burial appears to have begun after the addition of the chancel, and the two developments taken together clearly imply that the church was becoming more important both legally and in terms of its routine use. In the second phase it had cemetery facilities to offer the local population (for the extent of the population served, see p 67) and the slight increase in nave space resulting from the liturgical reordering might have allowed more people than the owner's immediate household to attend normal services. In the second phase of the first church, then, it was becoming more a public institution than a private convenience, and the building of the much more spacious second church – surely an abortive bid to achieve full parochial status – can be seen as a natural extension of this development.

The second church

The larger two-celled structure, which replaced the first church, offers little evidence for liturgical interpretation. No floor levels were preserved in the chancel, and the nave had few surviving internal features. There is no direct evidence in either compartment for the position of the altar at this period, though the change in the proportions of the chancel (length to width ratio internally 11:8) compared with that of the first church (8:11), as well as the gross increase in its length (4.56m as against 1.93m), suggest that the chancel of the second church was intended to accommodate the altar. Of the exact position of the altar within the chancel there is no indication.

The overall area of the nave was 2.5 times that of the first church (Table 6) but since the altar had been removed into the chancel, the whole of the nave would have been available for congregational use. Applying the calculation used above, the maximum capacity of the second church would have been 104 – a huge increase on the 29 of the enlarged first church.

The only significant feature in the nave is the posthole (G518) close to the west wall with its centre some 0.6m north of the longitudinal axis. The possibility cannot be excluded that this posthole is of later date. The interpretation of this feature is rendered difficult by the absence of any other posthole(s) or feature(s) associated with it.

In particular, evidence recovered during the excavation indicated that there was no earthfast post south of the axis to pair with it. Without assuming such a pairing, however, no interpretation is possible; it may be suggested that there was originally a second post, not earthfast but supported on a pad or base at ground level. This arrangement would correspond with that at the west end of the first church: the west gable and the postulated two posts could have carried a small bellcote approximately 1.6m square. If this were the case it would represent an interesting survival of the feature from the previous phase, but with a change from the hybrid form to a type more recognisable in terms of what has survived from the later medieval period.

The chancel arch of the new church was close to the previous one but not exactly in the same position (Figs 21 and 25). Liturgical continuity has been suggested as a reason for retaining the chancel arch in its original position despite sometimes complex developments in other parts of a church structure (Huggins *et al* 1982). In many churches, however, the chancel and body of the church were built independently of each other and this provides an equally good reason why the common wall, including the chancel arch (though not necessarily the original one), might be retained through many phases of reconstruction. At Raunds the circumstances are different; the second church completely replaced the earlier building and the nave east wall of the second church would have totally destroyed the earlier altar, if it had stood in the position postulated (p 8). Apart from any considerations of demography and social status, the building of the second church must represent a liturgical new start. Previous practice seems to have played no part in the design of the new building, and the proximity of the successive chancel arches must be fortuitous or the result of other factors which cannot be determined archaeologically.

6 An Anglo-Saxon church and churchyard

At Raunds Furnells we see – with a clarity hitherto unknown – the initiation, development and closure of a Christian graveyard. Not only is the graveyard well preserved but also the church and, beyond the ecclesiastical boundaries, the manor and village. The potential for interpretation of this church and churchyard is as yet by no means exhausted. It will only be so when it is integrated into a comprehensive interpretation of the development of the Raunds area, and the church and manor in late Anglo-Saxon England. Nevertheless, even at this stage, it has been possible to suggest interpretations which contribute to the archaeology of Anglo-Saxon churches, the archaeology of liturgy, and the archaeology of graveyards.

Furnells can be counted among a number of recent excavations which have substantially expanded our knowledge of the pre-Conquest church. Archaeological and documented evidence demonstrates in unison both the frequency of pre-Conquest church provision at the village level and its close association with manors and other sites of elevated status. Some churches are documented as private foundations (Morris 1983, 63ff), while others occur in a clear topographical association with manors or other centres of authority. Where the documented evidence cannot establish whether the manor was drawn to an existing church site, or whether the church was founded adjacent to the manor, the task must fall to archaeological evidence. At Furnells, the church can be seen as an integral part of a settlement that was formally laid out from the late seventh century and that developed topographically by steady adaptation of the enclosure established at that date. The church was founded close to a large timber building which was subsequently replaced by an aisled building. Once redundant, the church became an ancillary, presumably residential, building which continued in use alongside the now stone-founded manor which replaced the aisled building. Finally the remnants of the church were incorporated into the manor house itself during the late medieval period.

Who was responsible for founding the church and its graveyard? This development would seem an incontrovertible example of the seigneurial provision of a church. Indeed, as David Parsons has outlined (p 65), such a provision was one of the key attributes to be gained by those desiring the status of a thegn in late Anglo-Saxon England. The responsibility must then fall to a predecessor of the Burgred who held Furnells at the Norman Conquest. The grave under the cabled slab, with perhaps a cross at its head, is a clear candidate for the 'founder's grave'. It remained isolated and respected until the establishment of the second church, at which point the cross was broken up for use as building material.

The first tiny unicellular church was without a graveyard and must be viewed as a field chapel. The addition of a churchyard may also reflect the rising status of its owner. Alternatively it might be related to a more general reorganisation of burial and ecclesiastical provision in the later Anglo-Saxon period. With the establishment of the graveyard, one third of the thegn's tithe would have been diverted to the church (Laws of Edgar 959–63, Whitelock 1955, 395; 2). For a church without a graveyard, the tithe went to the mother church and the thegn paid the priest whatever he chose (Whitelock 1955, 395; 2.1). The minster church was probably at nearby Higham, but the ecclesiastical structure of East Northamptonshire has as yet to be fully studied (but see Franklin 1982).

Although privately founded, the church appears to have served a broader community than just those living within the manor house itself. Making assumptions about the length of use of the graveyard, and cutting through some of the more difficult problems of palaeodemographic estimation (Boddington 1982c), it may be argued that the population served by the church was in the order of 40 individuals, of whom about half were adults. The demographic structure was very typical of that expected for a pre-industrial population. This suggests that a representative cross-section of the local community was buried here. David Parsons' estimates of absolute maximum capacity for the first church (p 64) indicate that around half of this population (or all of the adults) could have attended the church at any one time, but 'shoulder to shoulder', in very cramped conditions. The provision of the second church, with its almost fourfold increase in capacity, must have been a welcome comfort for the congregation. Burial rite within the graveyard was varied. At the one extreme was the middle aged man buried in the 'founder's plot' marked by a decorated grave cover, perhaps also by a cross; at the other, humble villagers were buried, apparently in shrouds, with just a few stones for support or protection. This range of burial provision demonstrates that a wide social spectrum was buried within this churchyard.

Such a population, of c 40 people, is greater than might be expected for the manor house itself. It might, perhaps, be adequate to account for all the late Saxon settlement known and suspected from North Raunds village, though here it is somewhat on the low side. Certainly it is not large enough to have included the occupants of the remote dependent settlements, at least one of which has been demonstrated archaeologically to be of this date (West Cotton; Dave Windell in Dix 1986–7). Furthermore it is not known whether attendance and burial at the church were divided on geographical grounds – serving, for example, one area of the village – or, as seems more likely, on tenurial grounds, serving those under obligation to the manor; or whether in practice these two factors are largely coincident. Domesday records that four slaves, four villagers and six smallholders were attached to Burgred's manor (Thorn and Thorn 1979). The difficulties in interpreting this documentary source should not be understated but it may be noted that this number of individuals, with families, and perhaps also allowing for a bailiff and servants at the manor house, suggests a population of the same order of size as that attested by the skeletal population. Sixteen individuals are recorded from the dependent hamlets. If families are included, the total population of both Raunds and these settlements would have been too large to have been buried in this one churchyard alone.

Such a collation of documentary and archaeological evidence is, of course, tenuous. Nevertheless, it serves to define a scale of association between the excavated evidence and the Anglo-Saxon community. The buried population equates in size with the manor and its obligants rather than with North Raunds or the entire village or parish. It is therefore apparent that there must be more than one graveyard serving the Raunds population in the late Saxon period. Attention is naturally focused on the parish church of St Peter's, sited on the opposite side of the valley and just 260m distant, on land adjacent to the possible site of Burystead manor. Recent analysis by the Royal Commission on the Historical Monuments of England shows that this largely thirteenth-century structure conceals a large twelfth-century church (Hugh Richmond, pers comm); the origins of this before the twelfth century are unknown. There are, however, no known Anglo-Saxon architectural, cross or grave cover fragments from St Peter's. Previous interpretations of the Furnells church have favoured a model on the lines of the provision of two churches, one for each manor, as at nearby Aldwinkle (Cadman and Foard 1984; Beresford and St Joseph 1958, 53). Multiplicity of village churches is also a common occurrence in Norfolk (for example, Batcock 1988, Rogerson et al 1987). Such a model would envisage the Furnells church being made redundant in favour of an existing church at St Peter's during the twelfth century as a result of changes in manorial or ecclesiastical reorganisation. This may not, however, be the only explanation. It is, on the current reading of the documentary evidence, doubtful whether a manor house stood on the Burystead site adjacent to St Peter's in the late Saxon period (G R Foard pers comm). It is thus equally possible that there was only one church in the late Saxon village (Furnells), this being moved across the valley in a change of manorial arrangement during the twelfth century.

Dr Mike Franklin has briefly reviewed the documentary evidence for the Raunds churches (Franklin 1982, 31–6). At the Conquest the Bishop of Coutances held the six hides and one virgate previously held by Burgred in Raunds (ie Furnells). William Peverill claimed one hide and half a virgate held by him as a member of the manor of Higham that was previously held by Gytha. Franklin suggests that it is reasonable to assume that each of these land units had its own church. The churches of Higham and Raunds were supposedly given to Thornton Abbey at the time of its foundation by William, Earl of Aumale in 1139. While this is not mentioned in the abbey chronicle, it is clear that by 1189 they were regarded as part of the abbey's possessions; they were probably granted in the period 1139–57. But a church of Raunds was also given to Lenton Priory by William Peverill at its foundation, perhaps in the period 1121–38. Franklin concludes that the documentary evidence, while reasonably full, cannot adequately explain the two churches and the abandonment of the Furnells church. Both the documentary evidence and the dating evidence from Furnells and St Peter's are, however, not incompatible with Furnells church being replaced during the twelfth century by the new church of St Peter's.

These models of manorial and ecclesiastical provision are being addressed by the Raunds Area Project. It is therefore prudent at this stage to leave open the question of where the remainder of the late Saxon population at Raunds worshipped and where they were buried.

Burial at Furnells is secondary to the establishment of the church and it was tempting to see the first tiny building as representing a chapel for the exclusive worship of those residing within the manorial enclosure. If this was the case, however, this small building – just 5.5m long – would surely have been included within the enclosure itself. Instead, it is set in an external location, south of an access route leading to the site from the village and at a position where it could be seen from much of the North Raunds village area. It certainly cannot be argued that the church is set externally to allow for the subsequent introduction of a graveyard – for which there would not have been room within the manorial enclosure – as the church was set right against the manorial ditch and presumed bank. At this time, it would seem, there was no intention of providing a graveyard. The positioning of the church against a bank necessitated the infilling and recutting of the manorial ditch further west in order to accommodate the graveyard. This caused pressure on space within the manorial enclosure which was eventually eased by an expansion westwards. Although the ecclesiastical area was not bounded by ditches prior to the introduction of burial, the first church would appear to have had a sanctuary area defined by a variety of post markers. The archaeological evidence suggests that these posts were erected independently of each other. The character of the posts can only be a matter of speculation; perhaps they were wooden crosses erected by the congregation over a period of years, but more mundanely they may simply have been *ad hoc* markers delimiting the church area from the activities of the manor.

Access to the site from the east can be observed in the late seventh-century layout which had its entrance on its eastern side. This precise line of entrance was continued to the north of the graveyard in the tenth and eleventh centuries (Figs 5 and 25) and was later used by the central axis of the fourteenth-century east manor courtyard complex. It is in this topographical context that this first church should be viewed; it was a privately founded building set in a position which allowed public access. Further, it may be noted that the eastern access led directly to the hall in the tenth to early fourteenth centuries, rather than to any other building. As early as the seventh century a distinctive bow-shaped building sat within the eastern entrance. These factors all emphasise the long term provision of an important access route along the line of the northern edge of the cemetery.

Despite the tiny dimensions of the first church, the evidence it has provided of liturgical practice is of considerable interest. A burnt area might be associated with the consecration of the church; a pot used for wax production was reused as a *sacrarium*, then as a *piscina*; the new chancel was provided with a clergy bench while the altar stood west of the chancel arch. For the first church, and just possibly for the second, a bellcote was mounted on the west wall.

Little is known from documentary sources about the masons and builders of the first private churches. The method of construction of the Furnells church was certainly in stark contrast to the post-built hall erected at about the same period within the manorial enclosure, though largely local materials were used in the church construction. It is also fascinating to observe that even for the first tiny church, there was an evident desire for correct orientation; it was just 5–6° from true east and approximately 20–30° at variance with the existing buildings and enclosures on the site.

Christian cemeteries have often been viewed with some degree of indifference by Anglo-Saxon archaeologists and have not been thought to provide a range of socially indicative data comparable to that available from pagan period cemeteries with their accompanying artefacts. Close examination of the Furnells data has uncovered a wealth of information relating to funerary and social practice.

The wide variety of differing arrangements for burial suggests that responsibility for the deposition and covering of the corpse fell upon the deceased's kinsfolk rather than the clergy. Undoubtedly the incumbent of the church would have been present to perform the religious service – payment of soul-scot was made at the graveside (Whitelock *et al* 1981, 369) – but it would appear that the packing of the body into the grave and the marking of its position were not controlled by the church in any way. If this had been the case then a more uniform burial practice might be expected. Instead we are presented with an almost bewildering display of different grave arrangements which must largely result from spontaneous activities on the day of burial. This 'spontaneity' element makes all the more difficult the task of summarising and interpreting burial practice.

These difficulties of interpretation are compounded by both the partial survival of evidence and by the complexity of the processes of decay of the corpse. It is normally impossible in graveyard archaeology to develop a conclusive interpretation from a single occurrence of any specific phenomenon. Fortunately, the coherence of the patterning of many of the phenomena in the Furnells graveyard suggests that some interpretations are highly probable. The parallel-sided effect suggests that many of the corpses were wrapped in shrouds, or buried in narrow coffins, while burials with a non-parallel posture may have been dressed in clothing or loose shrouds. Bone tumble and stone arrangements indicate that many of them may have been buried beneath wood covers or encapsulated in wood coffins. Coffins were most frequent south and east of the church. For a small group of males – those exhibiting external tumble – burial was in all likelihood delayed, leading to advanced putrefaction before burial. The displacement of many of the larger bones of this male group suggests that they had been carried some distance to the cemetery. Their burial in the most popular area adjacent to the south and east sides of the church suggests that they may have been of some status within the local community. More normally, though, burial must have been soon after death, perhaps on the same day (Bullough 1983).

The treatment of several groups of individuals is of considerable interest. The most distinctively treated are the infants, who from sometime around the turn of the eleventh century were buried close to the church walls in the so-called 'eaves-drip' position. This pattern of burial was not uncommon at the very end of the Anglo-Saxon and at the beginning of the post-Conquest period (eg St Guthlac's, Hereford, Shoesmith 1980; Castle Bailey, Norwich, Ayers 1985; The Hirsel, Berwickshire,

Rosemary Cramp pers comm). It demonstrates the degree of emphasis being placed on proper baptism of infants at that period, which is reflected in the contemporary canon law (Johnson 1850). Rather than following the pattern of earlier periods, when infants were often not given proper burial, the Furnells evidence indicates considerable care being extended to the newborn. In contrast, less favour was shown toward female adults who tend to be displaced west and north of the church. This is a pattern of burial more known from Scandinavian countries (Gevjall 1960, Cinthio and Boldsen 1983–4) than English churchyards. In England there was neither legislation governing arrangements for burial of the sexes nor, apparently, any distinct social customs. Rather, it appears that the north side of the church was less popular for burial. That the north churchyard area was less favoured is clear from the higher density of burials, coffins, covers and markers south and east of the church. The concept of the north side of the church being the 'dark' side has been thoroughly explored by Muncey (1930) and by the Rev W L Gibson:

'The portion of churchyards lying towards the south, east and west are by the inhabitants of these neighbourhoods, and by those I believe of other places, held in superior veneration; being still emphatically and exclusively styled the 'sanctuary'. Hence it happens that there are scarcely any graves visible in that portion of our graveyards [that lie to the north of the church], except . . . where from the peculiarity of the situation, the principal approach to, and entrance into it, had always been from that side.' (Gibson1803)

It should be noted, however, that the north side of the Furnells church was in use for burial from the outset. The Furnells evidence does not support the frequently quoted folklore that burial on the north side did not begin until the south side was 'full'. It may have seemed more desirable to bury on the north side at Furnells as this lay alongside the access route to the manorial enclosure, reflecting what Gibson terms 'the peculiarity of the situation'.

Skeletal evidence records the presence of two lepers (5046, 5256), though the diagnosis for one of these is uncertain. Although these individuals were perhaps not severely disfigured, it is still of interest to note that they were not treated in any way differently from the other burials and that there is no evidence here of the isolation of lepers, commonplace from just two centuries later (Finucane 1981). In contrast, the man crippled by poliomyelitis and/or tuberculosis (5218) was buried with a stone in his mouth, a feature unique in this cemetery but which does occur in other cemeteries (for example, White 1988). He was also buried north of the church. One of the lepers (5046) was buried at the southern limit of the cemetery but there is no reason to suggest that this was in any sense a burial outside the consecrated area, as was perhaps the man interred in the cemetery ditch at North Elmham, Norfolk (Wade-Martins 1980).

Two skulls had cuts on the rear of the cranium. Both skeletons were male (5103/M/17–25; 5288/M/25–35; pp 123–4). One had external bone tumble, indicating delay before burial (5288); he was interred south of the church, near the doorway. Faye Powell's report, completed in 1982, interprets these as saw marks related to post-mortem examination or mutilation. In the inter-vening years since the preparation of this report it has been possible to compare the cuts with those on a group of burials from the pagan Anglo-Saxon cemetery at Eccles, Kent. This comparison suggested that the cuts result from sword blows (Keith Manchester, pers comm). The position of the cuts on both the Furnells burials is not incompatible with executions, but equally they might have resulted from combat. Certainly they appear to have been the cause of death of the individuals. This disputed interpretation demands further analysis of the cranial material. Unfortunately, these skeletons have since been destroyed in an accident (p 113).

Charcoal burials were common at the period of the Furnells graveyard but there were none at Furnells. There is increasing evidence that true charcoal burials, those on a thick bed of charcoal, were restricted to the more important or urban churchyards. They are of im-portance to us here, as it seems possible that the deposits of charcoal were placed in the coffins of cadavers for whom burial was to be delayed. At Furnells there were a few corpses who quite clearly were interred many days after death; in these cases the bones had become dra-matically displaced. The phenomenon of delayed burial is, at first impression at least, new to the later Anglo-Saxon period. There are no thick charcoal deposits in the burial grounds of pagan Anglo-Saxon England, nei-ther are there burials with tumbled bones. At that period burials were often interred away from an established burial ground, and there are many examples of individ-ual pagan inhumations and single family groups. In the Christian period burial would be expected to be in con-secrated ground and only at such locations could the proper religious liturgy be celebrated. There might thus be a delay in transport to a suitable graveyard. As Chris-tian graveyards must have been commonplace in most villages by the tenth century, delayed burial might indi-cate that the deceased was being transported to his 'home' cemetery. Alternatively it might indicate that the officiant was not on hand to celebrate the burial liturgy.

To what extent is the burial rite used in the cemetery part of a local tradition? No churchyard of the Anglo-Saxon period has yet revealed the sheer variety of stone arrangements present at Furnells. In the absence of cemeteries dated to the eighth and ninth centuries from the Raunds area, it is not possible to state whether the burials are part of a local tradition or a tenth- and eleventh-century peculiarity. Certainly, stone arrange-ments occur elsewhere. Primarily they are arrangements around the head – ear muffs or head supports. They occur in pagan contexts through much of southern Eng-land and by the tenth century are in use in churchyards throughout Britain. The examples are too numerous to list here, but amongst those recently published are St Peter's, Barton-on-Humber (Rodwell and Rodwell 1982), Castle Bailey, Norwich (Ayers 1985), Rivenhall, Essex (Rodwell and Rodwell 1985) and St Nicholas Shambles, City of London (White 1988).

After nearly two centuries of use, the Furnells church-yard was effectively full; few further graves could have been inserted without disturbance of previous inter-ments. Little is known generally of the processes in-volved in preparing a graveyard for its 'second generation' of burials. Here at Furnells the process was quite dramatic. Posts and markers were uprooted, crosses and coffins broken up, mounds levelled, and hollows filled with mortar and sand from the demolition of the first church. Few graves adjacent to the church can have remained marked after such a thorough reconfigu-ration of the graveyard surface. The shaft of a cross, which might have marked the founder's grave, was used for a door jamb in the new building. Perhaps the act of establishing a new generation was all the more dramatic at Furnells because it coincided with the reconstruction of the church and possibly with new ownership. It remains to be seen whether the preparation for a new generation of burial at other churches was quite as momentous.

The historical context of the Furnells churches is of some interest, particularly as it straddles the period from the Danelaw to the Norman Conquest. The parish of Raunds lies within the Danelaw established by treaty in 878, very much the period of construction of the first church. Regrettably the nature of the archaeological dating evidence does not allow precise correlations between historic and archaeological events. The church may have been established before, or after, the Danelaw – what is of note is that there is no evidence of disruption of ecclesiastical use of the site during the Danish period. In any event the period of independence of the eastern Danelaw was short, barely 40 years (Whitelock 1941) and, as John Godfrey has noted, it was the minsters and monasteries which fared worst under the Danish wars, 'while the parish churches . . . come off comparatively lightly' (Godfrey 1962, 283). Domesday records the transfer of the manor, eventually to become known as Furnells, from Burgred to the Bishop of Coutances at the Conquest (Cadman and Foard 1984). Such a large-scale reconstruction may represent the actions of a new owner concerned to replace a church which may well have long been considered too small for its congregation. The rough treatment of at least two Saxon crosses, which were broken up during the construction along with around half-a-dozen or more coffins, the occupants of which were unceremoniously dumped into pits in the north graveyard, might add support to such a hypothe-sis. There is also a lack of liturgical continuity from the first to the second church. It is, therefore, very tempting to assign the rebuilding of the church to this transfer of ownership at the Conquest. Unfortunately, the dating for the rebuilding is very poor. The rebuilding may date to the period of the Conquest or may be later. Whether the rebuilding is associated with a new owner and whether this is the transfer of ownership recorded at the Norman Conquest can only remain an open question.

The second church was well suited to congregational use as a potential parish church but this potential was not realised, with at least burial rights being removed – perhaps by the beginning of the twelfth century – and the church being converted to a new use some time after.

The church and churchyard at Raunds Furnells is a rare archaeological statement. It is rare because of the opportunity for total and careful excavation. It is rare also because of the early redundancy of the church, leaving its first generation burials largely undisturbed. Conveniently, we can see the preparation of the church-yard for its second generation of burial but that genera-tion is barely underway when burial on the site ceases.

The site is exceptional also for its context; the adjacent manorial complex and village have also been the subject of extensive archaeological excavation. No doubt as the Raunds Area Project progresses, and its constituent sites are prepared for publication, there will be cause to interpret further this particular unit of the landscape.

PART II   SPECIALIST REPORTS

7   Radiocarbon dates

by Andy Boddington

Nine samples were submitted to the Harwell laboratory for dating (Table 24). All were from the graveyard with the exception of <71> which is from the fourth layer in sequence within the first church chancel (SP4). Samples <71> and <119> are of charcoal, the others of human bone. Samples were obtained from Zones 1, 1A and 1B only. At the time of selection the zone pattern had not been recognised, hence these samples were primarily selected to date the church. In any event it is unlikely that internal phasing within the graveyard could have been determined from these dates on account of the short life of the grave-yard, about two centuries compared to the large standard deviation associated with the dates.

The dates were calibrated using the program CALIB (Stuiver and Reimer 1986). The results quoted in Table 24 are from 'Method B' which calculates the probability distribution around the radiocarbon age as a function of time. The relative probability areas provide an estimate of the importance of each age range. With the exception of the date for 5266, which is unacceptably early on archaeological grounds, the dates indicate a period of use in the tenth and eleventh centuries for the church and graveyard. The most probable 2σ range for an average of the cemetery dates (excluding the chancel sample and 5266) is Cal AD 978–1040.

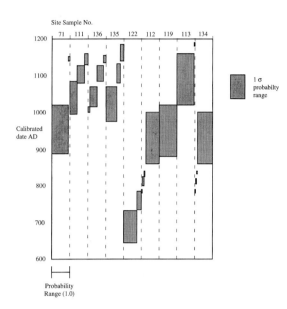

Fig 70   Radiocarbon dates from the church and graveyard; probability areas of 1σ range (Table 24)

Table 24   Radiocarbon dates from the church and graveyard

SP/Unit	Zone	Site (Harwell) sample number	Date BP	Standard deviation (σ)	One σ range	Probability area (1σ)	Two σ range	Probability area (2σ)
SP4/546	–	71 (5015)	1040	70	891–1037	0.96	781–789	0.01
					1142–1149	0.04	804–823	0.02
							827–841	0.01
							858–1159	0.96
SP5/5222	1	111 (5010)	970	70	996–1073	0.53	900–919	0.02
					1081–1130	0.33	943–1217	0.98
					1137–1155	0.13		
SP4/5299	1	136 (5011)	960	60	1001–1013	0.09	979–1216	1.00
					1016–1071	0.41		
					1083–1129	0.35		
					1137–1155	0.15		
SP4/5286	1/1A	135 (5012)	1000	70	978–1072	0.63	889–1194	0.99
					1082–1129	0.26		
					1137–1155	0.11		
SP4/5266	1A	122 (5013)	1320	70	644–734	0.73	581–592	0.01
					736–771	0.27	596–784	0.84
							786–883	0.15
SP4/5223	1	112 (5014)	1110	90	780–790	0.05	682–1042	0.97
					803–824	0.09	1092–1122	0.02
					826–842	0.07	1139–1152	0.01
					856–999	0.79		
SP4/5254	1A	119 (5016)	1080	70	879–1020	1.00	773–1045	0.96
							1089–1125	0.03
							1138–1153	0.02
SP4/5178	1A	113 (5019)	930	70	1022–1161	0.97	985–1230	0.98
					1181–1186	0.03	1243–1256	0.02
SP4/5298	1	134 (5020)	1100	80	782–788	0.03	710–749	0.03
					806–819	0.06	765–749	0.93
					830–838	0.04	1093–1121	0.02
					865–1001	0.85	1139–1152	0.01
					1013–1016	0.02		

8 The ceramic evidence

by Terry Pearson

The pottery was initially sorted in accordance with the stratigraphy and examined for change in composition and type variety between earlier and later pottery groups. It was possible to estimate the dating and development of the different ceramic types from the change of character apparent in successive stratigraphic groups.

There are eight assemblages of pottery of concern to us here:

(1) *Levelling for the first church* Pottery from layers beneath the church (SP2; Table 26)

(2) *Construction of the first church* A small set of pottery of late Saxon date related to the construction of the first church (SP3; Table 26)

(3) *Addition of chancel to the first church* A similar quantity of late Saxon material from the construction of the chancel (SP4; Table 26)

(4) *The churchyard* A large group of residual early–middle Saxon material derived from pre-churchyard contexts and included within the grave fills (SP20; Table 26)

(5) *Use of the churchyard* An absence of some late Saxon types which are well evidenced from the adjacent settlement. This negative statement reflects the construction of the churchyard boundaries and the consequent exclusion of contemporary ceramics from the graveyard and church zone.

(6) *Construction of the second church* A very small set of pottery from the construction and floors of the second church (SP5; Table 26)

(7) *Infilling of boundaries* A moderate quantity of pottery from the silting and infills of the churchyard boundaries (Table 26)

(8) *Conversion of the church* A later, small group of pottery related to the conversion of the second church to a manorial building (Tables 26 and 33)

The stratigraphic contexts for this material are summarised in Table 26. Pottery of the pre-church phases (*c* 450–850) will be further discussed, along with the later post-church material in the report on the remainder of the site (*North Raunds* forthcoming; see also Cadman 1983,107–22; Foard and Pearson 1985, 9–21). This present report is limited to the presentation of the data and discussion of the Saxo-Norman dating evidence for the church and cemetery, drawing where necessary on pottery groups from elsewhere on the Furnells site which have been included here to complete the ceramic sequence.

The radiocarbon dates for the graveyard and church have been detailed in Table 24. These dates are important to the arguments presented below because they provide a *terminus post quem* for sherds incorporated in soils used to level the area in preparation for the construction of the church.

The late Saxon pottery

The residual late Saxon ceramic assemblage from the church and cemetery is dominated by shell tempered St Neots type ware with a few sherds of the other late Saxon regional East Anglian pottery types – Stamford ware, Northampton ware and Thetford type ware. The bulk of the assemblage derives from contexts postdating the construction of the first church and predating the use of the cemetery. The radiocarbon dates indicate that the cemetery was in use during the tenth and eleventh centuries and the pottery suggests that burial may not have started until the second quarter of the tenth century.

New types of St Neots ware were introduced to the Furnells site from the middle of the tenth century. These were absent from the cemetery area, indicating that pottery was not being brought into the churchyard during the period when it was used for burial. In the light of this absence the church and cemetery sequence cannot be studied in isolation, hence its stratigraphic groups were compared against those from the rest of the site and associated coin dating evidence was available for the introduction and use of some of the common types. The sequence from the manor – the late Saxon halls and associated occupation – confirms the church and cemetery ceramic model.

St Neots type ware is present in quantity throughout the series, indicating that it was the more locally produced ware for this site and probably for the Raunds area as a whole. The composition of the groups show changes in the form of vessels and the technology employed in their manufacture. The introduction of the other regional types into the sequence can be seen against this background. This framework, based on a local tradition supplemented by non-local wares, demonstrates the development of trade in ceramics on the one hand and the evolution of the local St Neots type ware on the other. The sequence recovered suggests a model for the initial stages in the development of St Neots type ware which may be of more than local significance.

St Neots type ware

Pottery types R031, R055, R070, R075, R077, R093, R095, R144 A soft fired pottery with crushed shell temper petrologically defined by the presence of the fossil bryozoa (Hunter 1975; 1979, 230–40). The type has been fully described (Hurst 1955, 43–70; 1976, 320–23; Addyman 1965, 38–73; 1969, 59–93; 1972, 45–99). Although there is a lack of evidence for the early stages of the industry, its peak of production during the tenth century has been demonstrated (Hurst 1976, 323). Petrological studies of the fabric have shown that it is not possible to distinguish between different centres of production, though some regional differences are apparent (Hunter 1979, 230–40; 1975). The initial characterisation of this type identified a range of wheel-thrown types (Hurst 1955, 43–70). However, later work on the material from Eaton Socon led to the identification of handmade, 'proto-St Neots type ware' (Addyman 1965, 52–5; 1972, 78). The handmade types were of the same forms as the wheel-thrown types previously defined. Analysis of the groups at Eaton Socon suggested that the handmade wares were the precursors of the wheel-thrown wares (Addyman 1965, fig 13).

Study of the Raunds assemblage has shown that description of manufacturing techniques can be used to define the work of different potters and possibly the production centres of St Neots type ware (Foard and Pearson 1985, 13–16). The handmade pottery formed a higher proportion of the assemblage at Raunds than has so far been found elsewhere. This may well suggest that the manufacturing technique was as much a regional trait as it was a chronological development within the industry. Shell tempered or calcareous gritted hand-made wares continued to be present in the Raunds area throughout the Saxo-Norman period. This tradition of manufacture may have influenced the potters of the Lyveden/Stanion region who continued to produce handmade pottery from at least the early thirteenth to the fifteenth centuries (Pearson forthcoming). From the stratigraphic sequence of phases at Raunds it is possible to demonstrate the successive introduction of different forms of St Neots type ware (pp 77, 82–4).

Stamford ware

Stamford ware has been extensively described (Dunning 1956; Hurst 1957; Kilmurry 1977; Kilmurry 1980; Mahany *et al* 1982). A recent review of the Stamford ware fabrics (Leach 1987) provides a useful breakdown of the types and has been used as a basis for the classification of the Raunds sherds. Only a small quantity of Stamford ware was recovered from the church and cemetery. A rather larger group was found during the excavation of the surrounding settlement, though the proportion in relation to St Neots type ware was about the same in both cemetery and manor. While Stamford ware contributes little to the overall dating of the ceramic sequence, as the material consists largely of undiagnostic body sherds from unglazed jars or cooking pots, the fabrics can be ascribed to the late ninth and tenth centuries (Leach 1987).

Northampton ware

The excavation of a kiln in Horsemarket, Northampton (Williams 1974; McCarthy 1979) produced a quantity of pottery which has been identified as being of late Saxon date (*c* 850–1100). Major production was probably confined to the tenth century (Denham 1984). Five sherds of the base of a Northampton ware vessel were recovered from the fill of the ditch (G1293). This ditch was infilled prior to the creation of the churchyard, and the association of this type with St Neots and Stamford wares suggests that these sherds were deposited during the early tenth century.

Thetford type ware

Thetford ware was first distinguished from the earlier middle Saxon Ipswich ware, both of which were produced in Ipswich, by John Hurst (1956). Since this seminal work, the picture has developed with the publication of pottery from production sites at Thetford (Rogerson and Dallas 1984), Norwich (Atkin *et al* 1983;

Jennings 1981) and post-Norman Conquest kilns at the rural sites of Grimston (Clarke 1970), Langhale (Wilson and Moorhouse 1971) and Bircham (Rogerson and Adams 1978).

A few sherds of Thetford type ware have been found at Raunds and these from a limited range of forms – large jars with thumb impressed decoration. The type seems to have arrived at the site as individual vessels and occurs mainly in eleventh-century contexts. Two sherds are sealed by the east wall of the second church (SP5) within the top fill of the graves which underlie its foundations.

The twelfth-century pottery

A small quantity of twelfth-century pottery was recovered from the infill of the cemetery boundary ditches and from layers associated with the conversion of the church. These types of shell and limestone tempered fabrics (R100, R101, R122, R160) represent the introduction of new forms during the period between the Norman Conquest and the end of the twelfth century.

The thirteenth- to fourteenth-century pottery

Little thirteenth- to fourteenth-century pottery was recovered from the church and cemetery levels. These sherds were contamination from the period of secular use of the church and cemetery area. Sherds from the Northamptonshire industries at Lyveden and Stanion and Potterspury were represented in this material.

The chronological sequence

The chronological sequence of the church and cemetery is based on the stratigraphic evidence for the site. Table 25 summarises this sequence, equating the general activities with the specific structural phases.

Assemblage 1: Levelling for the first church

Prior to the construction of the first church, the church and cemetery area was perhaps in intermittent use for domestic occupation or other activities. The dating derives from the pottery which suggests that the main period for these activities was during the sixth to seventh centuries. A small quantity of seventh- to eighth-century pottery may be from the adjacent occupation. The features, including pits, a sunken featured building and postholes contained 199 sherds of early Saxon pottery (Table 27; SP16, SP17 and SP18). The similar quantity of contemporary pottery (172 sherds) recovered from the layers deposited during the levelling of the ground for the first church may indicate the extent of disturbance to the early levels caused by this activity (Table 27; SP2, SP2–3).

The small assemblage of St Neots type ware from these levels (SP2 and SP2–3), 17 sherds representing 15 vessels, is fragmentary and together with the absence of occupation of late Saxon date in the immediate area, suggests that the pottery found in these levels was introduced as rubbish in make-up soils derived from *adjacent* areas of domestic activity. Had complete vessels been brought to the site while the work was in progress and then broken, a higher vessel to sherd ratio would have been expected.

Table 25 The chronological sequence: sequence of events related to their specific structural phases

Assemblage	Structural phases	
Pre-church occupation	SP16} SP17} SP18}	Early Saxon phases
	SP19	Late features in SP1
	SP1	
	SP109	Ditch under churchyard (G1293)
	SP110	Ditch under churchyard (G633)
(1) Levelling for the first church	SP2 SP2–3	
(2) Construction of the first church	SP3	
(3) Addition of the chancel to the first church	SP4 SP3–4	
(4) Clearance for the churchyard	SP20 (residual)	
(5) Use of churchyard	SP20	
(6) Construction of the second church	SP5 SP3–5	
(7) Infilling of the churchyard boundary ditches	SP24/26 SP24 SP25 SP27	
(8) Conversion of the church into a secular structure	SP6 SP1–6	

The late Saxon pottery from these phases is all St Neots type ware. The dating of this type is difficult because it was produced over a long period of time and no site within the main area of its production has as yet produced any absolute dates (Hurst 1976, 323). The date of the introduction of this type has not been firmly established as sites within the heartland of its distribution cannot be dated earlier than AD 900. It has, however, been demonstrated that the ware was in full production during the early tenth century (Hurst 1976, 323) and, by implication, a ninth-century date for its first appearance has been suggested. St Neots type wares were found in Thetford and occurred in the earliest deposits, which were interpreted as commencing in the tenth century (Rogerson and Dallas 1984, 123). It would seem likely that St Neots type ware was introduced during the ninth century at the same time as the other Saxo-Norman types of Stamford and Thetford type wares (Hurst 1976, 318). This would account for its widespread appearance in early tenth-century contexts. For Raunds it is important to determine whether this pottery, derived from the levelling layers, occurs in the tenth-century period, during which St Neots type ware was being produced in considerable quantities, or whether it derives from the ninth century. It may reasonably be argued from the sequence of development of St Neots type ware forms and from the introduction of Stamford wares in succeeding phases, that the material in the levelling layers is indeed of the later ninth century. It is not, however, possible to be confident of this date given the small size of the church and cemetery assemblage.

A general model for the development of St Neots type ware forms has been produced by Hurst (1976, 320–323, fig 7.18). The early forms comprise small jars and bowls. The small jars representative of this phase from the church and cemetery can be matched to the early jars from the St Neots area (Addyman 1965, fig 8; 1968, fig 12; 1972, fig 14). The sherds from these levels all derive from small jars. The evidence from Raunds suggests that the small jar form was current for a period before the bowl form was introduced. Within the church and cemetery sequence the bowl form is first evident in the levels associated with the construction of the first church. The small group of pottery from the earlier level is not sufficient to suggest that the bowl form was not contemporary with the small jar. Indeed, the technological evidence (p 77) suggests that the production of the two forms was related. Two distinct manufactured types were present in this group (R031 and R055). The frequency of occurrence of these types is given in Table 27.

St Neots type wares
R031 Handmade, St Neots type ware (Figs 72:2; 73:8, and 74:12–15)
A fine crushed shell tempered fabric with an even fabric-body thickness of between 7 and 10mm. The orientation of the fabric grits in cross-section clearly reflects the coils of clay used in the construction of the vessel wall. The internal surface is corrugated with horizontal depressions similar to throwing rings. The external surface is uniformly smooth and even and not affected by the internal grooves. These features describe the process by which these vessels were made (Foard and Pearson 1985, 15, fig 7). The coiled vessel was probably constructed on a turntable. The uneven surfaces left after the coils had been pinched together were smoothed by revolving the turntable with the finger tips of one hand pressing into the internal surface while the external surface was supported and smoothed by the palm of the other hand. The colour of this type consistently contrasts with the wider range of R055. The fabric core is uniformly black in colour while the surfaces vary from a grey-buff to pink colour. In some cases the internal surface is black. In other respects the type is similar to that described by Hurst (1955, 44).

R055 Handmade, St Neots type ware (Figs 71:1; 72:3–7; 73:9–11; 74:16–49)
Fine crushed shell tempered fabric, fabric thickness varying from 4–6mm. Generally thinner and more finely made than R031. The pottery is still handmade on a turntable but the technique is refined to produce thinner walled vessels. The colour of sherds is variable, ranging from purplish-black to pink.

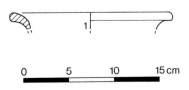

0   5   10   15 cm

Fig 71 St Neots type ware small jar from the levelling layers (SP2) for the first church (scale 1:4)

Table 26 Description of the sherds illustrated in Figures 71-75

No	Pottery type	Fabric	Form	Sherd	Description	Location
Figure 71: (Assemblage 1)						
1	St Neots ware	R055	Small jar	Rim	Fire blackened on rim	SP2, G2201, 2201
Figure 72: (Assemblage 2)						
2	St Neots ware	R031	Small jar	Base	Internally worn	SP3, G2188, 2194
3	" "	R055	Small jar	Rim	Grey-pink surfaces, worn internally	SP3, G2927, 2928
4	" "	R055	Small jar	Rim	Outer edge of rim fire blackened: ?lid seating	SP3, G1481, G1344
5	" "	R055	Small jar	Rim	Fire blackened on rim	SP3, G1481, 1344
6	" "	R055	Bowl	Rim	Smoke blackened externally and on rim	SP3, G1763, 1763
7	" "	R055	Bowl	Rim	Externally fire blackened to edge of rim	SP3, G2194, 2194
Figure 73: (Assemblage 3)						
8	St Neots ware	R031	Small jar	Base	Pink internal surface, leached	SP4, G1334, 1338
9	" "	R055	Small jar	Base	Black internal surface	SP3-4, G1744, 1777
10	" "	R055	Small jar	Rim	Pink-buff fabric	SP4, G700, 700
11	" "	R055	Small jar	Rim	Fire blackened on rim	SP3-4, G1745, 1745
Figure 74: (Assemblage 3)						
12	St Neots ware	R031	Small jar	Base		SP20, G2138, 5297
13	" "	R031	Small jar	Base	Internally burnt with encrusted deposit	SP20, G238, 5027
14	" "	R031	Small jar	Base		SP20, G172, 5015
15	" "	R031	Small jar	Rim	Externally fire blackened extending over rim	SP109, G2208, 1293
16	" "	R055	Small jar	Rim	Traces of fire blackening on rim and external body	SP1, G1636, 1637
17	" "	R055	Small jar	Rim	Heavily fire burnt externally and over edge of rim: the abrupt edge indicates lid seating	SP20, G220, 5024
18	" "	R055	Small jar	Rim	Heavy external fire blackening continuing over rim	SP20, G820, 5126
19	" "	R055	Small jar	Rim	Heavily fire burnt on and over rim	SP19, G2716, 2716
20	" "	R055	Small jar	Rim		SP20, G458, 5076
21	" "	R055	Small jar	Rim	External fire blackening extending over rim	SP20, G1134, 5214
22	" "	R055	Small jar	Rim		SP20, G917, 5159
23	" "	R055	Small jar	Rim	Fire blackened externally and extending over rim	SP20, G174, 5017
24	" "	R055	Small jar	Rim	Pink-buff surfaces	SP20, G411, 5068
25	" "	R055	Small jar	Rim	Slight smoke blackening	SP20, G1561, 5195
26	" "	R055	Small jar	Rim	Blackened surfaces	SP20, G1122, 5211
27	" "	R055	Small jar	Rim		SP20, G172, 5015
28	" "	R055	Small jar	Rim	Externally fire blackened	SP20, G903, 5155
29	" "	R055	Small jar	Rim		SP20, G270, 5036
30	" "	R055	Small jar	Rim	Orange-buff surfaces	SP20, G220, 5024
31	" "	R055	Small jar	Rim		SP20, G220, 5024
32	" "	R055	Small jar	Rim	Top surface of rim worn from lid	SP20, G1501, 5184
33	" "	R055	Small jar	Rim	Smoke blackened on edge of rim	SP20, G1501, 5184
34	" "	R055	Small jar	Rim		SP20, G820, 5126
35	" "	R055	Small jar	Rim	Narrow necked jar externally fire blackened	SP109, G2243, 1293
36	" "	R055	Small jar	Rim	Fire blackened externally with soot deposit on rim	SP109, G2243, 1293
37	" "	R055	Small jar	Rim	External fire blackening extending over rim	SP109, G2243, 1293
38	" "	R055	Small jar	Rim	Externally fire blackened	SP109, G2243, 1293
39	" "	R055	Small jar	Rim		SP109, G2243, 1293
40	" "	R055	Small jar	Rim	Externally fire blackened extending over rim	SP109, G2208, 1293
41	" "	R055	Small jar	Rim	Externally fire blackened on edge of rim	SP109, G2208, 1293
42	" "	R055	Small jar	Rim	Externally fire blackened extending over top of rim	SP109, G2035, 1293
43	" "	R055	Bowl	Rim	Slight external fire blackening	SP19, G1639, 1640
44	" "	R055	Bowl	Rim		SP1, G2451, 2451
45	" "	R055	Bowl	Rim	Rim broken horizontally following join between rim & body	SP20, G917, 5159
46	" "	R055	Bowl	Rim	Externally fire blackened	SP20, G993, 5166
47	" "	R055	Bowl	Rim		SP20, G1670, 5257
48	" "	R055	Bowl	Rim	Slight external fire blackening	SP109, G2243, 1293
49	" "	R055	Bowl	Rim/Base	Externally fire blackened	SP109, G1236, 1293
50	" "	R075	Small jar	Rim	Throwing rings visible on internal surface	SP20, G917, 5159
51	Stamford ware		Small jar	Rim	External fire blackening on rim	SP20, G220, 5024
52	Northampton ware		Small jar	Rim	Smoke blackened on edge of rim	SP20, G912, 5158
Figure 75: (Assemblage 6)						
53	St Neots ware	R055	Jar	Rim	Externally fire blackened	SP5, G499, 439
54	" "	R055	Jar	Base		SP5, G116, 116
55	" "	R144	Bowl	Rim		SP5, G541, 541
Figure 76: (Assemblage 6)						
56	St Neots ware	R093	Cylindrical vessel	Rim	Smoke blackened on edge of rim	SP25, G2365, 2362
57	" "	R051	? Handle (Unusual form)			SP24, G1351, 1259
58	" "	R051	Jar	Rim	Slight external fire blackening	SP24, G1351, 1259
59	Early Medieval	R100	Jar	Rim	Smoke blackened on edge of rim	SP25, G2365, 2365
60	" "	R100	Jar	Rim	Smoke blackened on edge of rim	SP24, G2858, 2842
61	" "	R101	Jar	Rim	Orange-buff surfaces	SP25, G2365, 2365
62	" "	R160	Jar	Rim	Thumbed decoration: externally fire blackened	SP24/26, G791, 788, 2326
63	" "	R160	Jar	Rim	Externally fire blackened	SP25, G2365, G2362
64	" "	R160	Jar	Body	Incised decoration: fire blackened externally	SP110, G633, 2039
65	" "	R122	Bowl	Rim	Thumbing round outer edge of rim	SP24, G1351, 1259
66	Thetford ware		Jar	Rim		SP24, G2852, 2842

Table 27 Distribution of pottery types by period. Assemblage 1: pre-church phases (SP16-18) and levelling for the church construction (SP2, 2-3)

Pottery type	Form	SP16	SP17	SP18	SP2	SP2 – 3
Pre-church	(All forms)	47	14	138	164	8
St Neots R031	Small jars	–	–	–	3	1
St Neots R055	Small jars	–	–	1	11	2
Total sherds		**47**	**14**	**139**	**178**	**11**

Assemblage 2: Construction of the first church

Pottery was recovered from levels stratigraphically related to the construction of the first church (SP3). Late Saxon St Neots type ware was recovered from:

– The wall foundation course (G1344)
– The pit at the west end of the nave (G2194)
– Layers within the church (G2129, G2691, and G2928).
– Contemporary external layers (G1763 and G1744)

Table 28 Distribution of pottery types. Assemblage 2: layers associated with the construction of the first church (SP3)

Pottery type	Form	SP3
Pre-church	(All forms)	43
St Neots type R031	Small jars	2
St Neots type R055	Small jars	17
St Neots type R055	Bowls	6
Total sherds		**68**

The small jar forms can be likened to those from the preceding phase and were present in all layers that produced pottery (Table 28). The fragmentary nature of the jar sherds, 19 sherds representing 17 vessels, is a further point of similarity which suggests that this material was cast up from the levelling soils. Not all the pottery was residual, however; the bowl form is a new addition to the range of pottery at this phase. A restorable complete St Neots type ware small jar was recovered from a pit set in the floor of the east part of the nave. This vessel (G745), described elsewhere (p 94), provides us with an example of the complete form of the early small jars common in this phase.

The bowl form was absent in the pre-church levelling phase (Table 27) but is present in small quantities in the layers associated with the construction of the church (Table 28). The introduction of the bowl form is generally seen as a development that took place in Thetford ware during the tenth century (Hurst 1976; Rogerson and Dallas 1984) and in Stamford ware (Kilmurry 1977), although it must be accepted that this dating may be due to a lack of securely dated groups belonging to the preceding century. Addyman has shown that the St Neots ware bowl form with the inturned rim was present in the earliest deposits in the St Neots area, although here also there was a dearth of dating evidence (Addyman

1965; 1969; 1972). The small jar forms of type R031 are not so refined as those of type R055 and it is assumed that these may represent different production centres, with the former type possibly being slightly earlier (or situated further away from Raunds). The bowl forms belong to type R055 and the analysis of the manufacturing method of the early bowl forms from Raunds has shown that it was a natural development of the method used in the construction of the small jar (p 90).

In summary, although the quantity of evidence is small, it would appear that the bowl form was introduced to Raunds later than the small jar. This statement can be supported by the stratigraphy on the church site – the bowl was not present in the levelling deposits – but cannot be confirmed on the adjacent settlement. In view of the small quantity of material recovered, the absence of the bowl form cannot be considered as evidence of its lack of production. Whether this observation is a reflection of the output of the industry or the tastes of the Raunds occupants is a question that cannot at present be answered.

While there was an absence of small finds from this phase, a fragment of bone comb was recovered from the external layers north and east of the church (G1744, [280]). The piece comprised a composite tooth segment with stubs of four broken teeth on each side beyond a zone decorated with ring and dot.

Assemblage 3: Addition of the chancel to the first church

Late Saxon pottery which relates to the addition of the chancel mainly derives from layers within SP3 and SP4. Deposits from SP3–4 are:

– Layers south and north of the SP5 church (G781, G1745; G1256, G1269, G1367, G1676)
– A layer within (G1777)
– The fill of a posthole outside the door of the church (G1733)

Within SP4, pottery derives from:

– Layers within the church (G136, G538, G546, G562, G700, G1338).
– Surfaces north of the nave (G450, G777)
– External layers (G2687)
– The fill of an abandoned grave (G1011)
– The posthole of a marker for a grave (G1291)

Table 29 Distribution of pottery types. Assemblage 3: layers associated with the addition of the chancel to the first church

Pottery type	Form	SP3 – 4	SP4
Pre-church	(All forms)	15	36
St Neots type R031	Small jars	8	5
St Neots type R055	Small jars	18	10
St Neots type R055	Bowls	1	1
Total sherds		**42**	**52**

This pottery group is similar to the earlier material associated with the construction of the first church (SP3), 43 sherds represent a maximum of 30 small jars and bowls

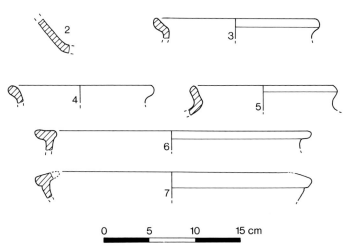

Fig 72   St Neots type wares from the layers associated with the construction of the first church (SP3; scale 1:4)

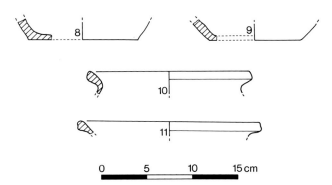

Fig 73   St Neots type wares from layers associated with the addition of the chancel (SP4 and SP3–4; scale 1:4)

(Fig 73). This fragmentary picture is in line with the condition of the sherds from the preceding phases.

Assemblage 4: The churchyard

The excavation of the cemetery recovered 1188 sherds of pottery from the grave fills, two-thirds of these belonged to the pre-church phase (823/1188/69) and one-third were of a late Saxon date (351/1188/30) and may have been contemporary with the first phase of the church (SP3). All this material predates the cutting of the churchyard boundaries, at which point the area was effectively sealed off and no more pottery was deposited until the conversion of the church building and the infilling of some of the boundaries. While it is possible that some pottery might have been introduced into the churchyard area after the cutting of the boundaries, perhaps in association with the burial rite, all the indications are that this was not the case. All the pottery from the graveyard is consistent with having been derived from pre-cemetery contexts.

The sequence starts with the earlier Saxon ditches which ran beneath the west part of the subsequent cemetery (Fig 5; SP110, G633 and SP109, G1293). These ditches were cut by the south cemetery boundary (SP27, p 14). With the construction of the first church, the south part of the enclosure ditch (G633) was infilled prior to the church construction, and the immediate

area was levelled (SP2, described above). The length of the earlier ditch (G633) which ran below the first church was infilled before the remainder of its length, which was not infilled until the area was cleared for the graveyard (Fig 5). Two sherds of pottery were recovered from the fills of this ditch below the first church. One of these sherds is early or middle Saxon in date and can be discounted as residual; the remaining sherd is of late Saxon St Neots ware (type R055) derived from a small jar and is consistent with the pottery from the levelling of the area prior to the construction of the first church. The similarity of the pottery assemblage from the remaining fills of the ditch to that from the later levelling for the cemetery suggests that with the establishment of the cemetery the southern part of the outer enclosure ditch was finally infilled. The character of the assemblage from the later ditch (SP109, G1293) is significantly different in that the pottery is less fragmentary and in greater quantity. This would suggest that it was infilled during clearance for the graveyard at the same time as the southern part of the outer ditch. At this point too, any bank present was levelled into the graveyard area. In addition, some soils may have been brought in to complete the preparation (below). The result of this process is that many of the graves contain late Saxon pottery, dating up until the creation of the churchyard. The stratigraphic evidence indicates that the soils resulting from the final levelling were in place over the churchyard before the commencement of burials. The absence of pottery which can be dated from the mid-tenth century onwards in association with this evidence suggests that a date for the creation of the cemetery may be put at c AD 925–950.

In keeping with its depositional history – first deposited in a ditch, then levelled into the graveyard, then incorporated into the grave fills – the assemblage was very fragmentary and widely distributed in the cemetery. In addition, the average sherd size was small and the majority showed evidence of post-breakage wear. After extensive comparison of sherds only two from different contexts were found to join, one from a fill of the inner manorial enclosure ditch (G1293) and the other from the construction levels of the second church (G499). The former sherd was extensively burnt over the edges and blackened while the latter showed no sign of this burning, suggesting that their depositional histories were quite different.

Table 30 shows the quantity of sherds of each pottery type recovered during the excavation of the phases associated with the clearance for the cemetery. Material from earlier phases (SP19, SP110 and SP109) has been included for comparison. Early Saxon pottery was present as residuals in all groups. Only about one-sixth of the early Saxon pottery occurred in non-residual contexts (SP16–18; 199/1254/16). The high quantity of residual sherds might reflect extensive disturbance of the pre-graveyard features. Alternatively, it is possible that this pottery was imported into the cemetery within soils used in its preparation. Analysis of the non-residual pottery from the pre-graveyard levels and that from the grave fills has shown that there are few fitting sherds and that different types were represented. This would seem to suggest that during the clearance of the graveyard, in preparation for burial, soil was imported into the graveyard area – presumably to help level the surface. Although there is a high proportion of residual early – middle Saxon pottery in the grave fills, there is rather less from the fills of the two pre-graveyard ditches (G633, G1293). While residual pottery outnumbers late Saxon pottery by about 2:1 in the grave fills (823/1174/70), in the two ditches the proportion is about equal (164/348/47). This perhaps reflects the levelling of the adjacent bank(s) into these ditches.

The late Saxon sherds represent one third of the assemblage (639/1926/33). The composition of this group is interesting as it reflects a range of the pottery types produced in East Anglia and the East Midlands at that time. The relevance of this group derives from its stratigraphic position between the construction of the first church and the use of the churchyard. The late Saxon pottery probably entered the churchyard as residuals in soils containing domestic waste. The overall homogeneous nature of the assemblage includes types which were probably current in the late ninth or early tenth centuries and excludes types which were otherwise common at Raunds during the second half of the tenth century. As such, a latest re-deposition date of AD 925–50 could be advanced on the basis of the pottery. The pottery types and forms which comprise this group would suggest that the clearance for the cemetery took place at one time rather than over a longer period as burials extended out towards the boundaries. There are some sherds which should be considered as typologically later intrusions, mainly comprising the Thetford type wares and one sherd of St Neots type. The remainder of the St Neots types are consistent with the earlier groups, although they probably continued to be produced well into the tenth century alongside the more developed types.

Table 30 Distribution of pottery types from contexts stated[1]

| Pottery type | Form | Early ditches | | Later pre-church features SP19 | Pottery from grave fills SP20 | Totals |
		SP110 G633	SP109 G1293			
Pre-church	All forms	33	131	183	823	1170
Late Saxon						
St Neots type						
R031	Small jars	3	20	11	57	91
R055	Small jars	15	123	62	262	462
R055	Bowls	3	10	1	13	27
R055	Lamp	0	0	0	1	1
R095	Small jar	0	2	0	0	2
R075	Small jar	0	1	0	1	2
R070	Small jar	0	0	0	1	1
Stamford wares	Jars	1	1	4	11	17
Northampton ware	Jars	0	5	0	1	6
Thetford ware	Large jars	0	0	0	4	4
13th – 14th century						
13th-century shelly	Jars	23	0	0	4	27
12th-century	Bowls	0	0	0	1	1
Lyveden/Stanion	Jars/jugs	0	0	0	3	3
Brill ware	Jugs	0	0	0	1	1
Potterspury ware	Jugs/bowls	0	0	0	4	4
Oxidised ware	Jugs/jars	0	0	0	1	1
Total sherds		78	293	261	1188	1820

[1]From the ditches below the church and cemetery (SP110, G633 & SP109, G1293); the later features in SP1 (SP19) and from the grave fills in the cemetery (Assemblage 4:SP20)

The Stamford ware fabrics were in production in the late ninth and early tenth century (Leach 1987, fabrics E/F and A/D?). The sherds in this group mark the earliest appearance of this type in the Raunds stratigraphy; they comprise a small percentage of the late Saxon assemblage from the churchyard clearance (11/351/3). They probably date to the latter part of the Stamford production period for these fabrics.

The largest late Saxon group of St Neots type wares are the small jars and bowls, types R031 and R055 (332/351/94). This group marks a continuation of the types present in the earlier phases. In addition, the sherds of a lamp and of an unusual inverted jar rim show that the range of St Neots type ware forms was starting to increase. Three new types of St Neots ware appear in the group (types R095, R075, R070); they are represented by five sherds and can be shown to be the products of a different manufacturing technique from the vessels of the larger group (5/1926/1). Although the source of these types cannot be identified, their infrequent occurrence at Raunds suggests that they are regional imports of St Neots type ware and so should be seen alongside the Stamford and Northampton wares.

St Neots type wares

R095 Wheel-thrown St Neots type ware

Finely crushed, shell tempered fabric with even fabric thickness varying from 2-4mm. This type is wheel-thrown and very finely made. A wide range of colour variation is apparent on the few sherds from Raunds, from purplish-pink to grey-black. The external surfaces are smoothed over but the throwing rings are still visible on the inside. Small jar forms.

R075 Wheel-thrown St Neots type ware (Fig 74: 50)

Fairly coarse, shell tempered fabric with even fabric thickness of 5–6mm. The type is wheel-thrown and well made with throwing rings and marks on the internal and external surfaces. An even colour range was achieved, predominantly buff-pink with slight grey patches. Small jar forms.

R070 Oolite tempered St Neots type copy?

Oolite tempered fabric copying St Neots ware small jars. Handmade, coiled, with uneven fabric thickness of 5–7mm. Reduced (black) fabric with smoothed external surface. Few sherds of this type have been found at Raunds and characteristics of the fabric are very similar to the early–middle Saxon types. The similarity of the form to the late Saxon St Neots type ware jars suggests that it could belong to the same tradition. However, until more is found its identification as an early–middle or late Saxon type should be questioned.

Stamford wares

The Stamford ware sherds in this group consist of fabric E/F, generally dated to the late ninth to early tenth centuries, and fabric A/D? (Leach 1987, 69–70) which was current during the tenth century. The occurrence of the E/F fabric range is a pointer to the early import of Stamford ware to Raunds, especially as this type is thought to have gone out of production during the early tenth century. The earliest date at which this type arrived at Raunds is clearly important to the dating of the

sequence, particularly the introduction of the St Neots wares. The earlier phases, from which came solely St Neots wares, suggest that this type was in circulation before the Stamford wares were introduced to the site. On this basis it is suggested that Stamford wares arrived at Raunds in the early tenth century; however, the resolution of this argument will ultimately rely on determining the date for the introduction of the St Neots type ware. The 19 sherds recovered from the graveyard represent a fragmentary group of the same number of vessels; one rim sherd of a cooking pot (fabric A) has been illustrated (Fig 74: 51).

Northampton ware

The six Northampton ware sherds from this phase represent a maximum of two vessels. Both are cooking pot forms, and one (Fig 74: 52) comprises the badly finished base typical of much of this type (Denham 1984, 55). This type is thought to have been in full production during the tenth century and the context of the sherds at Raunds would suggest that it reached there during the earlier part of the century.

Thetford type wares

The four sherds of Thetford type ware present a problem in that, while there is no apparent reason why they should not have occurred at Raunds during the early tenth century, their form would suggest a later date. All four sherds derive from three grave fills (G5285, G5297, G5209). The form of vessel represented by these sherds is the large jar with external applied and thumbed strips, normally associated with the later tenth or eleventh centuries. These four sherds represent a rare inclusion of contemporary late Saxon ceramics within the graveyard boundary, perhaps introduced at or shortly before the rebuilding of the church.

Twelfth- to fourteenth-century pottery

Thirty-eight sherds belong to the twelfth to fourteenth centuries and represent contamination of the cemetery contexts from the conversion of the second church (SP5) and its subsequent rebuilding as the later eastern manor. Of these sherds 23 fit together to form the side of a large cooking pot of twelfth-century date (Fig 76: 64). This vessel has been included to illustrate the type (R160) but derives from a disturbance in the top fill of G633.

Assemblage 5: The use of the churchyard

Radiocarbon determinations from charcoal and bone samples from graves (see p 72) indicate that the graveyard was in use in the tenth and eleventh centuries. In addition the general absence of pottery datable to the second half of the tenth and the eleventh centuries, apart from isolated instances noted above, is a further indication of the period of use. Large groups of pottery from the rest of the Furnells site can be dated to this period and their analysis has shown that the local traditions of St Neots type ware had changed significantly by this time. While the basic fabric remained unchanged, differences in the forms produced and the method of firing enabled the new types to be identified from body sherds as well as the diagnostic rim and base sherds.

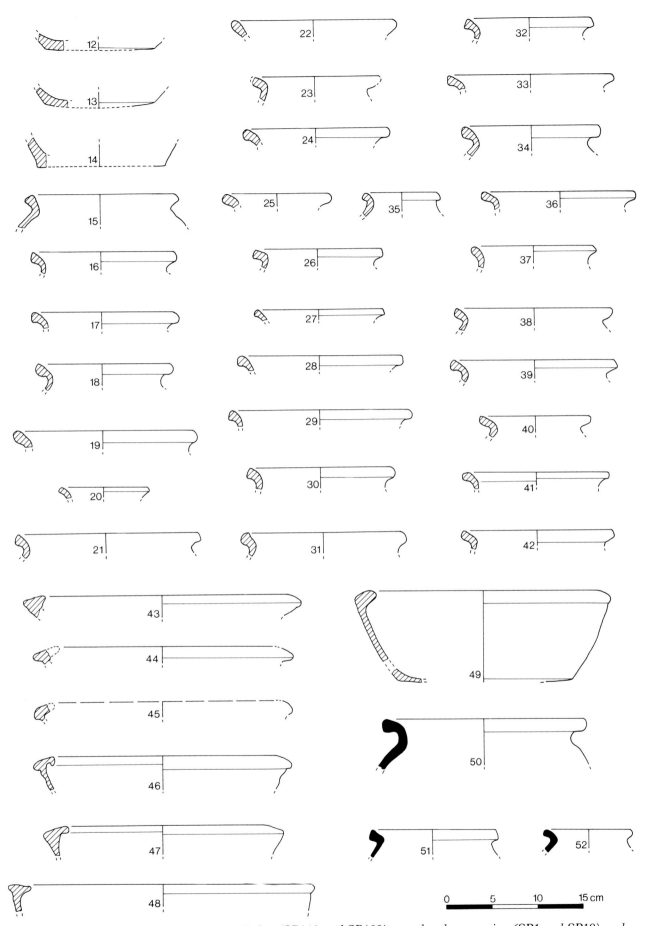

Fig 74 St Neots type wares from the early ditches (SP110 and SP109); pre-church occupation (SP1 and SP19) and from grave fills representing the clearance for the churchyard (SP20) [Nos 12–50]; Stamford ware (SP20) [51] and Northampton ware (SP20) [52] (scale 1:4)

Table 31 Distribution of pottery types. Assemblage 6: layers associated with the construction and use of the second church (SP5)

Pottery type	Form	SP3 – 5 layers[1,2]		SP5 walls[3]	SP5 construction trample[4]	SP5 floor[5]	SP5 layers[6]
Pre-church	All forms	0	5	39	2	1	8
St Neots type							
R031	Small jars	1	0	6	0	0	0
R055	Small jars	0	12	8	1	0	3
R055	Bowls	0	0	2	0	0	0
R144	Jars	0	0	0	1	0	0
R077	Jars	0	2	0	0	0	0
R093	Cyl.jars	0	24	0	0	0	2
Stamford wares	Jars	0	0	1	1	0	0
Medieval shelly	Bowls	0	1	2	0	0	0
Lyveden/Stanion	Jars/jugs	0	1	1	0	0	0
Potterspury ware	Jugs/bowls	0	1	0	0	0	0
Total sherds		**1**	**46**	**59**	**5**	**1**	**13**

[1]left column G559 east of church   [2]right column G542, G543, G1273, G1306, G772   [3]G116, G434, G469, G499
[4]G541, G556   [5]G429 west of nave   [6]G750

Assemblage 6: Construction of the second church

The pottery and small finds recovered from levels associated with the construction of the second church (SP5) form a mixed group which is difficult to interpret. The rebuilding clearly led to the redeposition of earlier materials as residuals. It would appear that some stratigraphically early deposits were contaminated with later pottery. The range of pottery recovered is shown in Table 31.

The range of St Neots type wares includes new types which, while present in the late tenth- to eleventh-century groups from the manor site, are absent from the earlier phases of the church and graveyard. The type R031 and R055 sherds can be considered as residuals in this group, although these fabrics and forms may have continued in production into the second half of the tenth century. St Neots type R093 represents a developed form of cylindrical vessel with flanged rim: (an example from infilling of the cemetery ditches is illustrated (Fig 76: 56; see reconstruction drawing in Fig 77, R093). The size and condition of these sherds suggested that

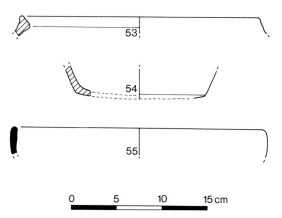

Fig 75   St Neots type wares from layers associated with the construction of the second church (SP5; scale 1:4)

they had been trampled into the destruction and construction layers. The condition of these sherds differs from the remainder of the assemblage in that they derive from one vessel. This narrow dispersal pattern would suggest the vessel was probably broken while in use on the site. The first datable occurrence of this type is in the fill of a gully from the adjacent settlement (SP115) in association with a coin of Edgar (AD 959–75). This was probably removed out of circulation shortly after AD 973 (Archibald forthcoming). This would suggest that the type was introduced in the middle of the tenth century, although the excavated evidence from Raunds indicates that it was not dominant until the late tenth or eleventh century.

St Neots type wares

R093 Wheel-thrown St Neots type ware (Fig 76: 56, Fig 77, reconstruction drawing)

Finely crushed, shell tempered fabric with even wall thickness varying between 5 and 6mm. The vessels are wheel-thrown. The internal surfaces tend to be unslipped with the grits protruding. Fewer shell grits appear on the external surface, which was slipped during the throwing process, probably incidentally, as the wet clay was drawn out over the grits during the smoothing of the surface. The colour range of this type is narrower, the majority of sherds being a grey-brown colour throughout with buff-orange-brown patches on the external, and less frequently on the internal surfaces. Throwing rings are visible on the internal and external surfaces. The bases may have been added separately as they show no sign of having been removed from the wheel head nor do they bear the marks of having been formed on the wheel internally. Indeed the uniform thickness of the fabric, with no thickening towards the outer edge, would suggest that they were not thrown. The rims were also made separately and added to the body. The principal form is a cylindrical vessel with flanged rim not unlike a 'top hat' when inverted.

Types R144 and R077 represent developments of the St Neots type ware tradition which at the manor site are associated with groups belonging to the first half of the eleventh century. These groups have been dated by the Stamford ware types that were present, particularly the type 5 pitcher, which has been dated to the later tenth and eleventh centuries (Kilmurry 1980).

R144 Handmade St Neots type ware (Fig 75: 55)
Smooth, soapy-surfaced fabric, with frequent crushed shell temper and isolated iron ore lumps. Variable fabric thickness 4–6mm, with thicker rims 8–10mm. Few shell grits appear on the surfaces which were incidentally slipped while the vessel was being made. The fabric is handmade with coil divisions visible in the cross-section. The colour range is from a fairly even brown-buff on the surfaces to the (darker) core which is grey. The principal form is a straight sided shallow bowl.

R077 Oolite and shell tempered St Neots type ware
Predominantly oolite tempered fabric with small amounts of larger shell grits. Even fabric thickness between 4 and 5mm with thicker rims and bases. Possibly wheel-thrown, but only the surface characteristics suggest that the fabric was made in this way as there is an absence of the throwing rings characteristic of this method of manufacture. The internal surface has grits protruding through the surface where the clay has shrunk back during firing. In contrast the external surface is smooth with an even clay covering. This slip is of the same clay as the body and shows where the external surface was smoothed over when wet, drawing the clay over the grits. The surfaces are predominantly orange to brown in colour with grey cores. Jar or cooking pot forms.

The twelfth- to fourteenth-century pottery is represented by six sherds and clearly represents contamination of the earlier deposits during the later modifications and rebuilding of the structure. The medieval shelly ware bowls were of a long lasting form which first appeared in the twelfth century but continued through to the early fourteenth (Baker *et al* 1979, 155–7; Steane and Bryant 1975, 61). This type probably developed out of the late St Neots tradition. The Lyveden/Stanion wares comprise jugs and cooking pot sherds. The manufacture of pottery at this production centre probably started in the late twelfth century and continued until the fifteenth (Pearson forthcoming). The sherds from this phase equate with material of thirteenth- and fourteenth-century date from the manor site. The Potterspury type wares first appeared in Raunds in post-1300 contexts and continued to be supplied until at least the late fifteenth century.

Assemblage 7: Infilling of the churchyard boundary ditches

A total of 248 sherds were recovered from the fills of the boundary ditches on the north and east (SP24), south (SP27) and west (SP25) of the graveyard. These ditches were only partially excavated which may account for the relatively low number of sherds found. Pottery was recovered from:

SP24 – North boundary ditch (G2858)
  – North boundary ditch (2nd recut; G1351)
  – North boundary ditch (3rd recut; G1349)
  – Post-north boundary ditch (G2932)

SP25 – West boundary ditch (G2365)
  – West boundary recut (G2361)
  – Clearance of the top of the west boundary ditch (G2169)

SP27 – South boundary ditch (G69)

The quantity of pottery types from the ditches is shown in Table 32. The west boundary ditch which separated the graveyard from the manorial compound produced most of the pottery while the north and south ditches produced very little (203/248/81 west; 22/248/9 north; 23/248/9 south). The composition of the overall assemblage is informative. Given its context, this material must be considered as essentially residual extending up to the infilling of the ditches. Discounting the pre-church Saxon pottery, the assemblage can be divided into three period components:

– The late Saxon group reflects the ceramic sequence associated with the church and cemetery rather than the more extensive range from that of the adjacent manor.
– The late eleventh- to twelfth-century material indicates the period of the conversion of the church and is presumed to date the infilling of the cemetery boundaries (in the twelfth century).
– The latest group of pottery can be attributed to the early thirteenth century and is seen as contamination from later activities, though it should be noted that there was continuing use of the cemetery boundaries on the west side and north east corner during the twelfth and thirteenth centuries (SP26, SP30, SP66 and SP67).

The late Saxon pottery
The late Saxon pottery in the fill of the ditch comprises 44% of the assemblage. The composition of this group reflects the range of pottery found in earlier levels belonging to the construction of the first church, the addition of the chancel and the levelling for the cemetery. These St Neots type wares (types R031 and R055: small jars and bowls) account for 82% of the late Saxon pottery in this assemblage and are identical to the material from the earlier levels. In the mid to late tenth century the evolved St Neots ware (type R093) began to displace the earlier types (p 75) and by AD 1000 formed a significant proportion of assemblages from the manor. Only four sherds of this type were recovered from the boundary ditches. The similarities and chronology of this group of pottery suggest that it may well have derived from the same agencies that introduced pottery into the cemetery at the time it was being prepared and laid out. If this is the case, the soils used to infill the ditches may have derived in part from the cemetery itself rather than from the manor. If this explanation is accepted then it suggests that the ditches were probably infilled from a bank – arguably formed from the upcast of the ditches – assuming that these were cut after the levelling and preparation of the graveyard.

R051 Later St Neots type ware (Fig 76: 57–58)
Finely crushed shell tempered fabric with soft slightly soapy to hard surfaces. Wheel-thrown with even fabric thickness. Predominantly buff to orange-buff coloured surfaces. The context of this and forms of this type

Table 32 Distribution of pottery types by period: from the infill of cemetery boundary ditches (SP25, 27 and 24)

SP Group	SP25 G2365[1]	SP25 G2361[2]	SP25 G2169[3]	SP27 G69[4]	SP24 G2858[5]	SP24 G1351[6]	SP24 G1349[7]	SP24 G2932[8]	Total
Pottery types (list below)									
Pre-church (All types)	1	46	22	11	0	2	2	0	84
10th to 11th century									
R031 St Neots type	0	5	2	1	0	0	0	0	8
R055 St Neots type	0	54	16	9	0	1	1	1	82
R093 St Neots type	0	1	0	0	0	3	0	0	4
R051 St Neots type	4	0	1	2	0	5	0	0	12
R098 Stamford ware	0	1	1	0	0	0	0	0	2
R074 Thetford ware	0	0	1	0	1	0	0	0	2
Late 11th to early 12th century									
R100	0	0	5	0	0	0	0	0	5
R101	0	0	9	0	0	0	0	0	9
R160	2	0	0	0	0	0	0	0	2
R122	0	27	1	0	2	1	0	3	34
13th century									
R114	1	0	2	0	0	0	0	0	3
R102	0	0	1	0	0	0	0	0	1
Total sherds	8	134	61	23	3	12	3	4	248

[1]*West boundary ditch* [2]*West boundary recut* [3]*General top of west ditch* [4]*South graveyard boundary*
[5]*North graveyard boundary* [6]*North graveyard boundary* [7]*North graveyard boundary G3176* [8]*Post-north boundary fill*

suggest an eleventh- to possibly early twelfth-century date. The small lug handle (Fig 76: 57) is an unusual form in St Neots type ware and may be of a later twelfth- or early thirteenth-century date.

The twelfth- to early thirteenth-century pottery

The twelfth- to early thirteenth-century pottery from the ditch fills accounts for 20% of the assemblage. This material can be generally ascribed to the period between the Norman Conquest and the beginning of the thirteenth century and consists of shell and oolite tempered fabrics (types R100, R101, R160 and R122) in cooking pot and bowl coarse ware forms, all of which were unglazed. The St Neots ware types continued in production well into the twelfth century. During the later stages, techniques of firing changed, producing a harder fired pottery than previously, and the jug form was introduced into the repertoire. The similarity of these shelly-oolite tempered fabrics to those from the thirteenth-century Northamptonshire pottery-manufacturing sites at Lyveden and Stanion has prompted speculation that some may have originated from there. This may, however, be spurious in that clays containing oolitic limestone extend for some considerable distance within the county and beyond (Brunier, see report in site archive). The excavations at Lyveden demonstrated the range of pottery produced during the thirteen to the fifteenth centuries (Steane and Bryant 1975, 61) and subsequent work in the nearby village of Stanion has increased our knowledge of the range of glazed wares. At Raunds, the Furnells manor site was dominated by the pottery from this centre of production and it accounted for over 95% of all the pottery used there during the thirteenth century.

Whatever the role of Lyveden/Stanion in the production of pottery in the twelfth century, it cannot be disputed that new pottery types were introduced from manufacturing sites which could not have been too far distant from Raunds. These new pottery types are quite dissimilar to the St Neots type wares in manufacturing technique, fabric, form and decoration, representing a new tradition which strongly influenced the later medieval industries in the county.

R100 Oolite tempered fabric (Fig 76: 59–60)
Fairly fine fabric with crushed oolite grits and occasional iron ore. The fabric thickness is variable due to the manufacturing technique. The pottery was handmade and coiled. Sherd breakage patterns and surface treatments suggest that while the body and base parts of the vessels were coiled, the rims and necks were made separately on a turntable before being fitted to the vessel at a point about 30mm below the neck. The external surfaces had been wiped while the clay was wet, producing a self slip that partially obscured the inclusions in the fabric in contrast to their exposure on the internal surface. The fabric is hard fired and the surfaces vary from harsh to smooth in texture depending on their treatment during manufacture and finishing before they were fired. In general the surfaces vary from buff to orange-brown, normally slightly darker externally, while the fabric core is grey to blue-grey in colour. The forms constitute a range of jar/cooking pot shapes in different sizes/capacities. The basic form is slightly baggy and squat, with strongly everted rims and incised wavy line decoration on the shoulder or upper body of the vessel.

R101 Oolitic limestone and shell tempered (Fig 76: 61)
Variable densities of inclusions are characteristic of this type. Rhomboidal oolitic limestone and shell fragments are visible on the surfaces. The fabric is hard fired, the surface textures varying from smooth to harsh. The pottery is handmade, coiled, with rims produced in a similar manner to type R100. The external shoulder and rim

of the vessels were smoothed over while the clay was wet, producing a self slip which obscured some of the grits. This was not a consistent feature of the production method. The surface colour is often extremely varied from buff-orange to grey. Cooking pot/jar forms similar to type R100 were produced. This type has many similarities with type T6 from Northampton (McCarthy 1979, 157).

R160 Shelly limestone tempered fabric (Fig 76: 62–64)
Coarsely crushed shell and limestone tempered with grits up to 6mm in size commonly visible on the surfaces and in the fabric section. Fairly hard fired with smooth to slightly soft surfaces. Handmade, coiled with divisions visible in the fabric section, demonstrating the hor-

izontal superimposition of the coils and the vertical pinching technique used to create a bond between them. The fabric walls are thickly made, averaging about 6mm on the body and base but slightly thicker on the rim. Dark brown surface with darker flecks and grey to black core. Everted rim cooking pots or storage jars. The shape of these vessels is different from those of types R100 and R101 in that they are not as wide or squat. Decoration consists of thumbing around the top edge of the rim giving a 'pie crust' finish.

R122 Coarse, calcareous gritted bowls (Fig 76: 65)
Sparsely to medium tempered fabric with shelly limestone grits. Medium hard fabric, sometimes with soapy surfaces. Handmade, coiled, in some cases possibly fin-

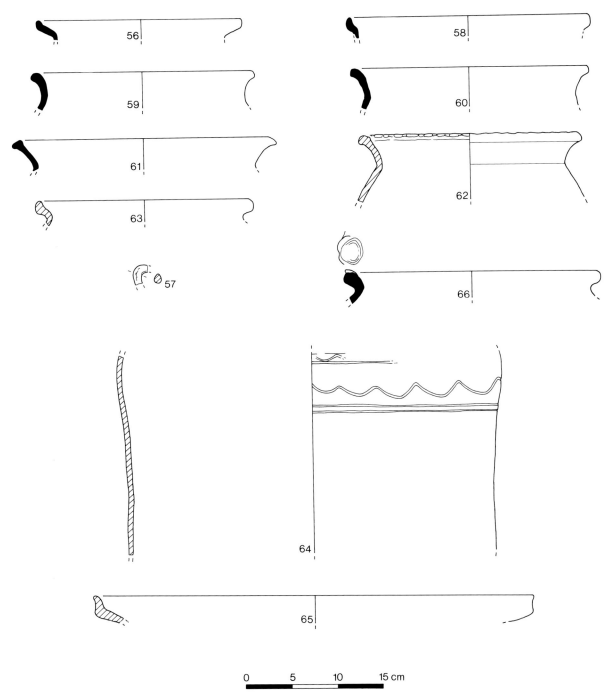

Fig 76   Pottery from the infilling of the church boundary ditches (SP24, SP27 and SP25; scale 1:4)

ished on a wheel or turntable. Surfaces smoothed over while the clay was wet producing a self slip which obscures to some extent the inclusions. The predominant form is that of a wide bowl with slightly everted rim. This form was produced at Lyveden throughout the thirteenth and into the fourteenth centuries (information from S Moorhouse), although there are differences in the fabric and its hardness. The occurrence of this type at Raunds suggests that it was in production during the later eleventh and twelfth centuries, which would agree with the suggested later dating from Bedford (Baker *et al* 1979, 155, type A10).

Thirteenth-century pottery

Only four sherds of later pottery were recovered from the ditch fills discussed; however, more material derives from the later use of these features. These consisted of thirteenth-century jars and jugs from Lyveden and Stanion (types R114 and R102). These sherds have been treated as contamination from the later use of these ditches, as three of the sherds were recovered from general clearing before the ditches were defined.

Assemblage 8: Conversion of the church

The small assemblage of pottery from the conversion of the church into a secular structure is not very informative as it covers a wide date range through to the thirteenth century. The contexts attributed to this stage were defined stratigraphically. Pottery was recovered from:

SP5–6 – Shallow pits east of the building (G547 and G764)

SP6 – Surface to the south of the SP5 church (G106)
– Wall across the SP5 church (G137)
– Posthole in Room 1 of East Manor (G288)
– Fills of the East Manor (G2462)

The pottery from these fills is shown in Table 33.

A total of 33 sherds was recovered; of these 23 (23/33/66) can be identified as residual, deriving from the earlier church levels, six sherds belonging to the eleventh to twelfth centuries and four sherds to the thirteenth century.

Three contexts produced pottery which could be attributed to the later eleventh to twelfth centuries. Within G137 a single late sherd could well date the construction trench for the wall across SP5 to within the twelfth century. Sherds were also recovered from G106, the surface to the south of the church, and G2462, eastern manor fills. In both these cases, however, the assemblages also contained later pottery of thirteenth-century date.

Discussion

Analysis of the ceramic evidence from within the confines of the churchyard boundaries allows the contexts to be placed within a relative chronology within the Saxo-Norman period. The key events of the church and graveyard sequence can be approximately dated as follows:

Late ninth–early tenth century AD	Foundation of the first church
Mid-tenth century AD	Addition of the chancel, beginning of burial
Late eleventh to mid-twelfth century AD	Building of the second church
Mid-twelfth to thirteenth century AD	Conversion to secular use

Of these, the last is the least secure as it is based on very little pottery evidence. In the event the small finds contribute little in the way of independent dating evidence and, apart from the radiocarbon dates for the burials and the stratigraphy, no other means of dating is available (Fig 77).

Within this period of the church and cemetery, the stratification reveals a clear sequence of introduction and change in both fabrics and manufacture and the pattern of development of St Neots type ware evidenced at Raunds makes an important contribution to the wider study of the regional Saxo-Norman pottery types.

Table 33 Distribution of pottery types by period. Assemblage 8: from features associated with the conversion of the second church (SP6)

Group	G547[1]	G764[2]	G106[3]	G137[4]	G288[5]	G2462[6]	Total
Pottery types							
Pre-church (All types)	0	2	0	3	1	0	6
Late Saxon							
R031 St Neots type	0	0	0	0	0	2	2
R055 St Neots type	0	1	0	3	0	3	7
Northampton ware	0	0	0	1	0	0	1
R051 St Neots type	0	0	2	1	0	1	4
Stamford ware	1	2	0	0	0	0	3
Late 11th to early 12th century							
R099	0	0	0	1	0	4	5
R122	0	0	1	0	0	0	1
13th century							
Lyveden/Stanion	0	0	3	0	0	1	4
Total sherds	1	5	6	9	1	11	33

[1]*Shallow pit east of church*　　[2]*Shallow pit east of church*　　[3]*Surface south of church*　　[4]*Wall cut across former nave*
[5]*Posthole in Room 1*　　[6]*East manor fill*

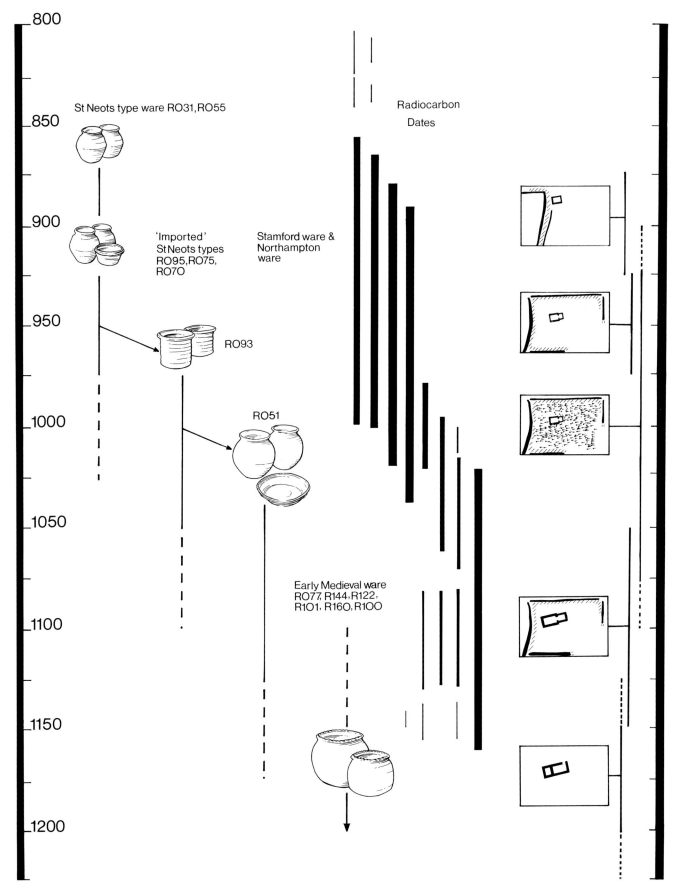

Fig 77   Diagram showing the introduction of the different pottery types to the church and cemetery by phase with the radiocarbon dates.

This contribution describes the evolution of the St Neots type wares that were supplied to Raunds during the early stages of the late Saxon period and marks the introduction of Stamford, Thetford type and Northampton wares. Two points are paramount in verifying the ceramic model of introduction and development of these wares. Firstly, whether the extent to which the pottery from the church and cemetery can be considered a representative sample and secondly, within what region a similar sequence has been identified. The series of late Saxon types was initially tested against the sequence excavated from the adjacent settlement. The latter assemblage was found to contain the same range of pottery although the overall quantities were greater. This established that the sequence from the church and cemetery was representative, but that there was a chronological discontinuity within its sequence representing the use of the graveyard, during which period it was bounded by ditches and banks and effectively isolated from the ceramic developments continuing on the rest of the site. Within a wider region late Saxon assemblages have been excavated at Northampton (McCarthy 1979), Bedford (Baker *et al* 1979) and St Neots (Addyman 1965). Although similar ceramic trends have emerged, these other sites lack the quality of stratigraphic evidence demonstrated at Raunds, hence the detailed sequence for the development and introduction of late Saxon pottery described at Raunds is at present unequalled.

The analysis of the pottery included the recording of the sherd size and degree of abrasion. Sherd size was calculated by the nearest fit method – fitting the sherd to a series of previously drawn out shapes (circle, rhomboid, square, and triangle, each with the same area) in graded sizes. Recording of sherd wear was aimed at looking at the degree of post-breakage wear. It was found that there was a higher degree of agreement between the results of different workers using a simple, three-stage classification. Three categories were used; 'good' where wear was visible, 'slight wear' where some rounding of the edges was apparent, and 'abraded' where the edges were badly worn. While these behavioural data have not yet been fully analysed, certain points emerged and have been used in the interpretation. These data are presented in the Level III finds catalogue; a synthesis together with comparable data from Furnells manor will be presented elsewhere.

In general the behavioural data have been used in the interpretation of the pottery in relation to the stratigraphic circumstances. The majority of the pottery had been introduced to the church and cemetery as residual material, particularly during the levelling phases. The distribution of late Saxon pottery in the graveyard provides some important data with respect to the way in which the levelling was carried out. Analysis of the pottery from the two pre-cemetery ditches, particularly G1293, showed that the average sherd size was higher and that the material was in better condition than that from the graveyard. In addition, there were more fits between sherds within the ditch fills than were found between sherds recovered from the cemetery. It was initially postulated that the pottery could have been deposited in the cemetery in soils used to infill the ditches and, from these dumps, spread across the churchyard. The distribution within the cemetery of the

pottery was plotted as the number of sherds per five square metres and the resultant pattern analysed. This suggests that the dumps of material were made to infill particular areas of the cemetery, rather than to form a general layer within the area which, in addition to the infilling of the two ditches, was probably carried out at the same time. The differences in condition of the sherds from the cemetery and ditches, with the former assemblage being more fragmentary, could be explained by the greater subsequent movement of the soils within the graveyard in contrast to the relatively stable environment of the ditch fills.

The table shows the number of sherds of each pottery type from the contexts of each stratigraphic horizon (Table 34). Type numbers have been omitted, apart from the different St Neots types, as this notation is used in the following discussion. The archaeology of the church and cemetery showed no evidence of late Saxon domestic occupation in the area defined by the cemetery boundaries. Although a pottery vessel was used in the church (p 58), the fragmentary nature of the remainder of the assemblage indicates that it was brought in from outside the churchyard enclosure. As has already been argued, the majority of the assemblage was probably derived from rubbish from the adjacent settlement which had become incorporated in soils that were imported into the cemetery during its preparation. It is also possible that some was used on the site during the various stages of the church construction, as indicated by the recovery of a large part of the St Neots type R093 vessel from SP5 (p 90). Following the introduction of the pottery into the area, it is interesting to look at the proportion that became reincorporated into subsequent levels through later activities. This is particularly important with respect to the pre-church pottery because of the numerically greater quantities that were recovered from the fills developed during the creation of the churchyard.

The main late Saxon pottery types used at Raunds consisted of St Neots type wares. The initial characterisation of this type (Hurst 1956) enabled its separation from other regional types but it has proved difficult to take this further to identify the products from different manufacturing sites. The wide distribution of the type and the general absence of excavated production sites has further complicated the problem. The archaeological evidence is limited by a lack of suitably stratified assemblages from within the heartland of its production. The Raunds sequence, providing both the stratification and a large assemblage, goes some way to remedy this. Its analysis has provided a model for the development of the industry within the region that supplied pottery to Raunds.

While the Raunds sequence supplied stratified clusters of material for which a relative chronology can be advanced, the problem of separating it into the products from different manufacturing sites remained to be investigated. Studies of the petrology of St Neots type wares showed that it was not possible to identify precise sources for the raw materials (Hunter 1979). The wide occurrence of the clays containing fossil shell and Bryozoa, the distinctive inclusion of this type, means that the same fabric could have been made in a region extending from Oxfordshire through to Lincolnshire. More subtle petrological divisions, reflecting more

Table 34 Distribution of pottery types: summary by period for church and graveyard

Assemblage (at right)	1	2	3	4 and 5	6	7	8	Total
Pottery types (listed below)								
Pre-church (All types)	371	43	51	1170	64	84	6	1789
Late Saxon								
St Neots type R031	4	2	13	91	7	8	2	127
St Neots type R055	14	23	30	490	27	82	7	673
St Neots type R095	0	0	0	2	0	0	0	2
St Neots type R075	0	0	0	2	0	0	0	2
St Neots type R070	0	0	0	1	0	0	0	1
St Neots type R144	0	0	0	0	1	0	0	1
St Neots type R077	0	0	0	0	2	0	0	2
St Neots type R093	0	0	0	0	43	4	0	47
St Neots type R051	0	0	0	0	0	12	4	16
Stamford wares	0	0	0	17	2	2	3	24
Northampton ware	0	0	0	6	0	0	1	7
Thetford ware	0	0	0	4	0	2	0	6
11th-12th century								
Shelly ware	0	0	0	28	3	50	6	87
13th century								
Lyveden/Stanion	0	0	0	3	2	4	4	13
Brill ware	0	0	0	1	0	0	0	1
14th century								
Potterspury ware	0	0	0	4	1	0	0	5
Oxidised ware	0	0	0	1	0	0	0	1
Total sherds	389	68	94	1820	152	248	33	2804

Assemblages
1 *Levelling for first church (SP2)*
2 *Construction of first church (SP3)*
3 *Addition of the chancel (SP4)*
4 & 5 *Churchyard levelling and graves (SP20)*
6 *Construction of the second church*
7 *Infill of boundary ditches (SP24, SP25, SP27)*
8 *Conversion of the church (SP6)*

localised sources such as other fossils and minerals, would probably not be sufficiently representative in individual sherds and therefore could not be applied with sufficient reliability to assemblages of material. The classification of the forms (Hurst 1956; 1976) outlined the main types of vessel produced but the possibility of regional or chronological bias provides a limitation which will not be overcome until the industries that comprise the tradition are better understood. Hurst has, however, shown that there are certain typological trends apparent in the evolution of the type and to a qualified extent these are confirmed by the Raunds assemblage. The Raunds sequence demonstrated changes in vessel shape through time. More importantly perhaps, changes in the way vessels were made, in combination with the forms, were found to provide a decisive means of sub-classification. This method in effect characterises the skills of the individual potter or group of potters rather than the identity of the manufacturing site. In essence, subgroups tend to be separated through time, although they may belong to the same industry, and represent the evolution of techniques or responses to new fashions or the introduction of potters with a different range of construction techniques. Each of the St Neots ware types described in this report embodied different techniques which in many cases resulted in subtle changes in the appearance of the sherds. The resultant picture in the early stages of the late Saxon period (late ninth to tenth centuries) suggests the existence of a local industry (R031/R055) which supplied the bulk of the pottery to the site with a small range of vessels which were probably imported from industries situated further afield. Numerically the quantity of these imported(?) types broadly equates with the quantity of other regional types brought to the site, such as the Stamford wares.

The ceramic model

The ceramic sequence derived from the stratified contexts describes the development of the local St Neots type wares alongside the introduction of other regional types reflecting the growth of economic trading links. The wider aspects of trade and economy will be considered in relation to the Furnells site. It is a conclusion of this analysis of the church and cemetery assemblage that the majority of the late Saxon pottery probably derived from adjacent settlement as domestic rubbish. It is important that the ceramic model, as far as it can be developed from the church and cemetery material, is described in more detail.

The earliest assemblage associated with the levelling of the area prior to the construction of the first church on the site comprised solely small jar forms representing two varieties (types R031 and R055) in the same basic shell tempered fabric. Two rim forms were evident, one with a rounded internal profile, and a second, slightly thicker, rim internally flattened probably as a lid seating. Examination of the sherds showed that the same basic method of manufacture was employed although the evidence for this was better preserved on the type R055 sherds.

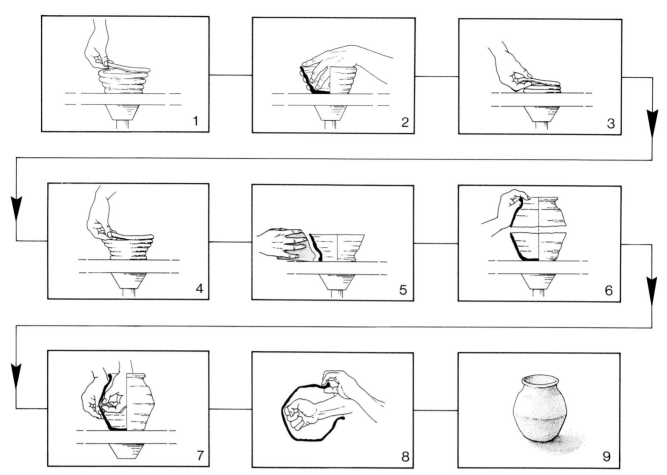

Fig 78   Construction method of the St Neots type ware small jars and bowls (types R031 and R055); the base and lower body were made in the same way for both forms [1 and 2], additional coils being added to form the bowl rim, which was then smoothed and finished. The rim and upper body of the small jar was coiled on a turntable [3 and 4] and probably finished with a template [5]. The upper body was then fitted to the lower body and base [6] and the join reinforced with a clay coil applied to the inside [7]: the jar was then inverted and the rounded base profile formed [8].

This evidence is identical to that of the early *sacrarium* vessel found below the floor of the first church (p 58). This vessel was complete and allowed the manufacturing techniques to be examined in detail (Fig 78). The technique involved the production of the vessel in two parts, the rim and upper body and the base and lower body, both of which were coiled on a turntable. The two parts were fitted together, forming a pronounced carination around the midpoint of the vessel. In some examples this was smoothed over and rounded to disguise the join. The concentric rims suggest that a template may have been used to achieve the consistent profile.

While the inturned rimmed bowl form was first apparent in the levels associated with the construction of the first church and the subsequent phase during which the chancel was added, it could have been introduced in the previous phase with the first appearance of the small jar. This form matches the shape and size of the base and lower body section of the small jars, which in addition to the stratigraphic evidence suggests the way in which this form may have developed. Indeed, the close association of the manufacturing methods used for both forms suggests that they were introduced at the same time (Fig 78).

The assemblage from the cemetery layers, which predates the commencement of burial in the area, demon-strates the continuation of the two basic forms. It has been argued that these deposits date to the first half of the tenth century on the basis both of the first appearance of Stamford wares and Northampton ware sherds and of the radiocarbon dates for the use of the cemetery. Some new St Neots type ware forms (including a lamp) are evident in this material, with size variation of the jar and bowl forms.

The next stage in the development of the St Neots type wares is marked by an absence of pottery from the cemetery. The dating for this period, during which burials took place, can be found from the radiocarbon dates. Pottery from the adjacent manor dated from the middle of the tenth century to the Norman Conquest demonstrates that new forms and new techniques of manufacture were introduced fairly rapidly. A few sherds of type R093, which is thought to represent a continued production of the main local St Neots type ware industries, were found in levels associated with the construction of the second church. In order to illustrate this phase, examples from a series of quarry pits on the manor site have been used in the chart (Fig 77).

Levels associated with the construction of the second church produced sherds of a shelly oolite fabric (R077) which is seen as a transitional type between the late Saxon St Neots type ware and the twelfth- to thirteenth-century shell tempered wares. This type is found alongside developed St Neots type wares (R051), and the two seem to have coexisted for some time during the later eleventh and early twelfth centuries. The infilling of the churchyard boundaries and the conversion of the church to a secular structure are associated with early medieval calcareous gritted fabrics (R100, R101, R160, R122) which introduce a new range of forms that depart from the styles of St Neots type ware. These types have been attributed to the twelfth century on grounds of their form and decoration, in addition to their clear separation from thirteenth-century deposits.

The ceramic assemblage from the church and cemetery provides a diverse range of information quite apart from its chronological significance. It is clearly important for establishing the chronology of the church and cemetery, but the sequence is equally crucial in the understanding and interpretation of the development of St Neots type wares. It is intended to pursue further the wider implications of this material.

9 The small finds

by Gwynne Oakley

The following is a synopsis of an analysis by Gwynne Oakley. Full details will be found in her main report (*North Raunds* forthcoming).

The graveyard

The small finds from the grave fills (SP20) are a fragmentary group and little dating evidence can be provided by them. Most are undatable but could belong to the early–middle or late Saxon period. The wide range of different types of objects suggests, like the pottery, that the artefacts are derived from domestic rubbish. None of these objects seems to have been deliberately buried with the deceased and the fragmentary nature of the domestic objects is largely consistent with their having been discarded with the pottery in soils which were used to level the cemetery area.

The objects are listed in Table 35. Details of specific objects of interest are catalogued below.

Tag or fastener (G5184 [260]; Fig 79) This hooked tag or fastener may be dated seventh to tenth/eleventh century by comparison with ornamental Anglo-Saxon metalwork published by Graham-Campbell (1982, 146).

Binding strip (G5016 [119]; Fig 79) This binding strip, which may represent a repair from a wooden(?) bowl, compares with an object from the Anglo-Saxon cemetery at Spong Hill in Norfolk (Hills *et al* 1984, 137).

Lead strip (G5210 [234]; Fig 80) One lead object was recovered, comprising a bent and twisted strip with triangular section, width 13mm, thickness 5mm, length 75mm. There are possible knife cuts near the twisted end. This object has been interpreted as possible waste from a window came.

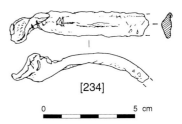

[234]

0   5 cm

Fig 80 Small finds from SP20: lead strip waste from possible window came (scale 1:2)

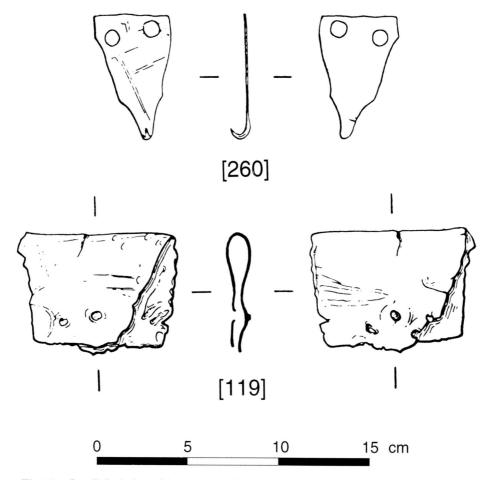

[260]

[119]

0   5   10   15 cm

Fig 79 Small finds from SP20: copper alloy tag or fastener [260] and copper alloy binding strip [119] (scale 1:2)

Table 35 Residual small finds in grave fills

Type	Additional description	Group	SP	Find
Iron				
Nails	Bent shank	G5028	20	[167]
		G5024	20	[168]
	Both ends broken	G5202	20	[249]
		G5274	20	[279]
Horse fittings	Bridle bit fragment, curved end	G5096	20	[203]
	Fiddle key nail	G736	20	[223]
	Part horseshoe with wavy edge, 2 fiddle key nails *in situ* and a calkin	G5206	20	[237]
	Clenched nail	G5144	20	[247]
	Bridle bit fragment, curved end	G5096	20	[248]
Knife blades		G5184	20	[259]
	A broken rod with triangular blade	G5266	20	[276]
		G5252	20	[308]
Pins or heckle teeth	Broken shaft	G5149	20	[255]
	Bent near point	G5166	20	[256]
		G5257	20	[271]
		G5324	20	[285]
Strips	Thin, irregular	G1512	20	[264]
	Thin, irregular	G5257	20	[273]
	Broken thin strap	G5002	20	[98]
Plate	Flat, possibly originally circular	G5186	20	[261]
Lead	Bent, twisted strip; waste from a window came?	G5210	20	[234]
Glass	Small, opaque green bead, probably Saxon	G5288	20	[283]
Copper alloy	Strip	G5019	20	[117]
	Strip	G5040	20	[186]
	Hooked tag or fastener	G5184	20	[260]
	Binding strip (from repair of wooden vessel)	G5016	20	[119]
Bone	Unworked	G5021	20	[122]
	Unworked	G5118	20	[224]
	Unworked	G736	20	[228]
	Pin fragment	G5221	20	[243]
	Unworked	G5181	20	[272]
	Pin	G5350	20	[328]

The churches

Four small finds were retrieved from the chancel of the first church:

Two arrowheads (G74 [206]; Fig 20, scale 1:2) These barbed and tanged arrowheads were found in demolition rubble against the plaster face at the back of the clergy bench. They are of late Neolithic or early Bronze Age date and are of Green's 'Green Low' and 'Sutton B' types (information from Gillian Wilson).

Knife fragment (G74 [85]) Fragment of eleventh-century knife from the same context.
Roman coin (G548 [195]) A radiate of Gallienus from a plaster layer in the chancel.

A further small find was recovered from the external surface north of the church:

Bone comb (G1744, [280]) Fragmentary, comprising a composite tooth segment with stubs of four broken teeth on each side beyond a zone decorated with ring and dot.

10 The *sacrarium* vessel

Description of the vessel

by Terry Pearson

The vessel is a small jar, height 185mm, rim diameter 127mm (Figs 81 and 82). The fabric is shell tempered and has soapy surfaces. The internal surface is rilled, similar to the effect of wheel-throwing finger marks, but the vessel is probably handmade. Examination suggests that it was made in two parts: the lower half up to the maximum girth, and the rim, neck and upper body made upside down and smoothed over later. The technique would seem to have been that it was handmade (coiled) in the two parts on a turntable at a speed sufficient to achieve concentricity of form. The evidence for the two part manufacture comes from the pattern of sherd breakage which demonstrates that the maximum girth is the weak area. The rilling marks on the internal surface are consistent with hand turning; the lack of any expression of the rills on the external surface, which is smoothed over, again indicates this method. The fabric, surface condition and form are consistent with examples of St Neots type ware which has generally been dated to *c* AD 850–1200.

There are several interesting characteristics of the form which are worth noting. The rounded rim profile is common in early examples; the neck is concave and is drawn out to the body forming a pronounced neckline. The body has a distinct carination, making the form almost biconical in shape. This feature was common in the middle Saxon period. It is unlikely that the method of manufacture dictated the shape in both periods which would suggest a continuity of ceramic tradition. Similar forms are found stratified at Furnells in the earliest levels producing St Neots type ware and do not occur in association with Stamford ware. It is generally accepted that Stamford ware was produced from the ninth century to the twelfth: at Furnells the earliest types would all tend to be of the period between the early tenth and the late eleventh centuries. The occurrence of these small jar forms in phases prior to the introduction of Stamford ware, and the general similarity of technique with comparable forms of the middle Saxon period, suggests a date at the beginning of the series – probably in the late ninth century.

Analysis of the sherds showed that the types of fracture could be divided into four categories relating to distinct zones of the vessel; the rim, the neck, the body and the base (Table 36). This breakage pattern could be used to reconstruct some of the events in the varied use of this vessel.

– Smoke blackening starts from a line 1cm above the base, indicating that the vessel had been set over a very hot fire.
– The vessel had been intensively burnt on the base causing both microfracture and larger cracks. The liquid contents had become deposited on the edges of the larger cracks and had then been burnt.
– Impact was clearly on the rim and downwards, initially on one side of the rim, while the pot was contained in the pit in the floor of the church. For this to have happened, the rim must have been raised slightly above the level of the surrounding ground surface.

It was noticed that there were two deposits on the internal face of the vessel, one burnt, black, and encrusted (see John Evans, below), the other white. The white deposit reacted with dilute hydrochloric acid and may be lime. It would appear to be below the black deposit and was probably incorporated in this system when it was burnt. Similar white deposits are found on a high proportion of St Neots type ware vessels of this period.

Table 36 Pattern of sherd breakage on the *sacrarium* vessel

Part of vessel	Number of sherds	Breakage of sherds
Rim	8	The rim sherds varied in length from 2 – 6cm and would be consistent with breakage from a point impact on one side of the rim downwards while the pot was held steady.
Neck	88	The neck sherds were all fragmentary and the majority were below 1sq cm in area. Over 70% of these sherds were laminated; they had fractured down the sherd core. This form of breakage would be consistent with an impact downwards on the rim.
Body	51	The primary fractures extend from the neck to the base and around the maximum girth of the vessel. These sherds are not laminated and vary from large to medium in size.
Base	23	Two forms of fracture were observed on the base. 1 *Earlier fracture*: examination of the base showed that it had been heated until it had started to form micro-cracks; several large fractures had also developed in the base allowing the contents to be deposited on the breaks. This must have occurred when the vessel was in use over a fire as the deposit on the breaks has also been burnt. 2 *Later fracture*: the base, weakened through burning, suffered later breakage.

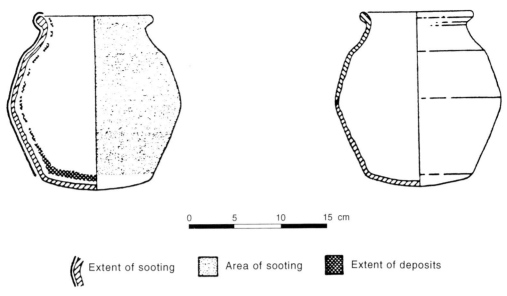

Extent of sooting   Area of sooting   Extent of deposits

Fig 81   Drawing of the sacrarium *pottery vessel*

Fig 82   Photograph of the sacrarium *pottery vessel*

The deposits on the interior surface of the *sacrarium* vessel

by John Evans

Two deposits, one white and one black, on the inner surfaces of the sherds were examined.

Method of analysis

The sample was gently crushed (to open up the vesicles) and placed in a Soxhlet apparatus. The residue was then extracted sequentially with hexane, chloroform, 2-propanol and water. Each extract was evaporated to dryness under reduced pressure. Any residues obtained were examined by infrared spectroscopy. The extracts, if sufficient in quantity, were then investigated using thin-layer chromatography (TLC). This technique is especially useful for the hexane (oils and fats) and chloroform (resins) extracts as it enables the various major constituent components of the oils to be detected. For instance, fats and oils are composed in part of triglycerides which are unique to a particular fat or oil.

The next stage of the procedure was to examine the residue by gas (GC) and high performance liquid chromatographies (HLPC). The actual procedure depended on the nature of the extract. For instance, the hexane extracts were hydrolysed and the resulting free acid methylated and/or naphthacylated esters were examined by HPLC. In this way it was possible to identify and quantify the levels present in the extracts. These data coupled with the TLC data enabled fats, etc to be identified with a reasonable degree of certainty. Examination of the aqueous extract for sodium chloride levels was also done routinely. In this way the use of salt for preservation, etc could be inferred.

The samples after extraction were divided into two portions. One portion was digested with hydrochloric acid in order to release amino acids from any proteinaceous material present. The liberated acids were then identified by appropriate chromatographic methods. Occasionally it was possible to isolate the protein by extracting the sample with a buffer and investigating the extract by electrophoresis. Additionally, the acid extract was investigated for calcium and magnesium levels. This information was used to indicate the original presence of aqueous systems. Where sufficient sample was available it was examined by scanning electron microscopy (SEM) for the presence of any identifiable biological debris. SEM is more useful than optical microscopy for this type of material as its coloration makes it difficult to view. Certain substances readily lend themselves to identification. Beeswax is very stable and its infrared spectrum very characteristic.

Summary

The sherds examined had two deposits, white and black. The white material was mainly calcium carbonate with traces of phosphate. No organic substances were detected. The calcareous deposit was most probably produced by the percolating ground water.

The black deposit was examined initially by infrared spectroscopy. The spectrum obtained suggested the presence of organic substances. The residue was extracted with a series of solvents of varying polarities and each extract was investigated by various chromatographic techniques and infrared and ultraviolet spectroscopy. The results of this investigation showed the presence of beeswax (30%), sucrose (5%), glucose (10%) and tartaric acid (2%). The remainder of the sample was composed of charcoal matrix. Citric acid was also suspected but not proven. No triglycerides or proteins were detected. Examination of the black material with a scanning electron microscope showed no vegetable matter. No structures apart from the vesicular nature of the residue were observed.

The presence of beeswax and sucrose suggests honey in the original contents. The presence of tartaric acid indicates a fermented substance, possibly wine as no vegetable matter was present, ie the tartaric acid did not result from the natural decay sequence of vegetable or fruit matter. The vesicular nature indicated that the organic phase had been burnt. Analysis of the surrounding soil gave no useful results.

In conclusion it would seem that a wine and honey mixture was burnt in the vessel.

Earth samples from the pottery vessel in the church

by Tony Gouldwell

Introduction

Two samples of sediment were submitted to the Environmental Laboratory, Department of Archaeology, University of Leicester, for the charcoal content to be examined and the likelihood assessed of a common origin for the two sediments. Sample <87> (AML 800732) comprised the soil (741) within the pottery vessel (G745) while sample <88> (AML 801000) was extracted from the burnt soil layer surrounding the vessel (G742).

Description of the samples

A textural description for each sample was made following Soil Survey field practice (Hodgson 1974). The following account applies to both cases, differences being indicated where appropriate.

The material arrived in a dry condition and had to be wetted for the relevant tests. Colour descriptions use Munsell Color (1975) conventions.

Colour (Dry) dark greyish brown (10YR 4/2), (wet) dark to very dark greyish-brown (10:YR 3.5/2).

Mottles Very pale brown, few, extremely fine, distinct. Charcoal inclusions give appearance of black, fine, prominent mottles.

Texture Variably sandy, with stones up to 5mm wide making manual assessment of texture of finer component difficult. Variation of grittiness within each sample seems to be as great as any apparent difference between samples.

Consistency Moderately firm, semideformable, uncemented, slightly sticky, slightly plastic.

After being shaken in water and allowed to settle, both samples settled out as a thin layer of silt/clay *c* 2–3% volume capping a column of gravel with grit sizes increasing progressively downwards.

Methods

As sample <88> was the larger, a random subsample of comparable size to the whole of sample <87> was taken by quartering and mixing a conical heap of the material, three times, finally appropriating quarters for examination. The samples to be used were then soaked in water in five-litre lipped buckets containing a little sodium carbonate to encourage disaggregation of silt and clay aggregates. The suspended solids were then washed through a series of nested sieves of mesh sizes 1.8mm to 355 microns to protect fragile macrofossils from damage by larger particles.

Standard paraffin flotation (Kenward 1974) was employed to separate macrofossils from mineral residue, using three paraffin soakings each followed by three flotations decanting into a 355 micron mesh sieve. Macrofossils were washed with detergent and stored under alcohol.

Charcoal fragments were examined using light under x10 and occasionally up to x100 binocular magnification. Flots and residues were similarly scanned under the low power for macrofossils.

Results

The weights of the samples processed were 924.4g (<87>) and 921.8g (<88>). Most of the wood charcoal remains were very small, their greatest lengths being about 2mm. Suitable breakages along the transverse, longitudinal or tangential planes were usually impractical without recourse to laborious techniques. Furthermore the transverse plane surfaces were often not large enough to permit an impression of vascular arrangement, being usually less than the size of a single typical pore group of, eg, oak.

Distinction between alder (*Alnus*), hazel (*Corylus*) and hornbeam (*Carpinus*) is not possible where adequate views of the vessel walls are not obtained. Identification of birch (*Betula*) is supported by the observation of minute pits (*c* 20–25 microns) in the vessel wall.

Table 37 shows those identifications of wood charcoal and cereal grains which were also made. These grains were blistered and often broken, obscuring identification.

Recent gastropod shell fragments were found in a sample of <88> residue, two of which were determined as *Vallonia exentrica*, a snail 2–2.2mm across which inhabits open, dry, calcareous sites and in this case is found within its normal British geographical range (Kerney and Cameron 1979).

Ancient fossil remains occur in the residues and are mostly fragmented. Echinodermata, Porifera and Foraminifera are present in both samples, suggesting an origin in a shallow marine environment.

Stones sieved from the samples were limestone (effervescence on addition of dilute hydrochloric acid) with maximum sizes of 18mm in sample <87> and 30mm in sample <88>.

Discussion and conclusion

The crumb structure suggests a former soil with limestone fragments and evidently associated fossils being intrusive. Also intrusive are tiny shell-tempered pottery sherds which implicate human agency in the introduction.

Texturally the samples appear very similar and a preliminary inspection of flotation residues shows comparable constituents of quartz grains, limestone particles, minute wood charcoal fragments and pottery sherds. The quantity of identified charcoal can be taken as significant in drawing comparisons between the two samples. All the recognisable wood remains are of common and widespread species.

Table 37 Charcoal identifications: samples <87> and <88>

Identification	Sample <87> Number	Size (mm)	Sample <88> Number	Size (mm)
Oak (*Quercus*)	7	5 – 18	1	7
Oak (*Quercus*)			6	<4
cf Oak (*Quercus*)	8	<4	*c* 5	<5
Ash (*Fraxinus*)	3	<4	3	<3
Alder, Hazel, Hornbeam (*Alnus, Corylus, Carpinus*)	6	<4		
Birch (*Betula*)	2	<3		
Unidentified diffuse porous	*c* 45	1 – 5	*c* 20	<3
Wheat (*Triticum aestivum*)	5			
cf Barley (*Hordeum vulgare*)	1			
Unidentified grain	2			

11 The building material

The worked building stone

by Paul Woodfield

The recovery of two quoins from the second church foundation and two or three building blocks emphasises the stone character of the first church and adds to our detailed knowledge of the building. A reworked fragment of an arch with interlace decoration, found in an unstratified context, might have been derived from the second church and a fragment of hood moulding may have been from a piscina from that church.

Catalogue

[58] Dressed stone (not illustrated)
Site location From the conversion phase (SP6) wall built across the nave of the second church (SP6, 50). It may therefore have had its origin in either the first or second church.
Stone type Blisworth limestone.
Description Fragment of stone dressed on bed with close herringbone axing. One edge dressed.

[132] Hood moulding (Figs 83 and 84)
Site location From a pitched stone floor laid within the sixteenth-century smithy (SP12, 48).
Stone type Blisworth limestone.
Description Hood moulding to an arch, the soffit having a diameter of *c* 600mm, thus narrower than a door: it may represent a feature such as a piscina. The lower arris has been cut back to form elongated nailheads. This ornamentation is likely to occur after AD 1100; the undeveloped form of the decoration suggests a date in the first half of the twelfth century, possibly earlier in the century rather than later.

[136] and **[148]** Chamfered stone (Fig 85)
Site location [136] lay on a surface south of the second church. This can be joined with an identical fragment from the west wing of the later manor ([148]). It seems most probable that they are from the first church, though the stratigraphic location of [136] is not secure.
Stone type Blisworth limestone.
Description Two chamfered stones, not quite fitting, with identical profiles. Length 390mm (together), height 72mm, width 136mm. The chamfer ends in a narrow fillet which has been subject to mechanical damage, suggesting that it was proud of the wall face which clearly commenced at the base of the chamfer. The soffit, however, shows no evidence of continuity of this plane and has a roughly-worked rebate. The stones might have formed a projecting architrave to an opening.

[175] Building block (not illustrated).
Site location From the conversion phase (SP6) wall foundation built across the nave of the second church (SP6, 442). It may therefore have had its origin in either the first or second church.
Stone type 'Barnack' limestone.
Description Building block, no mortar adhering. Average thickness 103mm. Burnt on all faces.

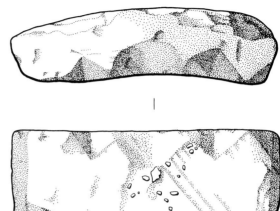

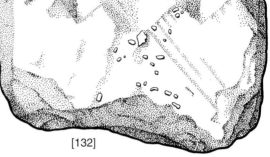

[132]

Fig 83   Hood moulding [132], possibly from conversion phase (SP6; scale 1:4)

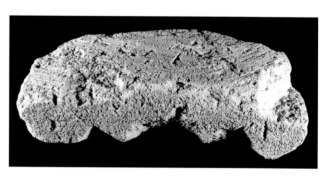

Fig 84   Hood moulding [132], possibly from conversion phase (SP6)

[177] Quoin (not illustrated)
Site location Reused in the foundation of the second church (SP5, 439).
Stone type 'Barnack' limestone.
Description Limestone casing to quoin, probably internal. Has been subject to prolonged burning.

[179] Building stone (not illustrated)
Site location Reused in the south nave wall of the second church (SP5, 469).
Stone type 'Barnack limestone'.
Description Building stone dressed on four sides, curiously long and narrow and slightly tapered from 80 to 95mm. Face and edges appeared weathered, perhaps a member of stripwork decoration. The eleventh-century context would not be inconsistent with this interpretation.

[181] Quoin (not illustrated)
Site location Reused in the foundation of the second church (SP5, 439).
Stone type Blisworth limestone.

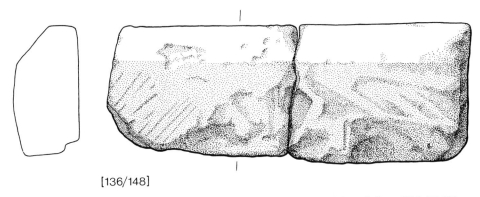

[136/148]

Fig 85   Possible architrave fragments from the first church, viewed from below ([136/148]; scale 1:4)

Description Building stone, with two dressed faces forming quoin with bull-nosed arris, dressed by coarse chiselling vertical to bed. Maximum thickness 83mm. Probably the jamb of an internal door or angle.

[303] Fragment from soffit of arch (Figs 86 and 87)
Site location This stone was probably recovered from a pitched stone floor (SP12, 46), laid at the time the east manor hall was in use as a smithy, ie during the sixteenth century.
Stone type 'Barnack' limestone.
Description An unstratified stone from the soffit of an arch with the arris chamfer worked with an incised interlacing zigzag of rounded ribbon, the enclosed field and angles left proud. Length 395mm, width 170mm, breadth 102mm. The decoration appears to relate to the curved intrados, of radius 1.7m, but the stone has been later recut without respect for the decoration, forming an approximate right-angled section on the back. The original intrados is chisel-worked to a fair finish. The style of decoration employing interweaving strings is unsophisticated in the English full Romanesque context suggesting a late eleventh century date.

Discussion

Perhaps of most interest in architectural terms is a stone from the soffit of an arch ([303], Figs 86 and 87) carved from 'Barnack' limestone. This was recovered from the 1975 trial trenching and most probably derives from a sixteenth-century pitched stone floor (SP12). Its decoration suggests an association with the second church. (A detailed description is given in the last catalogue entry above.)

Fig 87   Fragment from soffit of an arch ([303]), possibly from the second church

[303]

Fig 86   Fragment from soffit of an arch ([303]), possibly from the second church (scale 1:4)

The mortar from the first church

by John Evans

The samples recovered from the walls of the first church were in a degenerate condition; this factor limited the analysis to aggregate size measurement. From this analysis it was apparent that mineral additives had not been introduced into the sand used as aggregate. A group of quarry pits 40m south of the church are suspected on archaeological grounds to have been a source of aggregate at a later date (SP51/52). It is thought that similar pits may have provided for this church. Certainly the results from this analysis are not incompatible with the material having been derived from such pits. Analysis reveals that high levels of fine grains were present throughout the quarried material. Such high levels are usually detrimental to the strength of the mortar and may lead to rapid deterioration. Lower levels of fine grains were present in the church mortar, suggesting that if these pits were indeed the source of the aggregate then this problem of deterioration had been partly averted by a reduction in the fine content before inclusion in the mortar mix.

Geological identification of worked stone

by Diana Sutherland

Preliminary examination of the worked stone collected during the excavation confirmed that all examples were limestone, and that three different types could be recognised.

Cornbrash A golden, fossiliferous limestone from the cornbrash outcropping on the site.

Blisworth limestone (Great Oolite limestone) Also available on the site, occurring beneath the clay which underlies the cornbrash. It is a variable stone, being generally oyster-bearing but not necessarily oolitic. When it is oolitic and well cemented, a more robust form of Rounds Stone, it is difficult to distinguish from 'Barnack' Stone, a geologically different limestone imported to the site (see below). The more easily recognisable Blisworth limestone is of 'general building' type, such as is commonly used for rubble walling in the area at any period.

Table 38 Catalogue of 'Barnack' limestone

Stone	Group, Unit	Description
[300]	G5283, 1817	Thin-sectioned; grave cover
[305]	G5280, 1809	Thin-sectioned; grave cover or marker
[304=306]	G5282, 1814	Thin-sectioned; cover of coffin [1117]
[1117]	G5282, 296	Thin-sectioned; coffin
[177]	G499, 439	Macroscopic; dressed stone, burnt
[178]	G430, 430	Macroscopic. [178] & [179] form group represented by thin section of [189]; stone coffin fragment
[179]	G469, 469	Macroscopic; dressed stone
[180]	G499, 439	Macroscopic; carved stone
[182]	G499, 439	Macroscopic; stone coffin fragment
[187]	G499, 439	Macroscopic; dressed stone
[189]	G518, 516	Thin section, non-ferroan variant of 'Barnack' type; stone coffin fragment
[229]	G770, 770	Macroscopic; fragment of cross-head
[302=307]	G5282, 1814	Macroscopic; cross-shaft fragment
[164]	G249, 44	Macroscopic. Burnt but similar to [302]; cross-head fragment
[137]	G102, 102	Macroscopic identification with [139] very much like [178]-[189] group; stone coffin fragment
[139]	Unstratified	Macroscopic; stone coffin fragment
[175]	G137, 442	Macroscopic. Burnt. Probably 'Barnack' type; dressed stone
[93]	G90, 90	Thin section confirms similarity to [189]; dressed stone
[303]	G46, ?46	Macroscopic; lozenge decorated fragment of door arch

Table 39 Catalogue of Blisworth limestone

Stone	Group, Unit	Description
[136]	G120, 120	Oolitic, but ooliths are mainly flat type; as [148]
[148]	G120, 4	Oolitic, but ooliths are mainly flat type; well dressed, rectangular with chamfered edges
[181]	G439, 499	Oyster-rich, less oolitic, flatter type; dressed stone, worn corner
[301]		Fine grained, oyster rich, possibly sandy
[58]	G50, 137	Fine grained, noticeably oolitic, possibly sandy; dressed stone fragment with chevron marks on face
[132]	G46, 46	Oyster-packed; fragment of door arch with 'dog-tooth' decoration
[334]	G2005	Though somewhat 'Barnack'-like, oyster rich and ooliths of flat type; Blisworth limestone; squarish fragment of worked stone with prominent tool marks

Lincolnshire limestone ('Barnack' type) The majority of the better-quality worked stones belong either to this type or to the similar-looking robust variety of Raunds Stone. Both may be described as well-cemented, shelly, oolitic limestone, often cross-bedded and weathering to a ribbed surface; for positive identification, thin sections of representative stones were examined.

Results of thin-section study

'Barnack' limestone This consists of several varieties, of which the 'rag' is most like the Raunds samples. It is conspicuously shelly (25–45%), the shells including fragments of oyster and other bivalves and turreted gastropods. Ooliths (25–40%) occur in pockets between shells: many are spherical, dusky brown structures, variably layered, but there are also flatter, ovoid superficial ooliths grown on shell material. The matrix to the rock is medium to coarse-grained crystalline calcite (a ferran calcite which takes a blue stain). There are a few sand grains with calcareous coating. Such grains are more abundant in oolitic, less shelly 'Barnack' samples.

Blisworth limestone From Raunds this is variable, and it is the more oolitic type that resembles the 'rag' of the Lincolnshire limestone. The shells do not appear to be diagnostic, for they include oysters, other bivalves, and gastropods similar to those in 'Barnack' limestone. The matrix is similar, ferran calcite cement. A distinction can be made, however, on the basis of ooliths: in the Raunds stone, the flatter, ovoid superficial ooliths are more abundant than true spherical ooliths. Specimen [247], Blisworth limestone from the small quarry in the south-west of the site, is shelly rather than oolitic. Specimen [146] appears very similar, and the chip was not therefore sectioned.

Archaeological samples sectioned

The grave cover ([300], G5283) is very similar to 'Barnack' ragstone in all respects. It contains abundant shell fragments, including oysters, other bivalves and many turreted gastropods: the ooliths are round, almost round, and oval in section in much the same proportion as 'Barnack'; the cement is a mosaic of medium-grained, crystalline ferran calcite. Find [801] (from the western manor) is a rock that superficially resembles 'Barnack', but is considered to be an example of local Blisworth limestone. It is oolitic, but on examination the ooliths are found more often to be oval, with a shell nucleus. Shell fragments include the usual bivalves and occasional gastropods, in a ferran calcite cement.

Conclusions

It has been confirmed that both 'Barnack' type Lincolnshire limestone and Blisworth limestone are used for dressed and worked stones on the site, along with rubble Cornbrash limestone. Finds [907] and [1092] are shelly oolitic limestones which require further examination through thin sectioning.

12 The monumental stone

by Rosemary Cramp

Evidence was recovered for several stone coffins, three stone grave covers and two or three crosses. Most were fragmentary but one coffin and two covers were complete.

Catalogue

Coffins

[1117] Complete coffin (Fig 88)
Site location South of the first church
Dimensions Length 2.10m; width 0.78m; depth 0.38m
Stone type 'Barnack' limestone
Description This is a tapered form of coffin, with a rounded head recess (Willmore 1940, fig 20).

[304/306] Coffin cover for [1117] (Fig 89)
Site location Found broken and inverted above coffin during the 1975 trial trench: coffin covering was completed with cross-shaft fragments [302/307], and rough stones.
Dimensions Two large fragments, 0.53m and 0.44m long
Stone type 'Barnack' limestone
Description From a tapered stone, about 30–40mm narrower than the coffin on which it was found. Rough finished on one face, trimmed flat on the other.

[137] Coffin fragment (not illustrated)
Site location Discovered reused as part of the south wall of the eastern manor (G102)
Stone type 'Barnack' type
Dimensions Length 203mm; depth 75mm; greatest height 75mm
Description A fragment of the upper side wall of a stone coffin, broken on all sides. A small section of the chamfered upper surface of the wall survives.

[139] Coffin fragment (Fig 90)
Site location Unstratified
Dimensions Length 262mm; depth 120mm; height 85–90mm
Stone type 'Barnack' limestone
Description This is the broken fragment of the upper corner of the coffin. Part of the chamfer of the upper edge survives, and part of the internal cut for the head. The rest of the fragment was dressed for reuse.

[178] Coffin fragment (not illustrated)
Site location Built into the south nave wall of the later church (G499, 430)
Dimensions Length 285mm; height 90mm; depth 78>74mm
Stone type 'Barnack' limestone
Description Part of the chamfered upper edge survives.

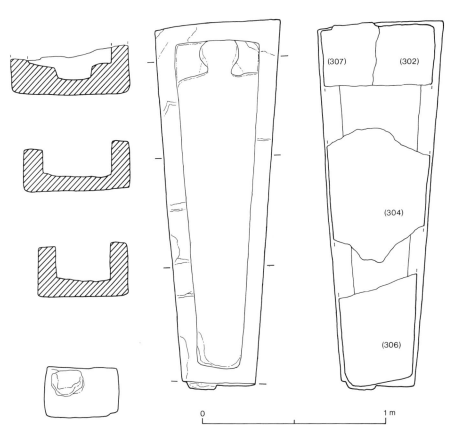

Fig 88 Stone coffin with cover in position ([1117]; scale 1:20)

Fig 89   Stone coffin with cover in position as found ([1117])

[182]   Coffin fragment (not illustrated)
Site location Built into the foundations of the north chancel wall of the later church (G499, 439).
Dimensions Length 210mm; depth 76mm; height 75mm
Stone type 'Barnack' limestone
Description Upper fragment of the side of a stone coffin with chamfered upper edge: possibly part of [139] and the other fragments listed above.

[187]   Coffin fragment (not illustrated)
Site location From the foundations of the later church west side of nave (G499, 430)
Dimensions Length 255mm; depth 90mm; height 75mm
Stone type 'Barnack' limestone

[189]   Fragment of a coffin in two joining fragments (not illustrated)
Site location Found as the packing of a posthole in the western part of the nave of the later church (G518, 516)
Dimensions Length 170mm; width 120mm; base thickness 82–85mm; wall thickness 32–40mm
Stone type 'Barnack' limestone
Discussion Although this piece has been cut down for reuse, the 'depth' of the wall is identical with [139] and so it is possibly part of that or a similar monument.

Summary of coffins
If one allows for the slight discrepancy in cutting which is inevitable in a coffin wall, then [137] and [182] could be part of the same monument, since they are near

equivalents in wall width and angle of chamfer. [178] is of a comparable width but has a different chamfer, and so is probably part of a different piece. [187] and [189] are closer in dimensions and type than to any other, and could possibly be part of the same monument – if roughly constructed – but are more plausibly part of two different ones. We have then, along with the complete coffin ([1117]) and the fragment of another with a head recess ([139]), evidence for what could be a minimum of five or a maximum of seven coffins.

Cross fragments
Three fragments of cross-head and two of shaft were recovered.

[164]   Part of the central portion of a cross-head
(Figs 90 and 91)
Site location Discovered as part of the wall foundations of the late thirteenth- to fourteenth-century west wing of the eastern manor (G249, 44)
Dimensions Height 204mm; width 225mm; depth 78–70mm. Depth of carving *c* 7mm
Stone type 'Barnack' limestone
Description The stone has been cut down for secondary use, and only part of one of its original faces survives. There is a central boss enclosed in a diamond-shaped strand, which is nipped together and then expands into a triangular shape. Part of a curving strand survives in the angle between the arms (see reconstruction drawing Fig 63).

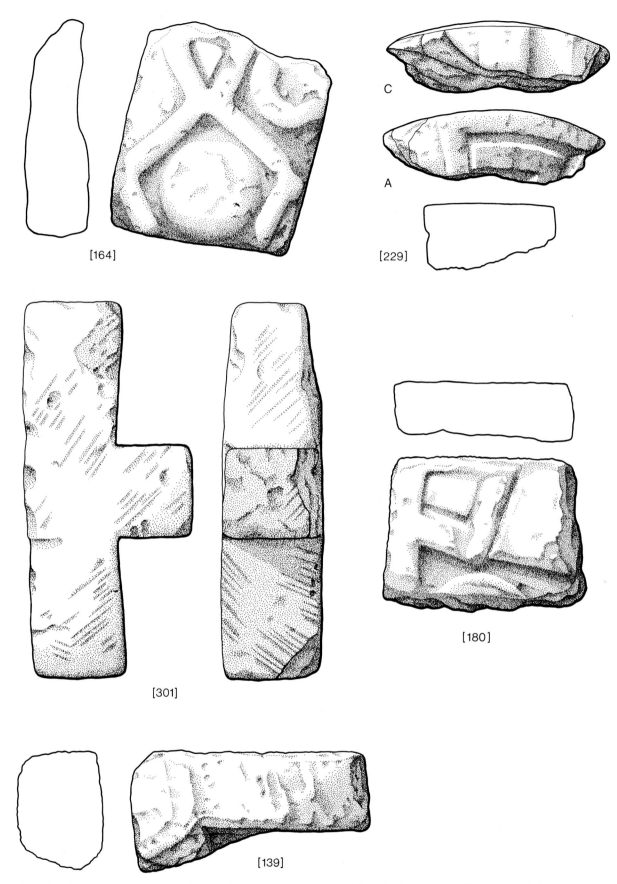

Fig 90   Monumental sculpture ([164], [180], [229], [301]) and coffin fragment ([139]): scale 1:4

Discussion Cross-heads such as this are known from the Midlands and East Anglia and are usually reconstructed as capping a short stemmed cross-shaft (Fox 1922, pl I Fulbourn, or pl VII Barnack). The excavators' reconstruction is discussed under [302], and in the discussion (p 112).

[229]   Fragment of a cross-head (Fig 90)
Site location Discovered as part of the external surface to the early church (G770, 770)
Dimensions Height 185mm; width 71mm; great depth 175mm
Stone type 'Barnack' limestone
Description Face A: broad; a corner of the flat band framing for the arm of the cross survives enclosing an angular strand of interlace. Face C: broad; this face is smoothly dressed and plain except for a vertical band in low relief. Face E: top; this curving surface is smoothly dressed but undecorated. It is difficult to reconstruct the form or the ornamental detail on this fragment although one face could be reconstructed as an arm outline enclosing a plait or twist, and the other as a simple cross in low relief. It is unfortunate that the central portion of the cross-head [164] has been so trimmed that it is impossible to say whether or not it fits this arm.

[301]   Cross-head fragment (Fig 90)
Site location Unstratified
Dimensions Length 395mm; width 100–105mm; height 180mm
Stone type 'Barnack' limestone
Description This piece has been broken along one long face and it is difficult to determine whether it should be considered with the existing longest span vertical or horizontal. The surfaces of the unbroken faces are all tooled with a fine diagonal tooling. Otherwise the piece is plain. On the whole this piece looks more credible in a vertical position, since the outward splay of the vertical 'arms' would make better sense if it were an upright grave marker.

Fig 91   Fragment of cross-head ([164])

It is just possible that it is a finial cross from a church, in which case the horizontal format would be possible. It is not possible to date such an anonymous piece but it is worth noting that the tooling is the same as on the plain tapered grave covers.

[302/307] Two joining fragments of a cross-shaft (Figs 92 and 93)
Site location Discovered together with other plain fragments ([306] and [304]) lying above the head of the stone coffin ([1117]) of an adult male. The neat trimming of two faces of this stone have suggested to the excavators an intermediate structural use for the cross before its final use as part of a coffin lid (G5282, 1814).
Dimensions Of both fragments together; height 600mm; width at base 335mm, at band 340mm, at top 310mm; depth 90–100mm
Stone type 'Barnack' limestone
Description Face A: broad; no ornament survives on or above the band. Below the flat band, however, mouldings survive and enclose a panel of what may be plausibly reconstructed as a four strand plain plait with median incised strands and cross joined terminals. Face B (not illustrated): narrow; dressed smooth. Face C (not illustrated): broad; split away. Face D: narrow; no classifiable ornament survives above the projecting band although part of the edge mouldings enclosing a curving strand survives. The broad flat moulding of the band encloses an angular closed circuit motif (Cramp 1984, G.1.25.5). Below there is a half section of what seems to be a four strand plain plait.
Discussion The motif on the band on face D is so similar to that on the centre of the cross-head ([164]) that they are plausibly to be considered as part of the same monument. The dimensions of the presumed head, and the width of the shaft, as well as the range of ornament, are comparable with a group of East Anglian crosses first defined by Fox; for example those from Whissonsett, Cambridgeshire, or Willingham, Norfolk (Fox, 1922, pl I and II). Nearer at hand in Cambridgeshire, the Helpston cross-head (Irvine 1889, 179 and pl I) is very similar to Furnells [164] and could have capped a similar shaft. Fox considered that each of these crosses must have been rather short, ranging in size from 2ft 8in (0.81m) to 4ft (1.22m). The Furnells cross has been reconstructed as taller than that (Fig 63). Since its ornament is more varied than the formulaic group with a simple zigzag on the narrow faces, it could be that this is an earlier and more individual piece. In the light of its stratigraphic position in the site sequence it is perhaps preferable to compare it with other East Midland monuments such as the crosses at Creeton, Lincolnshire, and that at Sproxton, Leicestershire, which has comparable banding on the shaft. The Sproxton shaft is 6ft 6in high (1.98m), with a head diameter of 1ft 9 in (0.54m). The projecting band is 7in high (0.18m) and this is comparable with Furnells (Routh 1938–9).

Grave covers
[180]   Fragment of grave cover (Fig 90)
Site location Built into the foundations of the west nave wall of the later church (G499, 439)
Dimensions Length 210mm; width 160mm; depth 65mm. Depth of carving 6mm
Stone type 'Barnack' limestone

Description The original surface survives on (part only of) one face. The ornament consists of a flat band border on the left enclosing two crossing strands and a loop of what could be interlace. The pattern is truncated by its trimming for reuse: two edges are roughly chamfered.

Discussion This fragment could have been split from the upper surface of a grave slab. The carving is in a grooved technique.

[300]   Grave cover in four joining pieces
(Figs 94–96)

Site location Discovered in the trial excavations of 1975 apparently overlying a stone arrangement at its west end. The stone covered a grave of an adult male (5283) and is considered by the excavators to be primarily associated with that grave. The wider end of the slab was orientated west over the head of the burial.

Dimensions Length 1.2m; width 0.5>0.32m; depth 115>70mm

Stone type 'Barnack' limestone

Description The surface of the slab is very worn, especially in the area of the cross at the wider end, and at the centre. The slab is bisected by a stem which joins three cross-heads: all are carved in shallow relief. At the wider end the upper cross is firmly outlined. The vertical arm is wedge shaped (type B, Cramp 1984; fig 2) and the horizontal arms are squared (type A, Cramp 1984). In the centre of the slab is a cross set in a circular frame (type E 10, ibid). At the narrower end is a cross of the same type as at the 'head'. On either side of the stem of the cross there are panels of plait, four strand at the wider end and three strand at the narrower. The narrow sides are chamfered outwards to the base and are more smoothly dressed than the underside.

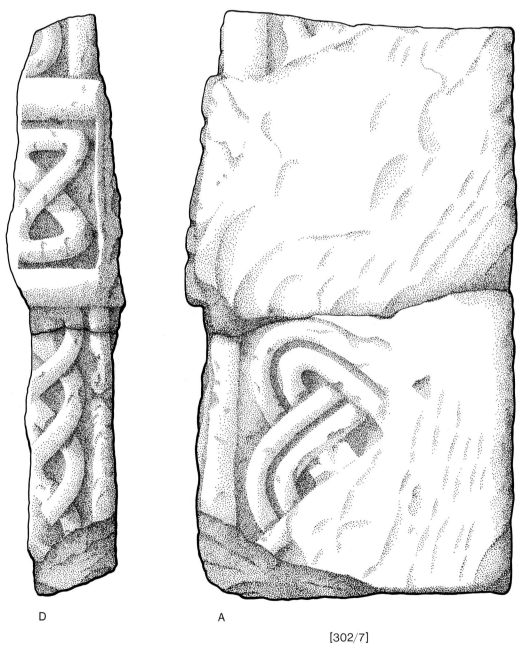

D   A

[302/7]

Fig 92   Two joining fragments of cross-shaft ([302/7]; scale 1:4)

Fig 93 Two joining fragments of cross-shaft ([302/7]; Face D)

Discussion This is the most elaborate grave cover from the graveyard and the excavators believe that its position determined the graveyard layout throughout its period of use (pp 51, 67). Certainly the surface of the slab exhibits considerable evidence of wear or weathering. If (as the excavators postulate on p 52) the cross [302/7] was set at the head of the slab, then it would have been a very notable monument indeed. When considered in relation to other surviving grave covers from eastern England, this is a well designed and well constructed example. It falls between Fox's type 4 and type 6 (Fox 1922, pls IV and V). In layout it is very like Little Shelford in that the crosses at each end are the same type and the panels, of

four strand plait at the head and three strand below, are identical. On the other hand the central double outlined cross is different, and the fact that it is a free-armed type may put it early in the sequence of 'Barnack' type slabs. Although there is no secure dating for slabs of this type, grave covers with crosses at each end of a stem seem to come into fashion towards the end of the pre-Conquest period (see Sockburn 25, Cramp 1984, pl 153) but there seems little doubt that tapering grave covers are a later fashion in England than the straight rectangular type. Plain tapering covers can be dated no more closely than the eleventh–thirteenth centuries and the decorated form continues into the later Middle Ages. This slab could reasonably date to the tenth century.

[305] Grave cover (Figs 97–99)
Site location Discovered in a recumbent position over an infant burial with Face A uppermost. The excavators have postulated that this is a secondary position (G5280, 1809).
Dimensions Length 1.1m; width at top 0.58m, at base 0.32m; depth 0.14m–0.11m.
Stone type 'Barnack' limestone
Description The stone is trapezoid in shape, smoothly dressed on all faces and chamfered on both broad faces. Face A: broad. At the broader end of the slab is an encircled St Andrew's cross in low relief. The cross may be analysed as constructed with two stretched loops or with broad median incised strands, interlinked with a ring which is also median incised. Face C: broad. At the broader end is an irregular deeply incised cross, type 1A. No arm is of the same length and the tooling is rather slapdash. On the other hand this face has been carefully dressed and chamfered.
Discussion The excavators originally speculated that this piece may have had two periods of use – a first use as an upright slab and a second as a recumbent cover (the position in which it was found). That the stone was designed as an upright grave marker is a possibility, since both faces are finished in an identical way and the crosses on both faces are placed at the upper broader end. Such short thick slabs are known elsewhere in eastern England and are usually considered to have been upright grave markers (see Gilmour and Stocker 1986, figs 47 and 49). On the other hand the chamfered edges, so common on plain and decorated recumbent monuments, appear rather odd on an upright stone. It is possible, then, that this was always a recumbent grave cover. It is, of course, also possible that the incised cross was never meant to be visible to anyone except the deceased.

Discussion

Burial in stone coffins in Anglo-Saxon England must always have been the prerogative of the rich and powerful. Moreover, with the decline in stone technology in the post-Roman period, even important rulers or ecclesiastics were buried in wooden coffins, some of which could be elaborately equipped with metal fittings. Alongside the tradition of wooden coffins, which only a few modern graveyard excavations have picked up, there appears to have been persistent memory of rich Roman burials. Bede's account of the death and, in the late seventh century, subsequent translation of the abbess Æthelthryth is a case in point (Bede, *Hist Ecc*, IV, 19).

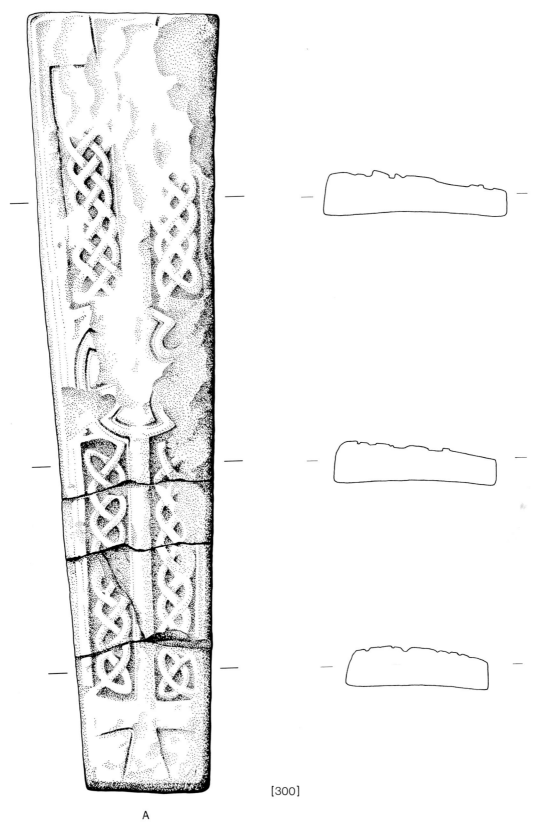

[300]

A

Fig 94   Carved limestone grave cover ([300]; scale 1:10)

The abbess was originally buried at her own request in a wooden coffin alongside the community. Sixteen years later it was decided to re-inter the bones in a stone coffin in the church. Members of the community were therefore sent to seek blocks of stone. This sounds as if they intended to produce the type of box coffin known

from late eighth-century examples, such as those from Breedon in Leicestershire, or Hovingham in Yorkshire. In the event the monks found a complete coffin, possibly Roman, and she was reburied in that within the church. It seems probable that Roman tub-like coffins may have inspired some pre-Conquest types, such as those

Fig 95   Upper surface of grave cover ([300])

Fig 96   Lower surface of grave cover ([300])

from Muchelney, Somerset (Willmore, 1940, 142, and fig 2A) or the later coffin from St Alkmund's, Derby (Radford 1976).

In fact, there is more evidence for burial in stone coffins in the Midlands than elsewhere in Anglo-Saxon England since there are coffin sides from Breedon, Wirksworth and Bakewell, Derbyshire, and the niches in the ring crypt at Brixworth would seem to be formed for supporting coffins. Tapering coffins with head-recesses are, however, normally considered to be post-Conquest in date. The Furnells coffin [1117] is therefore of great chronological importance in establishing this type in a pre-Conquest context. That coffin was covered by a made up lid, two fragments of which appear to have been from its original

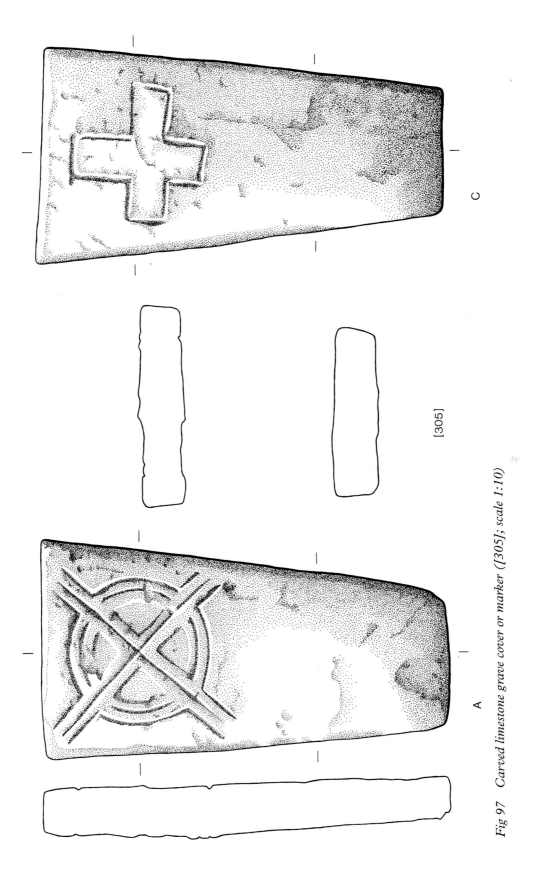

[305]

Fig 97   Carved limestone grave cover or marker ([305]; scale 1:10)

Fig 98   Face A of grave cover or marker ([305])

Fig 99   Face C of grave cover or marker ([305])

plain cover ([304/306]). The number of coffins at Furnells, between four and six, confirms the importance of the burial ground in the pre-Conquest period.

The development of the mass produced grave slab in late Anglo-Saxon England has yet to be fully chronicled. At the time when Christianity was generally accepted in Anglo-Saxon England, flat slabs, many with long stemmed central crosses, were a common form of grave cover in Merovingian Gaul. Perhaps the Romano-British tradition of the upright stele inhibited the acceptance of large recumbent monuments and encouraged

the development of crosses, although in the Anglo-Saxon kingdom of Northumbria both crosses and small recumbent monuments (name-stones) occur, particularly in monastic cemeteries. In the Midland kingdoms, during the period late seventh to early ninth centuries, there is considerable difficulty in pointing to any grave-yard monuments. It is possible that when such did develop they copied established Northumbrian types. Arguably the earliest large-scale slab with a relief central cross is the Herebericht slab from Monkwearmouth, which is plausibly of eighth-century date (Cramp 1984, pl 110, 604). Rather later in the eighth century are two slabs from Kirkdale, Yorkshire. One is carved as a skeuomorph of a textile covering with tasselled edges and is surely meant to be seen as a draped coffin cover. The other (which is incomplete) has a stemmed cross flanked by plant scrolls and there could have been a cross at the other end, now missing (Collingwood 1927, figs 21 and 22). These are, however, one-off pieces and none is tapering in shape as is the Furnells slab.

It seems from present evidence that all over England by the early tenth century recumbent slabs were becoming popular (Kendrick 1938, pl XCIX; Kendrick 1949, pl XLV, 3). The tapered form of a slab such as those previously analysed by Fox from Cambridge Castle (Fox 1922, pl IV) are dated by their stratigraphy, both in Cambridge and at Peterborough Cathedral, to the tenth/eleventh century. More recently slabs recovered from the excavations of St Mark's, Lincoln, have been similarly dated (Gilmour and Stocker 1986). Unfortunately the stones of this last group were discovered in reused positions. The Furnells decorated slab [300] is therefore of crucial chronological importance in providing early evidence for the use of the tapering recumbent slab of the 'Fenland grave-cover type' – a type which has recently been the subject of detailed reappraisal (Everson and Stocker, forthcoming). This is a monument type which occurs also in Northamptonshire at Oundle but has a wide distribution to the east. It would appear that all these slabs derive from quarries of shelly oolite from the Barnack area, and they are differently detailed from another group of Ancaster stone slabs mainly found in mid Kesteven, which have heavy cabled edges and more elaborate interlace patterns. The Furnells slab would seem to reflect the ability of local dignitaries to afford elaborate grave covers, perhaps after the late Saxon stone industry developed under lay control. 'Barnack' stone had been used for high quality carving of, for example, the Breedon monuments as early as the late eighth/early ninth century, and it remained an important source for East Midland buildings and monuments after the Norman Conquest (Butler 1964). The Furnells material not only enlarges the range of 'Barnack' monuments but also enables us to compare urban or monastic cemeteries with those of the rural proprietary churchyard. The former were more closely packed together, whether lay or clerical. The excavators' assumption that grave 5283 (slab [300]) provided a focus for the graveyard throughout its period of use (pp 51, 67) implies that a leading or founding family was able to enforce respect for a primary grave. This was marked not only with a slab but also possibly with a cross ([164], [302/7]) which is a notable variant on the East Midland type. Very few crosses have been associated with burials anywhere in Anglo-Saxon England and the importance of the Furnells evidence lies in the excavation of monuments in situ within a burial ground where most graves were not marked by any elaborate marker. The status of slabs is then clear, and it is thus possible to consider the monuments in something more than a typological or iconographic context.

13 The human remains

by Faye Powell

Introduction

Bone survival at Furnells was particularly good, though in some cases extensive crushing or decay of bone had occurred (pp 32–4). The complete and meticulous excavation of this graveyard provides an invaluable set of skeletons, which the report below demonstrates is a rich source of data relating to the anthropology and health of this late Saxon population.

The skeletal material was examined in the period 1979 to 1981 using standard pro-formas which are lodged with the archive (see Chapter 1). In addition the computations for the osteometric analysis are available at the same source. Since 1982 the skeletal collection has been on temporary loan to the School of Archaeological Sciences, University of Bradford where it is undergoing further osteological research. During 1983, the building in which the collection was housed was partly destroyed by an explosion at a nearby Liquid Petroleum Gas Station. Part of the skeletal collection was lost in this blast.

Demography

A total of 376 numbers were allocated to skeletal remains (5000–5372, 5094b, 5094c, 5176b). One infant from David Hall's 1975 trial trench was not retained and is not included in this analysis (5372). Another infant comes from a pre-graveyard context but, as this factor was not initially recognised, it is included in the analysis below (5367). A number of burials were found to be not *in situ* – being either reburied in pits, reburied in later graves, disturbed by later grave fills, or disturbed by the second church foundations. Adjustments for these *ex situ* graves could be made where the bones could be clearly identified as those missing from an *in situ* burial nearby. With these adjustments, the total number of individuals was found to be 363, 339 *in situ* in their original graves and 25 in disturbed contexts.

Of this total 100 were male and 82 female: 181 individuals could not be sexed. This last figure consists largely of sub-adults; only nine adult individuals could not be sexed, these because of their fragmentary nature. There were 191 adults, 170 sub-adults and two individuals whose age could not be determined. In the osteometric, morphological and pathological analyses below the figures differ slightly from those used in the demographic analysis. This is because the association of a number of the disturbed burials with their *in situ* remains was not made until the skeletal report was nearing completion. Thus the total number of burials considered below is 374 and not 363 as given above. This has introduced very little distortion into the data as the material not *in situ* was usually fragmentary and unsuitable for osteological analysis.

Table 41 Age ranges and sex totals

Group	Age range	Totals
Infant	Neonate – 1	66
Young child	0 – 6	108
Child	1 – 12	89
Adolescent	12 – 17	11
Sub-adult	Neonate – 17	170
Young adult	17 – 35	102
Old adult	35+	75
Adult	17+	191
Male	Adult	100
Female	Adult	82
All		**363**

Table 40 Explanation of the statistics used in the life tables

Symbol	Explanation [1]
D(X)	The raw osteological data
d(X)	The raw osteological data expressed as a percentage
l(x)	Survivorship – summarises mortality *prior to* age x. The survivorship of the assessed Raunds population at age 17 is 54%, hence 46% of the population die before that age.
q(X)	Probability of death in age interval X - summarises the mortality *during* an age interval. Thus the probability of those at Furnells who live to age 17 not reaching their 25th year is 0.32; expressed another way, 68% of those who reach the age of 17 live on to at least the age of 25. The probability of death cannot be accurately established for the oldest age interval as the length of this interval is not known.
q⁻(X)	As the osteological age intervals used are of unequal lengths the probabilities of death statistics are not directly comparable across age ranges. To make them approximately comparable $q(x)$ is divided by n, the number of years in the age interval.
e(x)	Expectation of life at age x – summarises mortality *after* age x. At Furnells a person reaching the age of 17 would expect to live, on average, a further 17.7 years – to the age of 34.7. Most commonly used as $e(0)$, the expectation of life at birth.
C(X)	The age profile of the population (%)

[1] *after Boddington 1987c*

Table 42 Life table for all aged burials

Age	D(X)	d(X)	l(x)	q(X)	q'(X)	e(x)	C(X)
NN[1]	21	6.4	100.0	0.06	0.064	20.4	0
0	45	13.7	93.6	0.15	0.147	21.8	4.2
1	7	2.1	79.9	0.03	0.027	24.5	3.9
2	35	10.7	77.8	0.14	0.034	24.2	14.2
6	32	9.8	67.1	0.15	0.024	23.7	18.3
12	11	3.4	57.3	0.06	0.012	21.2	13.6
17	57	17.3	53.9	0.32	0.040	17.4	17.7
25	45	13.7	36.6	0.37	0.037	15.7	14.5
35	32	9.8	22.9	0.43	0.043	12.2	8.8
45	43	13.1	13.1	1.00	0.067[2]	7.5	4.8

Total 328

[1]*Neonate*

[2]*Estimated maximum age = 60 years*

Age and sex were determined from as wide a range of criteria as possible. Only adult individuals (17 years or over) were sexed, as it was felt that the sexing criteria for sub-adult skeletons were at the time of writing insufficiently precise. Full details of the criteria utilised for age and sex analysis may be found in Microfiche 1.

As can be seen clearly from the table and graphs, the period of infancy, birth to two years, held the greatest risk of death (Table 42; Figs 100, and 101). When this age range is broken down more closely we see that in the first year of life the risk of dying (15%) is over twice that of birth (6%) or during the second year of life (3%). While birth is indicated as a time of relatively high risk of death, other subsequent factors seem to play a more important role in causing infant mortality. The first year of life is a potentially dangerous period because of the many new elements an infant is being subjected to. Two different nutritional sources, that from the mother and subsequent weaning, and the development of immunity to infection are just two examples of such normal pressures on an infant and may have been partly responsible for the high infant mortality apparent in the Furnells sample.

The adult female distribution of mortality peaks in early adulthood, while that for children peaks in early life. During the 17–25 year age range, 44% of all adult females died. There is a gradual decline in the risk of dying in the next two age ranges, with about a fifth of all females dying in old age. The period of least risk of death, age range 35–45 years, is a period when childbearing is considered least likely. It is noted that 71% of all females recorded from Furnells died during the childbearing age range of 17–35 years. While all the female deaths in early adulthood cannot be attributed to pregnancy or childbirth, childbirth is generally considered to be a particularly dangerous time in a female's life. Most first pregnancies might be expected to occur during the 17–25 year age range; usually this is associated with a higher risk of death than subsequent pregnancies. This is in keeping with the Furnells evidence where nearly half of all females (44%) died during this age range. It cannot be established whether these women were dying during childbirth or subsequent to the birth. The low number of neonates found does suggest, however, that the majority of the pregnancies continued through to full term. The smaller, though still not insignificant, number of females dying in the subsequent age range, 25–35

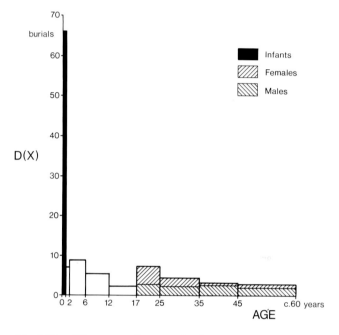

Fig 100   Histogram of age at death

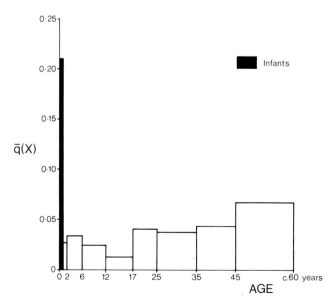

Fig 101   Histogram of probability of death

Table 43 Life table for adult males[1]

Age	D(X)	d(X)	l(x)	q(X)	q⁻(X)	e(x)
17	22	22.4	100.0	0.22	0.028	21.8
25	23	23.5	77.6	0.30	0.030	16.6
35	25	25.5	54.1	0.47	0.047	11.6
45	28	28.6	28.6	1.00	0.068[1]	7.5

Total 98

[1]*Estimated maximum age = 60 years*

Table 44 Life table for adult females[1]

Age	D(X)	d(X)	l(x)	q(X)	q⁻(X)	e(x)
17	34	44.1	100.0	0.44	0.055	15.9
25	21	27.3	53.9	0.49	0.049	14.5
35	7	9.1	28.6	0.32	0.032	13.5
45	15	19.5	19.5	1.00	0.067[1]	7.5

Total 77

[1]*Estimated maximum age = 60 years*

years, would suggest a continuing risk from the hazards associated with childbirth. Certainly their probability of death (q⁻=4.9%) is rather greater than that for males of the same age (q⁻=3.0%). The hazards experienced are as likely to be the result of poor medical attention and hygienic standards as the experience of childbirth itself. This high mortality of females in early adulthood can be associated with the high infant mortality during the first year of life. If a mother died at childbirth or within the first year of an infant's life, the vital nutritional standard of the infant would fall dramatically, hence increasing the risk of infant mortality.

The pattern of male deaths shows a more regular form. Risk of dying gradually increased with age. The graph shows a 'plateau' at the age ranges of 25–35 years and 35–45 years when the probability of dying was very similar for both age ranges (q⁻=2.8% and q⁻=3.0% respectively). The majority of the males survived to over 45 years and the male pattern of death may be contrasted with that of the females. For the males the risk of death increased with age, while for the females it decreased so that females who survived to the age of 35 years were then at less risk than their male counterparts.

In conclusion, it may be said that two periods, infancy and – for females – early adulthood, were times of relatively high risk of death. For infants the cause of this higher probability is thought to have been poor standards of nutrition and hygiene at an age when risk of infections and bacterial/viral disease is at its highest. Adult females showed high mortality during the childbearing years, particularly in the younger age range of 17–25 years, the age range at which the first pregnancies presumably occurred. Pregnancy and childbirth is not thought to have been the only, or even the primary, cause of high mortality. Poor medical and hygienic standards, during or after the pregnancy, are likely to have contributed largely to the death rate. The rate of male mortality was observed to increase with age, suggesting that normal biological deterioration, rather than any specific external factor, was the main cause of death.

Morphology

Morphology is the study of form. Observable traits, or morphological variation, in the human skeleton can be formed by hereditary (ie genetic) or external (environmental) factors. These traits can be 'continuous' – which, when observable, vary in shape or degree – or 'discontinuous' – which are either present or absent. Cranial wormians are an example of a continuous trait, these being extra ossicles found within a cranial suture. Such bones can be small, large, singular, plural or completely absent. An example of a discontinuous trait is the septal aperture, a small hole which sometimes occurs just above the distal articular surface of the humerus. It is either absent or present. These variations are not pathological. They are normal variations in the human skeleton which may be related to adaptability and/or heredity. Variations occur in the skeleton just as they do in the soft tissue, for example blue or brown eyes, blonde or dark hair.

Variation is observed and recorded in order to study patterns of the form in the human skeleton, temporally and geographically. Variation occurs in every bone of the skeleton and at several locations on the bone. While variation is a specialised study in itself, there is a reduced standard series of traits for which observations and comparison can be made, on a general level, with other samples of skeletal material (Table 45). Comparison of variability of these more obvious traits with other skeletal series can lead in future to a more detailed study of morphological variation in the Furnells material.

A summary of percentage occurrence of morphological traits by age and sex is given in Table 45.

Metopic suture (Table 52)
In utero, the frontal bone of the foetus is formed in two halves, both of which have usually fused by birth. The suture that joins the two halves is called the metopic suture. Often remnants of the suture are found in the skulls of young children; however, the retention of this suture, in varying stages of the fusion, can be found in adult crania. As can be seen from the table, only a minority of

Table 45 Summary of occurrence of morphological traits (%)

Trait	Male	Female	Sub–adult	Adult	All
Metopic suture	7.6	11.3	13.7	9.7	10.3
Coronal wormians	2.2	1.6	0	2.0	1.6
Parietal wormians	5.1	6.3	5.1	3.2	3.6
Lambdoidal wormians	26.3	37.5	13.3[2]	31.3[2]	27
Inca bone	1.1	3.0	8.2	1.9	3.4
Parietal foramina L	50.6	52.4	54.0	51.6	52.2
Parietal foramina R	44.3	58.7	39.2	50.7	47.8
Supra-orbital rim L (notch)	66.7	54.1	55.2	61.4	59.6
Supra-orbital rim L (foramen)	24.7	29.5	12.1[2]	27.1[2]	22.8
Supra-orbital rim L (smooth)	8.6	16.4	32.8[2]	11.7[2]	17.7
Supra-orbital rim R (notch)	65.8	57.4	55.4	62.9	60.7
Supra-orbital rim R (foramen)	22.4	31.1	19.6	25.7	24.0
Supra-orbital rim R (smooth)	11.8	11.5	25.0[2]	11.4[2]	15.3
Supra-scapular border L (notch)	85.7	90.0	70.6	86.1	81.1
Supra-scapular border L (foramen)	7.1	0	0	5.6	3.8
Supra-scapular border L (smooth)	7.1	10.0	29.4	8.3	15.1
Supra-scapular border R (notch)	88.9	81.8	90.9	86.2	87.5
Supra-scapular border R (foramen)	0	9.1	0	3.4	2.5
Supra-scapular border R (smooth)	11.1	33.3	9.1	14.3	12.5
Humerus: septal aperture L	8.1	18.8	6.3	13.5	11.8
Humerus: septal aperture R	3.8[1]	17.7[1]	8.5	10.4	9.9
Tibia: 'squatting' facets L	42.6	60.0	0	51.0	49.0
Tibia: 'squatting' facets R	47.2	56.3	25.0	51.4	50.5

[1] *Difference between male and female values significant at the 5% level*
[2] *Difference between sub-adult and adult values significant at the 5% level*

skulls possessed a metopic suture (10.3%). If the sample is divided into 'adult' and 'sub-adult', 9.2% of all adults and a larger proportion, 13% of sub-adults retained the suture. When the adult group is further divided into sex categories, the male figure is 7.6% and the female figure is 10.5%. It would appear from this that the retention of the metopic suture, being highest in sub-adults, may be due to developmental factors. It would also appear to be sex related, occurring more often in the female crania, though this trend is not statistically significant.

Cranial wormians (Tables 53–55)
Wormians are extra small bones found within cranial suture lines. They are usually preformed in membrane and later ossify when the sutures close. The occurrence of cranial wormians has been shown (El-Najar and Dawson 1977) to be genetically controlled rather than due to environmental stresses (eg cranial deformation). Coronal wormians are rare in the crania from Furnells. Only 1.6% displayed this trait, two males and one female. Parietal wormians are also uncommon: 3.9% showed the presence of these ossicles. Wormians of the lambdoidal suture are, however, much more common than those in the other two sutures, occurring in over a quarter (27.4%) of the skulls observed. The frequency of the trait is higher in females than males, 37.5% of the female crania possessing lambdoidal wormians compared with 26.3% of the male crania, though this trend is not statistically significant. Of the total of sub-adult crania observed, 13.3% displayed the trait. The statistically significant lower figure for the sub-adult group may suggest that ossification of cranial wormians is occurring later in life, during adulthood when the sutures begin to fuse. It is not possible to say that wormian bones, or their precursors, are not present in the children's crania as the material may have been cartilaginous and hence lost to the archaeological record.

'Inca' bone (Table 56)
An 'inca' bone is a large single wormian usually found at lambda, the junction of the sagittal and lambdoidal sutures. Its name originates from the relatively high frequency with which it was found in skeleton populations of the pre-Columbian Andes, as observed by early skeletal biologists. The frequency with which it occurs in this sample of 207 crania from Furnells is low. Only 3.4% or 7 individuals: 3 adults and 4 children.

Parietal foramina (Tables 57, and 58)
The parietal foramina are small holes, usually one for each parietal, found on either side of the parietal suture, near the lambdoidal suture. These foramina allow blood vessels to pass from the scalp through the superior longitudinal sinus within the cranium. Their existence is not always constant and may be absent, unilateral, or large in form. Of the 408 crania observed for this trait, the left parietals displayed a frequency of 51.7% and the right 52.7%. The female adult crania have a higher frequency than the male, of 55.6% and 47.5% respectively.

Supra-orbital rim (Tables 59–64)
The supra-orbital artery passes above the eyeball just under the superior edge of the orbit. Sometimes this artery leaves no trace on the rim of the bone but often it passes through a notch or foramen. The notch was the most frequently observed variant in this sample of 399 left and right orbits, at 60.1%. Of the adult group only, 51.6% possessed notches on both left and right sides. The smooth edge was the least frequent, occurring in 16.5% of the sample and the foramen occurred in 23.3%.

Supra-scapular border (Tables 65–70)
On the upper border of the scapula, near the coracoid process, the supra-scapular nerve passes over the

scapula. Usually, a notch is formed to provide a channel for this nerve vessel. Occasionally, the ligament which bridges this channel ossifies, forming a foramen. Sometimes, no evidence of the nerve is found on the bone and the border is smooth. The scapula is an extremely fragile bone and often only the denser glenoid fossa rather than the body of the scapula itself survives. However, 93 fragments of the superior scapular border did survive. The notch was by far the most common variant with a frequency of 84%. The foramen was rare, being observed only twice, giving it a frequency of 3.2%. The smooth border was observed eight times, a frequency of 12.9%. The foramina were observed only from the 45+ years age group, suggesting that the ossification of the ligament is a development of older age.

Septal aperture (Tables 71, and 72)

A thin lamina of bone separates the olecranon and coronoid fossae at the elbow joint. Occasionally, there is a 'communication' between these fossae, forming a septal aperture or supra-trochlear foramen. This is usually manifested as a small hole or multiple holes. Of this sample of 407 humeri, the trait occurs slightly, but not significantly, more frequently in the left compared with the right humerus. It does, however, occur more frequently in the female humeri than in the male, with frequencies of 18.3% and 6.1% respectively. The trait, however, is not generally dominant and occurs in only 10.8% of the sample.

'Squatting' facets (Tables 73, and 74)

The term 'squatting' may be misleading. While squatting may play a part in forming these facets, or extensions to the distal articular surface of the tibia, it is not solely responsible (Trinkhaus 1975). Other factors, such as locomotive stress, are also important and neonates, as well as populations generally accepted as non-squatting, still display the trait to some degree. The name comes from the early skeletal biologists' belief that the trait was to be found only in 'primitive' societies where squatting was considered to be the 'normal' posture of semi-relaxation. The facets were observed moderately more frequently in female tibiae than in male with 58.1% and 45.0%, respectively. The highest frequency was found in females aged 35–45 years (75.0%). The lowest frequency was in males aged 45+ years (29.6%). The articular surface of the male tibia apparently becomes more defined with age, while the female sample shows an irregular distribution. The cause of these facets is not understood but has been suggested to be due to stress or flexion of the lower limb (Trinkhaus 1975). The male frequencies, decreasing with age, would reflect this suggestion, flexion becoming more difficult with age. The relatively high female frequencies may suggest different occupational or habitual posture from the males, continuing throughout their lives.

Osteometric analysis

Osteometric analysis is the study of the size and shape of the skeleton. For any individual, growth and size are genetically determined, though environmental factors play an important role in the development of the skeleton. Such factors can affect the outcome of the genetic potential. Hence by studying the skeleton it is possible to observe the results of this interplay of genetics and environment. Within this report osteometrics are used for descriptive purposes only; their ultimate value, however, lies in their use for studying variability within the population group and variability between skeletal populations.

A standard series of measurements on the cranial and post-cranial skeleton was selected in order best to describe, metrically, the skeletal remains and at the same time provide an efficient and useful base from which future comparative statistics could be calculated. A total of 102 measurements were taken for each individual; 30 cranial and 36 for each side of the post-cranial skeleton. Indices calculated were those for platymeria and platycnemia; an estimate of stature was calculated for each adult when possible (summarised in Table 46). The majority of measurements were lengths, breadths, heights, and diameters and were taken from standard landmarks on the skull and post-cranial skeleton. The measurements were chosen to standardise with other workers and for their easily recognisable descriptive elements. A full list of measurements may be found in Tables 83–85.

With the vast majority of data provided, computer assistance was required and most generously and ably produced by Andy Boddington at the Northamptonshire Archaeology Unit using the SPSSG package. Age and sex cross-tabulations were generated giving the actual number and percentage of individuals of each age and sex category.

Osteometrics were determined where possible for all individuals aged 2 years and older. Summarising statistics were generated for each age and sex group and for the adult males and adult females. These summaries are detailed in Microfiche 1, Tables 86–90.

Table 46 Summary of stature measurements

Sex	Height Mean	s	Observations
Male	167	6.7	50
Female	162	7.3	33

Pathology

Despite the complexity of the study of the pathology of such a large and varied group of individuals, such a study can provide invaluable information, both directly about the health of the individuals themselves, and indirectly about the types of conditions and diseases to which the population as a whole was subjected. In the report below, a summary noting prevalence and frequency of disease is given along with comments on the more general implications. Selected detailed descriptions are appended where they are of interest.

Osteoarthritis

This is by far the most common disease present in this series, there being 745 separate incidents observed, by element. Virtually every one of the 197 adults over the age of 17 years showed some degree of osteoarthritic degeneration in one or more elements. No degeneration due to osteoarthritic causes was observed in any child or adolescent.

Table 47 Osteoarthritis: age and sex distribution

Age	Male	Female	Unsexed	Totals
Sub–adult	–	–	1	1
17–25	11	9	0	20
25–35	23	16	0	39
35–45	26	6	1	33
45+	24	15	0	39
Adult	0	0	4	4
Totals	84	46	6	136

The distribution of osteoarthritis throughout the skeleton was not regular. The area most affected was the lower vertebral column, particularly the thoracic and lumbar vertebrae. It was in this area that the exostoses and degeneration were observed to the greatest degree. The number of incidents observed in the vertebral column was 288 (38.7%); 92 and 93 observations were made at the thoracic and lumbar regions, respectively.

The next two areas of relatively high prevalence were the shoulder and hip. At the shoulder joint itself, the glenoid fossa of the scapula was the area in which osteoarthritic lipping could be observed most frequently, though the shoulder girdle in general is markedly affected. The clavicular facets for the sternum and scapula, and the head of the humerus, were moderately affected.

Osteoarthritis of the upper limb in general was restricted to the shoulder and elbow joints. The radius and ulna showed degeneration at their proximal articular surfaces. The wrist joint was relatively free from degeneration, as can be seen from the low frequency of the 'hand' category (Table 50). This class includes the carpals, metacarpals, and phalanges.

The lower limb was affected by osteoarthritis primarily at the acetabulum of the innominate. The knee and ankle joints, though often the site of fracturing, showed a relatively low prevalence of the disease, as can be seen from the 'tibia' and 'fibula' classes. It would appear that the osteoarthritic affect of the trauma to the lower leg was most commonly found in the hip and lower back areas.

The osteoarthritis observed was in the majority of cases due to chronic degeneration of the joint due to wear and tear. The more severe cases were usually associated with injury.

5062: Male, 25–35 years. The condition of the left shoulder and right hip of this individual was particularly unusual (Figs 102 and 103). Osteoarthritis of both joints was severe. While the origin of the osteoarthritis of the hip was probably traumatic (see also *Trauma*, below) the origin of the shoulder osteoarthritis is unknown and it is not known if the two conditions were associated. The glenoid fossa of the left scapula showed marked exostosis and degeneration with some slight eburnation, indicating the destruction of the cartilage and at least some movement at the joint. The head of the left humerus showed corresponding eburnation but with complete cystic degeneration of the articular surface. The shaft of the left humerus was 100mm shorter than the right, being 214mm and 314mm respectively. The dimensions of the other areas of measurement (ie maximum, minimum shaft diameters and epicondylar breadth) were similar. The bones of the lower arm, the ulna and the radius, showed no disparity in size. It might be suggested that the shortening of the limb may have been due to poliomyelitis. The right hip joint was very badly affected, with extensive exostosis and degeneration causing much deformation. The acetabulum was grossly extended and shallow, suggesting a dislocation or relocation of the femoral head. Eburnation of the surface was apparent, as was corresponding eburnation of the femoral head, indicating continued movement despite destruction of the cartilage. Exostosis of the femoral head was massive, with the extra bone growth extending to the trochanters. The femoral neck was much reduced, possibly due to a telescopic fracture. The excess bony formation at the femoral head was notably callus bone as opposed to the compact bone usually found in osteoarthritic 'lipping'. While slight lipping was observed at other joints, osteoarthritis due to wear and tear of the joints was not developed to any degree. This localisation of severe osteoarthritis can possibly be attributed to injury, affecting only the right hip. (For descriptions of burials 5009, 5010, and 5016, see Microfiche 1.)

Trauma

Injury may have been more common than the skeletal evidence suggests, as only evidence for severe trauma would be apparent. The injury to the bone that was observed was usually manifested as fracture of the shaft or dislocation of a joint. Twenty-seven separate incidents were observed in twenty-four individuals (6.5% of the total number of individuals). The fibula and radius sustained the most injuries with 23.1% and 15.4% of all trauma respectively. These injuries were fractures of the distal shafts of the Pott's and Colles' type. The cause of these types of fracture is usually a fall. In the case of the Pott's fracture to the fibula the fall is to one side with the foot remaining still, causing pressure to the distal shaft and so lateral fracturing. Colles' fracture to the radius is usually caused by a fall forward with the hand outstretched. The pressure is parallel to the shaft rather than perpendicular to it.

Table 48 Trauma: age and sex distribution

Age	Male	Female	Unsexed	Totals
17–25	2	2	1	5
25–35	5	4	0	9
35–45	4	0	0	4
45+	4	1	0	5
Adult	0	0	1	1
Total trauma	15	7	2	24
Trauma not observed	88	73	12	173

The humerus, ulna, femur and hands all received trauma to the same degree, with a frequency of 11.5%. The injury to the hands was usually in the form of dislocation of the phalanges. The feet, clavicle and tibia were the least affected by trauma with frequencies of 7.7%, 3.9% and 3.9% respectively.

Evidence for injury was most often found in males over the age of 25. Trauma was observed in over twice as many males as females, though the overall frequency of trauma is low and the difference in the frequency of trauma between the sexes is not statistically significant.

Fig 102   Shortened left humerus of burial, possibly resulting from poliomyelitis (5062/M/25–35)

Fig 103   Pelvis of burial showing extensive exostosis and degeneration, possibly resulting from injury (5062/M/25–35)

5160: Female, 45+ years. The right humerus, ulna, and radius displayed extreme ankylosis and lipping of the elbow joint at the trochlea and capitulum, olecranon process and radial facet, and radial head, respectively. There was no eburnation of the trochlea but marked eburnation of the capitulum. It is probable, therefore, that movement was limited to rotation in the forearm but without any upward or downward movement. The head of the radius showed corresponding eburnation. This osteoarthritis was localised and was probably traumatic in origin, being caused by a heavy blow to the joint.

(For descriptions of burials 5009, 5016, 5019, 5051, 5062, 5064, 5078, 5087, 5100, 5108, 5136, 5142, 5144, 5201, 5205, 5222–3, 5242, 5247, 5261, 5286, 5299, and 5369 see Microfiche 1.)

Osteitis

The prevalence of osteitis was relatively low, occurring in 7.5% of the sample. Osteitis, while found in only 28 individuals, was found in 64 separate incidents; therefore, once allowed to develop it spread or affected several parts of the skeleton.

Infection was most commonly observed in the tibia, fibula, and femur, with frequencies of 34.4%, 25% and 11% respectively. The clavicle and ulna, though not with high frequencies, have a relatively higher prevalence than most elements, possibly because of their proximity to the surface.

Table 49 Osteitis: age and sex distribution

Age	Male	Female	Unsexed	Totals
6–12	0	0	2	2
12–17	0	1	2	3
17–25	2	5	0	7
25–35	5	3	0	8
35–45	3	0	0	3
45+	2	1	0	3
Adult	0	0	1	1
Total osteitis	12	10	5	27
Osteitis not observed	91	70	9	170

Table 50 Frequency of disease and trauma (%)

Bone	Osteoarthritis	Trauma	Osteitis
Clavicle	7.9	3.8	6.3
Scapula	10.5	0	0
Humerus	7.7	11.5	0
Ulna	5.4	11.5	6.3
Radius	5.1	15.4	0
Innominate	9.4	0	4.7
Femur	4.8	11.5	10.9
Tibia	1.5	3.8	34.4
Fibula	0.3	23.1	25.0
Patella	2.8	0	0
Hands	1.3	11.5	1.6
Feet	1.1	7.8	1.6
Manubrium	2.0	0	0
Ribs	0	0	1.6
Vertebrae:			
Cervical	8.3	0	0
Thoracic	12.3	0	1.6
Lumbar	12.5	0	0
Sacral	5.5	0	0

Five incidents of osteitis may have been associated with trauma to the affected bone. Osteomyelitis, being due to the staphylococcus bacillus, was evident in two young individuals, an adolescent female (5175) and a child aged 10–12 years (5200); both were affected in the lower limb.

Two other burials are of particular interest (5046 and 5218). Burial 5046 has been diagnosed as leprous. The lower limb changes in the tibiae, fibulae, tarsals and metatarsals were characteristic and changes of facies leprosa were also observed (Dr K Manchester pers comm). An X-ray by Dr Manchester revealed a femoral fracture due to pyogenic infection. A third burial (5256) had some features characteristic of leprosy and might also have been leprous. Burial 5218 showed characteristics of tuberculosis and poliomyelitis (Fig 53). It was felt that the individual might have had poliomyelitis as a child, hence the lack of development of the left humerus and right femur, and developed tuberculosis later in life (Dr K Manchester and Professor J M Reverte, pers comm).

5046: Male, 17–25 years. Extensive and extreme infection was found in the right femur, tibia and fibula and in the left tibia. There was also degeneration of the pubic symphysis due to osteitis. The right femur showed osteitic development with periostitis (inflammation of the periosteum, the membranous covering of all bone) of the distal shaft but not affecting the condyles. The tibia displayed moderate osteitis of the proximal and distal shaft while the right fibula displayed gross osteitis of the whole shaft. The left tibia was observed to have gross osteitis and periostitis of the whole shaft. The cause of this widespread infection of the lower limbs and pubic symphysis is not known; however, the infection must have been prevalent for some time before death considering the degree of destruction and its extent. The lower limb changes were characteristic of leprosy; facies leprosa was also observed.

5074: Male, 25–35 years. Periostitis was observed at the distal shaft, posteriorly, of the left femur, along the linea aspera. The left tibia and fibula were also affected, with marked periostitis of the tibia condyles and proximal shaft and moderate osteitis of the fibula shaft.

5218: Male, 17–25 years. Evidence for severe infection, possibly the early stages of tuberculosis, and/or poliomyelitis, was found in this individual. Complete destruction as a result of osteitis was observed of the left glenoid fossa and the head of the left humerus (Fig 53). The shaft of the humerus was much shortened but not atrophied. The right leg was also markedly affected. The right femur was much shortened and atrophied from lack of use. The proximal end was normal in size but the distal end showed complete destruction with much cyst formation in the condyles and articular cartilage, with fusion of a much distorted patella. The right fibula showed erosion of the proximal articular surface due to osteitis. The right foot displayed marked degeneration of all the bony material. There was complete fusion at facet joints and bodies of the third and fourth cervical vertebrae with slight skewness to the left side. The eleventh and twelfth thoracic vertebrae showed marked degeneration of their centra and intervertebral facets. The eleventh thoracic vertebra was wedge-shaped due to

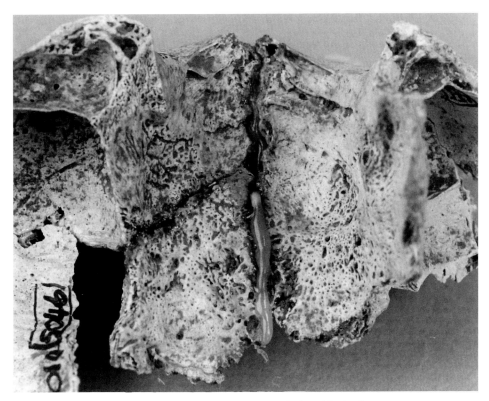

Fig 104   Nasal surface of palate showing characteristics of facies leprosa (5046/M/17–25)

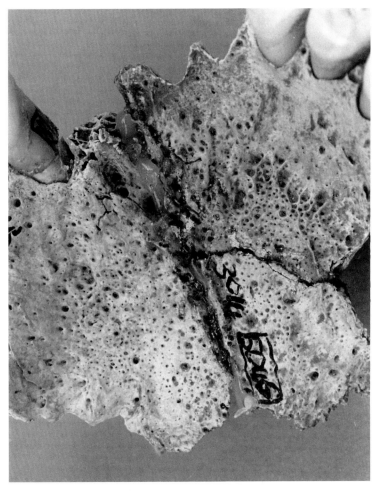

Fig 105   Oral surface of palate showing characteristics of facies leprosa (5046/M/17–25)

Fig 106   Tibia and fibula showing gross osteitis characteristic of leprosy (5046/M/17–25)

Fig 107   Close up of tibia and fibula showing gross osteitis characteristic of leprosy (5046/M/17–25)

collapsing of the centrum. The adjoining surface of the tenth and twelfth centra showed cyst formation, indicating degeneration of the intervertebral cartilage. The external surfaces were also badly pitted with evidence of non-specific osteitis. Ankylosis had begun. The other thoracic vertebrae showed only slight osteoarthritic lipping. There was partial sacralisation of the fifth lumbar vertebra. This individual was, uniquely for this graveyard, buried with a stone in his mouth (p 42).

5256: Male, 25–35 years. A patch of osteitis was observed on the lateral surface of the right ilium, anteriorly. Both lower limbs were badly affected by osteitis. The femoral shafts were slightly thickened distally with marked periostitis. Both tibiae displayed marked periostitis of the mid-shaft and the distal shafts medially and laterally. There was destruction to the lateral articular surface. Both fibulae shafts, mid- and proximally, showed marked periostitis. The nature of the infection was similar to that of 5046 (above) and may have been due to leprosy.

(For descriptions of burials 5006, 5009, 5028, 5046, 5074, 5112, 5123, 5136, 5142, 5156, 5159, 5175, 5195, 5200, 5201, 5204, 5205, 5207, 5231, 5242, 5253, 5299, 5311, 5335 and 5348, see Microfiche 1.)

Table 51 Orbital osteoporosis: age and sex distribution (%)

Age	Left orbit			Right orbit		
	Male	Female	Unsexed	Male	Female	Unsexed
Neonate–2	–	–	0	–	–	55.6
2–6	–	–	47.8	–	–	50.0
6–12	–	–	50.0	–	–	47.8
12–17	–	–	55.6	–	–	0
17–25	22.2	39.1	–	21.1	48.0	–
25–35	20.0	21.4	–	15.8	21.4	–
35–45	25.0	57.1	–	16.7	25.0	–
45+	15.8	23.1	–	5.6	27.3	–

Orbital osteoporosis (cribra orbitalia)

This manifested itself by sieve-like perforations of the roof of the orbit. This anomaly has been attributed to enlarged lachrymal glands (Brothwell 1981) or a nutritional, in particular an anaemic, deficiency (Cybulski 1977). Anaemia is the most widely accepted cause.

From Table 51 orbital osteoporosis can be seen to have occurred with relatively high frequency, 29.3% of the observable population (108 individuals). Osteoporosis was not observed in infant orbits, probably because the perforations had not had time to develop before death. It was markedly frequent in children from the ages of 2 years to adolescence, nearly half the adolescents displaying the trait. Females also showed a high prevalence, relative to males. This distribution would corroborate the suggestion that a nutritional deficiency, in particular anaemia, was the cause of this pitting of the orbits. Children and, in particular, adolescents have high nutritional requirements, with the growth and development of their bodies. Females too have high nutritional standards to be met in order to produce healthy offspring and to survive to produce more.

Other diseases and anomalies

The category of 'other' in this report refers to any disease or anomaly other than osteoarthritis, trauma, infection or dental hygiene.

Button osteomae, or possible ossified sub-periosteal haematomae, were observed in four individuals, all adults, and were found only on the skull, usually the frontal or parietals (5010, 5018, 5134, 5224).

Spina bifida was observed most often in the sacrum but once at the sixth cervical vertebra. The bifurcation was usually complete but affected only one or two vertebrae at a time, usually the first, fourth, or fifth sacral vertebrae. It was observed in five adult individuals (5026, 5029, 5040, 5118, 5184).

Sacralisation of the fifth lumbar vertebra was quite common, occurring in six instances (5061, 5122, 5159, 5207, 5223, 5247), as was lumbarisation of the fifth sacral vertebra, with three occurrences (5158, 5202, 5236). The sacralisation in some instances, however, could be attributed to osteoarthritic changes and as such was not true 'sacralisation'. Supernumerary sacral vertebrae were also observed in one instance (5085) while supernumerary lumbar vertebrae were observed twice (5219, 5321).

Cleft palate was observed in one child, aged approximately 8–9 years (5281). In the same individual, imperfection extended to other lateral incisors which had grown as one tooth with the central incisors.

5118: Male, 45+ years. The second lumbar vertebra displayed a non-fused spinous process. The non-fusion may have been congenital or possibly traumatic as no other vertebrae displayed this trait. The fourth and fifth thoracic vertebrae were found to be fused together. The point of fusion was at the left intervertebral facets. The left inferior articular surface of the fifth thoracic vertebra was split with a fracture reaching up to the spinous process. The fracture may have been traumatic in origin with complete healing.

(For descriptions of burials 5010, 5018, 5026, 5029, 5040, 5061, 5085, 5122, 5134, 5150, 5158, 5159, 5184, 5187, 5202, 5207, 5219, 5223, 5224, 5236, 5247, 5281, 5321 and 5331, see Microfiche 1.)

Cranial cuts

Attempts had been made to remove the upper portion of the cranial vault of two skulls, 5103 and 5288. Saw marks and complete cuts were observed, with no apparent bone growth to indicate healing. The purpose of this post-mortem mutilation is not known but another instance was observed by the author in a cranium from the Roman Victoria Road site at Winchester. The technique at both sites was similar. This same 'decapitation', in late eighteenth-century skeletons, has been attributed to post-mortem examination or autopsy (see also p 70).

5103: Male, 17–25 years. The occipital bone was found to show cut and saw marks at the nuchal crest. The edge was smooth and clearly sawn; however, the occipital bone was fragmentary. The posterior fragment of the occipital survived but showed no corresponding signs of sawing.

5288: Male, 25–35 years. The left temporal had been sawn in two places: along the temporal line, partially through, then broken, and above and partially through the mastoid process, just superior to the auditory meatus. The second sawing had been completely through the bone. The saw marks were post-mortem, through relatively fresh bone as no splintering had occurred. It is possible that this mutilation of the bone may have been for purposes of post-mortem examination.

Dental disease

This can be classified into three categories; caries, periodontal disease and abscess. Caries and abscess were not observed in children's teeth; however, alveolar resorption and calculus build-up, associated with periodontal disease, were found occasionally in adolescents and children aged approximately 6–12 years.

Caries was found in relatively few instances. Table 77 shows the distribution of caries cavities throughout the maxillary and mandibular teeth by sex and age. There would appear to have been no difference between the sexes in the frequency of the disease, and the increasing frequency with age was also the same for both sexes. The drop in frequency in the male age range of 45+ years was probably due to the relatively high percentage of ante-mortem tooth loss at that age (Table 77). Caries was most often observed in the molars, both on the neck and occlusal surfaces. It was rarely found in the premolars, canines and lateral incisors, and never observed in the central incisors.

Periodontal disease was frequently observed in the form of alveolar resorption and the associated calculus build-up (Table 79). Alveolar resorption was found to a marked degree in half (49.7%) the maxillae and mandibles observed. Over one-third (36.1%) displayed the resorption to a moderate degree and only 14.2% showed very slight alveolar resorption. Virtually all adult maxillae and mandibles showed some degree of resorption. Ante-mortem tooth loss was, in the vast majority of cases, associated with alveolar resorption due to periodontal disease.

Calculus build-up was present most commonly to a moderate degree (Table 80). Where alveolar resorption was observed, calculus build-up was also found in almost every case.

Abscesses in the alveoli, like caries cavities, were observed in relatively few instances (Table 78). They were found in all areas of the maxilla or mandible, however, the most frequent site was the first molars on the buccal side. Both males and females developed abscesses with the same frequency, generally increasing with age.

The relatively low frequency of caries cavities with a high frequency of periodontal disease would suggest a diet low in sugars and carbohydrates and relatively high in proteins, the two diseases being mutually exclusive and caused by emphasis on the one food rather than the other (Hillson 1979).

Conclusion

The total buried population was found to be 363. Of the adults 100 were male, 82 female and 9 remained unsexed due to the fragmentary nature of their remains. Males hence predominated over females generally. The remaining 172 burials were sub-adult individuals of under 17 years of age. Mortality peaked in infancy; 20% did not survive the first year of life. This correlates with the peak of mortality in female adulthood, where the effects on longevity reduced the female life expectation at age 17 to just 15.9 years, compared with 21.8 years for males.

Morphological variation has been recorded and utilised in a broad descriptive manner in this text; along with the osteometrics it has potential for the analysis of the population characteristics of the contributing community and for comparison with material from other cemeteries.

Degenerative joint disease was the most commonly observed pathology; while evident throughout the skeleton, its highest prevalence was in the vertebral column. In contrast osteitis was observed least frequently, though two cases of particular interest occurred in association with leprosy and one with poliomyelitis. Osteoporosis of the orbits was observed in one-third of the population. The idea of its association with anaemia is reinforced by its higher prevalence in the female skeleton. Dental disease was by far the most apparent in the form of alveolar resorption and associated calculus build-up caused by periodontal disease. Ante-mortem tooth loss was from this cause in most cases. Caries, by contrast, was found in relatively few instances, as were periodontal abscesses.

Bibliography

Abbreviations
BAR   *British Archaeological Reports*
CBA   *Council for British Archaeology*
DoE   *Department of the Environment*
RCHME   *Royal Commission on the Historical Monuments of England*

Addyman, P V, 1965 Late Saxon settlements in the St Neots area,
   1: the Saxon settlement and Norman castle at Eaton Socon, Beds,
   Proc Cambridge Antiq Soc, **58**, 38–73
—, 1969 Late Saxon settlements in the St Neots area, 2: the Little Pax-
   ton settlement and enclosures, *Proc Cambridge Antiq Soc*, **62**, 59–93
—, 1972 Late Saxon settlements in the St Neots area, 3: the village or
   township at St Neots, *Proc Cambridge Antiq Soc*, **64**, 45–99
Anderman, S, 1976 The cnemic index, a critique, *Am J Phys Anthropol*, **44**, 369–70
Anderson, J E, 1963 The people of Fairty: an osteological analysis of
   an Iroquoian ossuary, *Bull Nat Mus Canada*, **193**, 28–129
—, 1969 *The human skeleton, a manual for archaeologists*, National
   Museum of Man, Ottawa
Anon, 1848 On the uses of piscinas, *Ecclesiologist*, **8**, 329–60
Archibald, M, forthcoming *Coins and tokens: Furnells*, in Audouy,
   forthcoming
Atkin, M, Ayers, B and Jennings, S, 1983 Thetford-type ware pro-
   duction in Norwich, *East Anglian Archaeol*, **17**, 61–97
Audouy, M, forthcoming *North Raunds, Northamptonshire: excavations
   1977–87*
Ayers, B, 1985 Excavations within the north-east bailey of Norwich
   Castle, 1979, *East Anglian Archaeol*, **28**, 1985
Baker, D, Baker, E, Hassall, J, and Simco, A, 1979 Excavations in
   Bedford 1967–1977, *Bedfordshire Archaeol J*, **13**
Barlow, F, 1979 *The English Church 1000–1066*, London
Batcock, N, 1988 The parish in Norfolk in the 11th and 12th
   centuries, in Blair (ed) 1988, 179–90
Bass, W M , 1971 *Human osteology, a laboratory and field manual*,
   Missouri Archaeol Soc, Columbia, Missouri
Baud, C A, 1982 La taphonomie, *Historie et Archaeologie*, **66**, 33–5
Bell, R D, Beresford, M W, *et al* 1987 Wharram Percy: the church of
   St Martin, *Soc Medieval Archaeol Monogr Ser*, **11**
Bennett, K A, 1965 The etiology and genetics of wormian bones,
   Am J Phys Anthropol, **23**, 255–60
Beresford, M W, and St Joseph, J K S, *1958 Medieval England, an
   aerial survey*, Cambridge
Berry, A C, 1974 The use of non-metrical variations in the cranium in
   the study of Scandinavian populations, *Am J Phys Anthropol*, **40**,
   345–58
Berry, A C, and Berry, R J, 1967 Epigenetic variation in the human
   cranium, *J Anat*, **101**, 361–79
Biddle, M, 1968 Excavations at Winchester 1967, sixth interim
   report, *Antiq J*, **48**, 250–84
—, 1970 Excavations at Winchester 1969, eighth interim report, *Antiq
   J*, **50**, 277–326
Binding, G, 1975 Quellen, Brunnen und Reliquiengräber in Kirchen,
   Zeitschrift für Archäologie des Mittelalters, **3**, 37–56
Blair, J (ed), 1988 *Minsters and parish churches: the local church in
   transition 950–1200*, Monogr 17, Oxford Univ Comm Archaeol
Boddington, A, 1987a Raunds, Northamptonshire: analysis of a
   country churchyard, *World Archaeology*, **18**, 412–25
—, 1987b Chaos, disturbance and decay in an Anglo-Saxon cemetery,
   in Boddington *et al* (eds) 1987, 27–42
—, 1987c From bones to population: the problem of numbers, in
   Boddington *et al* (eds) 1987, 180–97
—, 1990 Models of burial, settlement and worship; the Final Phase
   reviewed, in *Anglo-Saxon cemeteries: a reappraisal* (ed E Southworth),
   177–99, Stroud
Boddington, A, and Cadman, G E, 1981 Raunds, an interim report
   on excavations 1977–80, *Anglo-Saxon studies in archaeology and
   history*, 2, BAR British ser **92**, 103–22, Oxford

Boddington, A, and Morgan, M, 1979 *The excavation record,
   part 2: inhumations*, Northamptonshire County Counc Occas Pap
   3, Northampton
Boddington, A, Garland, N, and Janaway, R (eds) 1987 *Death, decay and
   reconstruction: approaches to archaeology and forensic science*, Manchester
Brothwell, D R, 1971 Palaeodemography, in *Biological aspects of
   demography* (ed W Brass), 111–30, London
—, 1972 Palaeodemography and earlier British populations, *World
   Archaeol*, **4**, 75–87
—, 1981 *Digging up bones*, British Museum (Natural History), London
—, 1987 Decay and disorder in the York Jewbury skeletons, in
   Boddington *et al* (eds) 1987, 22–6
Brothwell, D R, and Krzanowski, W, 1974 Evidence of biological
   differences between early British populations from Neolithic to
   medieval times, as revealed by eleven commonly available cranial
   vault measurements, *J Archaeol Sci*, **1**, 249–60
Brown, M M, and Gallagher, D B, 1984 St Cuthbert's church,
   Ormesby, Cleveland: excavation and watching brief 1975 and
   1976, *Yorkshire Archaeol J*, **56**, 51–63
Bullough, D, 1983 Burial, community and belief in the early medieval
   west, in *Ideal and reality in Frankish and Anglo-Saxon society* (ed
   P Wormald), 177–201, Oxford
Butler, L A S, 1964 Minor medieval monumental sculpture in the
   East Midlands, *Archaeol J*, **121**, 111–53
Cadman, G E, 1983 Raunds 1977–1983; an excavation summary,
   Medieval Archaeol, **27**, 107–22
Cadman, G E, and Audouy, M, 1990 Recent excavations on Saxon
   and medieval quarries in Raunds, Northamptonshire, in *Stone :
   quarrying and building in England AD 43–1525* (ed D Parsons)
Cadman G E and Foard G, 1984 Raunds: manorial and village
   origins, in *Studies in Late Anglo-Saxon settlements* (ed M Faull),
   81–100, Oxford
Carter, D R, and Spengler, D M, 1982 Biomechanics of fracture, in
   Bone in clinical orthopaedics (ed G Sumner-Smith), 305–34
Cinthio, H and Boldsen, J, 1983–4 Patterns of distribution in the early
   medieval cemetery at Löddeköpinge, *Pap Archaeol Inst, Univ Lund*,
   n ser **5**, 116–27
Clarke, H, 1970 Excavations on a kiln site at Grimston, Pott Row,
   Norfolk, *Norfolk Archaeol*, **35**, 79–95
Collingwood, W G, 1927 *Northumbrian crosses of the pre-Norman age*,
   London
Cowan, T W, 1908 *Wax craft: all about beeswax*, London
Cramp, R J, 1984 *Corpus of Anglo-Saxon stone sculpture in England 1:
   County Durham and Northumberland*, British Academy, Oxford
Cunliffe, B, 1976 Excavations at Portchester Castle 2: Saxon, *Soc
   Antiq Res Rep*, **33**, London
Cybulski, J S, 1977 Cribra orbitalia, a possible sign of anaemia in
   historic native populations of the British Columbia coast, *Am J Phys
   Anthropol*, **47**, 31–40
Denham, V, 1984 The pottery, in Williams *et al* 1984, 46–63
DoE 1975 *Principles of publication in rescue archaeology*, London
DoE 1982 *Report of the CBA/DoE working party on the publication of
   archaeological excavations*, London
Dickinson, G, *et al*, 1983 *Rutland churches before restoration: an early
   Victorian album of watercolours and drawings*, London
Dix, B (ed) 1986–7 (1988) The Raunds Area Project: second interim
   report, *Northamptonshire Archaeol*, **21**, 3–30
Dunning, G C, 1956 Trade relations between England and the
   Continent in the late Anglo-Saxon period, in Harden (ed) 1956, 218–33
Durandus, G See Neale, J M and Webb, B
El-Najar, M Y, and Dawson, G L, 1977 The effect of artificial cranial
   deformation on the incidence of wormian bones in the lambdoidal
   suture, *Am J Phys Anthropol*, **46**, 155–60
Everson, P, and Stocker, D, (forthcoming) *Corpus of Anglo-Saxon stone
   sculpture, 5, Lincolnshire*, British Academy, London
Feasey, H P, 1906 The Paschal candle, *Ecclesiastical Rev*, **34**, 353–71
Finnegan, M, 1978 Non-metric variation of the infra-cranial skeleton,
   J Anat, **125**, 23–37

Finucane, R C, 1981 Sacred corpse, profane carrion: social ideals and death rituals in the late Middle Ages, in *Mirrors of Mortality* (ed J Whaley), London

Foard, G R, 1978 *Archaeological priorities: proposals for Northamptonshire*, Northamptonshire County Council Occas Pap

Foard, G R, and Pearson, T, 1985 The Raunds Area Project: first interim report, *Northamptonshire Archaeol*, **20**, 3–22

Fox, C, 1922 Anglo-Saxon monumental sculpture in the Cambridge district, *Proc Cambridge Antiq Soc*, **21**, 15–45

Franklin, M J, 1982 Minsters and parishes: Northamptonshire studies, unpubl PhD thesis, Univ Cambridge

Frere, W H, 1901 *Pontifical services: illustrated … with descriptive notes and a liturgical introduction*, Alcuin Club Collect, **3**, London

Gevjall, N-G, 1960 *Westerhus: medieval population and church in the light of skeletal remains*, Lund

Gibson, W L, 1803 Observations on the remains of a stone cross, or pillar, in the hundred of West Flegg, in the county of Norfolk, *Archaeologia*, **14**, 40–54

Gilmour, B J, and Stocker, D A, 1986 St Mark's church and cemetery, *Archaeol Lincoln*, **13:1**, CBA, London

Glazema, P, 1949 Oudheidkundige opgravingen in de nederlands hervormde kerk te Oosterbeek (Gld), *Bull Koninklijke Nederlandse Oudheidkundige Bond*, 6 ser, 2, 33–84

Godfrey, J, 1962 *The church in Anglo-Saxon England*, Cambridge

Graham-Campbell, J, 1982 Some new and neglected finds of 9th century Anglo-Saxon ornamental metalwork, *Medieval Archaeol*, **26**, 144–51

Greenwell, W (ed), 1853 *The pontifical of Egbert, Archbishop of York, AD 732–766*, Surtees Soc, **27**, Durham

Haddan, A W, and Stubbs, W, 1871 *Councils and ecclesiastical documents relating to Great Britain and Ireland*, **3**, Oxford

Harden, D B, (ed) 1956 *Dark-Age Britain*, London

Henderson, W G (ed), 1873 (1875) *Liber pontificalis Chr Bainbridge archiepiscopi Eboracensis*, Surtees Soc, **61**, Durham

Hess, L, 1946 Ossicula wormiana, *Human Biol*, **18:6**, 1–80

Hills, C, Penn, K, and Rickett, R, 1984 The Anglo-Saxon cemetery at Spong Hill, North Elmham, Part 3: catalogue of inhumations, *East Anglian Archaeol*, **21**

Hillson, S W, 1979 Diet and dental disease, *World Archaeol*, **11**, 147–62

Hodgson, J M, (ed) 1974 *Soil Survey Field Handbook*, Soil Survey Tech Monogr, **5**, Harpenden

Holt, C A, 1978 A re-examination of parturition scars on the female pelvis, *Am J Phys Anthropol*, **49**, 91–4

Hope, W H St J, 1899 *English altars from illuminated manuscripts*, Alcuin Club Collect, **1**, London

Houghton, P, 1974 The relationship of the pre-auricular groove of the ilium to pregnancy, *Am J Phys Anthropol*, **41**, 381–90

Howell, W, 1969 The use of the multivariate techniques in the study of skeletal populations, *Am J Phys Anthropol*, **31**, 311–14

Huggins, P, Rodwell, K, and Rodwell, W, 1982 Anglo-Saxon and Scandinavian building measurements, in *Structural Reconstruction* (ed P Drury), 21–66, BAR, 110, Oxford

Hunter, R, 1975 Neutron activation analysis of St Neots type ware, unpubl MA dissertation, Univ Bradford

—, 1979 St Neots type ware, in Williams 1979, 230–42

Hurst, J G, 1955 Saxo-Norman pottery in East Anglia, part 1: general discussion and St Neots ware, *Proc Cambridge Antiq Soc*, **49**, 43–70

—, 1956 Saxo-Norman pottery in East Anglia, part 2: Thetford ware, *Proc Cambridge Antiq Soc*, **50**, 42–60

—, 1957 Saxo-Norman pottery in East Anglia, part 3: Stamford ware, *Proc Cambridge Antiq Soc*, **51**, 37–65

—, 1976 The pottery, in Wilson (ed) 1976, 283–348

Hurst-Thomas, D, 1976 *Figuring anthropology*, New York

Irvine, J T, 1889 Saxon monumental slabs found at Peterborough Cathedral, *J Brit Archaeol Assoc*, **45**, 79–80, 180

Jennings, S, 1981 Eighteen centuries of pottery from Norwich, *East Anglian Archaeol*, **13**

Johnson, Rev J, 1850 *A collection of the laws and canons of the Church of England*, Oxford

Kendrick, T D, 1938 *Anglo-Saxon art to AD 900*, London

Kenward, H K, 1974 Methods for palaeo-entomology on site and in the laboratory, *Sci in Archaeol*, **13**, 16–24

Kerney, M P, and Cameron, R A D, 1979 *A field guide to land snails of Britain and north-west Europe*, London

Kilmurry, K, 1977 An approach to pottery study: Stamford ware, *Medieval Ceram*, **1**, 51–62

—, 1980 *The pottery industry of Stamford, Lincolnshire, c AD 850–1250*, BAR Brit Ser, **84**

Knight, J K, 1976–78, (1981) Excavations at St Baruc's chapel, Barry Island, *Trans Cardiff Naturalists' Soc*, **99**, 28–63

Leach, H N, 1987 Stamford ware fabrics, *Medieval Ceram*, **11**, 69–74

Lehmann-Brockhaus, O, 1955–60 *Lateinische Schriftquellen zur Kunst in England, Wales und Schottland vom Jahre 901 bis zum Jahre 1307*, vols 1–5, Prestel Verlag, Munich

Levett, J, 1634 *The ordering of bees: or, the true history of managing them …*, London

Liebermann, F (ed), 1903 *Gesetze der Angelsachsen 1*, Savigny Foundation, Halle

List, K, 1967 Die karolingische Kirche in Höllstein (Krs Lörrach), *Nachrichtenblatt der Denkmalpflege in Baden-Württemberg* **10**, 31–5

Lockton, W, 1920 *The treatment of the remains at the eucharist after holy communion and the times of the ablutions*, Cambridge

Lovejoy, C O, Burnstein, A H, and Heiple, K G, 1976 The biomechanical analysis of bone strength, a method and its application to platycnemia, *Am J Phys Anthropol*, **44**, 489–606

Loyn, H, 1971 Towns in late Anglo-Saxon England, in *England before the Conquest, studies in primary sources presented to Dorothy Whitelock* (ed P Clemoes and K Hughes), 115–28, Cambridge

LRO 44/28/1318 *Cossington churchwardens' accounts, 1534–1601*, Rothley Temple MSS, Leicestershire Record Office

LRO DG36/140/6 *Melton Mowbray churchwardens' accounts*, 1553, Leicestershire Record Office

Luard, H R, (ed) 1869 *Annales monastici*, **4**, Rolls ser, 36.4., London

Mahany, C, Burchard, A, and Simpson, G, 1982 Excavations in Stamford, Lincolnshire, 1963–1969, *Soc Medieval Archaeol Monogr Ser*, **9**

Mant, A K, 1987 Knowledge acquired from post-war exhumations, in Boddington *et al* (eds) 1987, 65–78

Martène, E, 1736–38 *De antiquis ecclesiae ritibus*, 2 edn, Antwerp

Masali, M, 1969 Body size and proportions as revealed by bone measurements and their environmental adaptation, *J Hum Evol*, **1**, 187–97

McCarthy, M, 1979 *Pottery synthesis*, in Williams 1979, 225–30

McKern, T W, and Stewart, T D, 1957 The innominate bone, in *Skeletal age changes in young American males*, [US Army] Technical Rep, Headquarters Quartermaster Research and Development Command, Natick, Massachusetts

Meaney, A L, and Hawkes, S C, 1970 *Two Anglo-Saxon cemeteries at Winnall, Winchester, Hampshire*, Soc Medieval Archaeol Monogr Ser, **4**

Meaney, M, Hawkes, S C, and Mellor, M, 1980 Late Saxon pottery from Oxfordshire: evidence and speculation, *Medieval Ceram*, **4**, 17–27

Mellor, M, 1980 Late Saxon pottery from Oxfordshire: evidence and speculation, *Medieval Ceramics*, **4**, 17–27

Morris, R, 1983 *The church in British archaeology*, CBA Res Rep, **47**, London

Muncey, R W, 1930 *A history of the consecration of churches and churchyards*, Cambridge

Munsell Color 1975 *Munsell soil color charts*, Munsell Color, Baltimore, Maryland

Neale, J M, and Webb, B (eds), 1843 (repr 1973) *The symbolism of churches and church ornaments: a translation of the first book of the Rationale Divinorum Officiorum*, Green, Leeds (repr AMS Press, New York) 1973

Nichols J 1795–1815 *History and antiquities of the county of Leicester*, vols 1–4, London

Parsons, D, 1986 Sacrarium: ablution drains in early medieval churches, in *The Anglo-Saxon church* (eds L A S Butler and R K Morris), 105–20, CBA Res Rep, **60**, London

Pearson, T, forthcoming The medieval pottery industries at Lyveden and Stanion, Northamptonshire

Pocknee, C E, 1963 *The Christian altar: in history and today*, London

Putschar, W G J, 1976 The structure of the human symphysis pubis with special consideration of parturition and its sequelae, *Am J Phys Anthropol*, **45**, 589–94

Radford, C A R, 1976 The church of Saint Alkmund, Derby, *Derbyshire Archaeol J*, **96**, 26–61

Rahtz, P, 1978 Grave orientation, *Archaeol J*, **135**, 1–14

Reynolds, N, 1976 The structure of Anglo-Saxon graves, *Antiquity* **50**, 140–3

Rodwell, W J, 1981 *The archaeology of the English church*, London

Rodwell, W J, and Rodwell K, 1977 *Historic churches, a wasting asset*, CBA Res Rep, **19**, London

—, and —, 1982 St Peter's church, Barton-upon-Humber, excavation and structural study, 1978–81, *Antiq J*, **62**, 283–315

—, and —, 1985 *Rivenhall: investigation of a villa, church and village, 1950–1977*, CBA Res Rep, **55**, London

Rogerson, A, and Adams, N, 1978 A Saxo-Norman pottery kiln at Bircham, *E Anglian Archaeol*, **8**, 33–44

Rogerson, A, and Dallas, C, 1984 Excavations in Thetford 1948–59 and 1973–80, *E Anglian Archaeol*, **22**

Rogerson, A, *et al* 1987 Three Norman churches in Norfolk, *E Anglian Archaeol*, **32**

Rohault de Fleury, C, 1883 *La messe, études archéologiques sur ses monuments*, **3**, Paris

Routh, T E, 1938-9 The Rothley cross-shaft and the Sproxton cross, *Trans Leicestershire Archaeol Soc*, **20**, 66-76

Salzman, L F, 1967 *Building in England down to 1540: a documentary history*, rev edn, Oxford

Serjeantson, R M, and Longden, H I, 1913 The parish churches and religious houses of Northamptonshire, their dedications, altars, images and lights, *Archaeol J*, **70**, 217–452

Shoesmith, R, 1980 *Excavations at Castle Green: Hereford City excavations*, 1, CBA Res Rep, **36**, London

Sjovold, T, Swedborg, I, and Diener, L, 1974 A pregnant woman from the Middle Ages with exostosis multiplex, *Ossa*, **1**, 3–23

Steane, J M, and Bryant, G F, 1975 Excavations at the deserted medieval settlement at Lyveden, *J Northampton Mus*, **12**

Steinbock, R T, 1976 *Palaeopathological diagnosis and interpretation*, Thomas Springfield, Illinois

Stuiver, M, and Reimer, P J, 1986 CALIB, *Radiocarbon*, **28**, 1022–30

Swedlund, A C, and Armelagos, G J, 1976 *Demographic Anthropology*, Dubuque, Iowa

Sylvester-Bradley, P C, and Ford, T D, 1968 *Geology of the East Midlands*, Leicester

Taylor, H M, 1969 The Anglo-Saxon cathedral church at Canterbury, *Archaeol J*, **126**, 101–30

—, 1973 The position of the altar in early Anglo-Saxon churches, *Antiq J*, **53**, 52–8

—, 1978 *Anglo-Saxon architecture*, **3**, Cambridge

Taylor, H M, and Taylor, J, 1965 *Anglo-Saxon architecture*, **1** and **2**, Cambridge

ter Kuile, E H, 1964 Les églises carolingiennes d'Osterbeek et de Tienhoven, *Opus musicum, een bundel studies aangeboden aan Prof Dr M D Ozinga*, ed H W M van der Wijck *et al*, 13–30, Assen, Netherlands

Thorn, F, and Thorn, C (eds), 1979 *Domesday Book: Northamptonshire*, Chichester

Torgersen, J, 1951 The developmental genetics and evolutionary meaning of the metopic suture, *Am J Phys Anthropol*, ns **2**, 193–210

Trinkhaus, E, 1975 Squatting among the Neanderthals: a problem in the behavioural interpretation of skeletal morphology, *J Archaeol Sci*, **2**, 327–51

Trotter, M, and Gleser, G C, 1952 Estimation of stature from long bones of American Whites and Negroes, *Am J Phys Anthropol*, **10**, 463–514

Trotter, M, and Gleser, G C, 1958 A re-evaluation of estimation of stature based on measurements of stature taken, *Am J Phys Anthropol*, **16**, 79–123

von Endt, D W, and Ortner, D J, 1984 Experimental effects of bone size and temperature on bone diagenesis, *J Archaeol Sci*, **11**, 247–53

Wade-Martins, P, 1980 Excavations in North Elmham Park, 1967–72, vols 1–2, *E Anglian Archaeol*, **9**

Wasserschleben, F W H, 1851 *Die Bussordnungen der abendländischen Kirche*, Halle

Weaver, D S, 1980 Sex differences in the ilia of known sex and age samples of foetal and infant skeletons, *Am J Phys Anthropol*, **52**, 191–5

Weaver, L, 1915 *Memorials and monuments*, London

Weiss, K, 1972 On systematic bias in skeletal sexing, *Am J Phys Anthropol*, **37**, 239–49

—, 1973 Demographic models for anthropology, *Am Antiquity 38 (2)*, Memoir 27

White, W J, 1988 Skeletal remains from the cemetery of St Nicholas Shambles, City of London, *London and Middlesex Archaeological Society*, London (*monograph report*)

Whitelock, D, 1941 The conversion of the eastern Danelaw, *Sagabook*, **12**, 159–76

— (ed), 1955 *English Historical Documents c 500–1042*, Oxford

Whitelock, D, Brett, M, and Brooke, C N L (eds), 1981 *Councils and Synods with other documents relating to the English church*, Oxford

Williams, J H, 1974 A Saxo-Norman kiln group from Northampton, *Northamptonshire Archaeol*, **9**, 46–56

—, 1979 *St Peters Street, Northampton: excavations 1973–1976*, Northampton Development Corporation Monogr, **2**

Williams, J H, Shaw, M, and Denham, V, *1984 Middle Saxon palaces at Northampton*, Northampton Development Corporation Monograph, **4**

Willmore, H H, 1940 Stone coffins, Gloucestershire, *Trans Bristol Gloucester Archaeol Soc*, **61**, 135–77

Wilson, D M, (ed) 1976 *The Archaeology of Anglo-Saxon England*, Cambridge

Wilson, D M, and Moorhouse, S, 1971 Medieval Britain in 1970, *Medieval Archaeol*, **15**, 124–79

Wood, M, 1965 *The English Medieval House*, London

Index

Raunds Furnells and Furnells are not indexed, as they form the basis of this report. Likewise, Anglo-Saxon and Saxo-Norman are not indexed. Where there are several entries, the main ones are indicated in **bold**. Tables 52-91 are contained in Microfiche 1. References to the microfiche indicate the number (1 or 2) and the frame or page number (such as Mf 2: 19).

ablution drains/water 8, 62, 64
adolescents (graves/burials/skeletons)
    Table 41, Mf 1: 1-11
  crushed bone 32
  dental disease 124
  depth Table 11
  distribution Fig 68, Table 22
  disturbed Table 11
  orbital osteoporosis 123
  osteoarthritis 117
  osteomyelitis 120
  in plots 50
  stone arrangements Table 17
adults (graves/burials/skeletons) 4, 6, 26, 31, 113, Fig 9, Tables 7–8, 41, Mf 1: 1, Mf 2: 1
  button osteomae 123
  cranial wormians Tables 45, 53–5
  crushed bone 32–3, Table 13
  decayed Table 13
  dental disease 124, Tables 76–80
  depth 27, 31, Fig 28, Table 11
  dimensions 31
  distribution Figs 9, 68, Table 22
  disturbed 32, 45, Table 11
  grave covers 51–2
  'inca' bone 116, Tables 45, 56
  metopic suture 115–6, Tables 45, 52
  non-parallel Table 9
  osteitis Table 49
  osteoarthritis 117, Table 47
  parallel Table 9
  parietal foramina Tables 45, 57–8
  in plots 50
  septal aperture Tables 45, 71–2
  spina bifida 123
  'squatting' facets Tables 45, 73–4
  stone arrangements 39, 40–2, Figs 54–5, Table 17
  supra-orbital rim 116, Tables 45, 59–64
  supra-scapular border Tables 45, 65–70
  trauma Table 48
  tumbled bones 36, Table 9
  see also females, males
aisled building/hall 66, Fig 3
altars 58
  Barton-on-Humber 61
  censing 62
  first church **8**, 21, 61, **63**, 64, 65, 68, Fig 24, Table 11
  second church 66
anaemia 123, 124
architrave (first church) 8, 21, 98, Fig 85, Table 11
archive 3–4, 113

ash (charcoal) Table 37
ashes (in consecration ceremonies) 62
barbed and tanged arrowheads 21, 93, Fig 20
'Barnack' limestone 101
  architrave 8, Table 11
  arch soffit 99
  blocks 8, 98
  coffins 43, 102–3, Table 38
  cross-heads 103, 105, Table 38
  cross-shafts 105, Table 38
  dressed stone Table 38
  in first church 8
  grave covers 45, 101, 105–6, 107, Table 38
  grave markers Table 38
  quoins 8, 98, Table 11
  thin sections 101, Table 38
Barton-on-Humber
  altar 61
  chancel burials 63
  head pillows 48
  stone arrangements 70
  wooden coffins 42
bead (glass) Table 35
bellcote
  in first church 8, 18, 21–2, 25, **64–5**, 66, 68, Fig 24, Table 11
  in second church 10, 66, 68, Table 11
bench see clergy bench
birch (charcoal) Table 37
Blisworth clay 5, 31, 32, 33, 47
Blisworth limestone 5, 100, Table 39
  architrave 98, Fig 85
  blocks 22
  chamfered stones 98, Fig 85
  dressed stone 98, Table 39
  in first church 8
  hood moulding 98
  quarries 14, 22, 49, 101
  quoins 98, Table 11
  in second church 14, 22, 49, Table 2
  stone arrangements 38
  thin sections 101
bone
  comb 77, 93
  pins Table 35
bones/skeletons Mf 2: 45–55
  adolescents *see* separate entry
  adults *see* separate entry
  anaemia 123, 124
  button osteomae 123
  children *see* separate entry
  cleft palate 123, Mf 1: 13
  cranial cuts 69–70, 123–4
  cranial wormians 115, **116**, Tables 45, 53–5, 75
  crushing 32–4, 113, Fig 35, Tables 5, 12–13
  decay/decayed 32, 33–4, 36, 47–8, 52, 113, Figs 36, 49, Tables 5, 12–14
  dental disease 124, Tables 76–80
  diseases *see* separate entry
  disturbance/disturbed 32, 50, 52, Fig 34, Table 5
  females *see* separate entry
  'inca' bone 116, Tables 45, 56, 75
  infants *see* separate entry
  injury *see* trauma

leprosy 69, 120, 123, 124, Figs 104–7, Mf 1: 7, 9
males *see* separate entry
measurements 117, Tables 83–91
  stature 117, Table 46
metopic suture 115–6, Tables 45, 52, 75
morphology 115–7, 124, Table 45
neonates *see* separate entry
orbital osteoporosis 123, 124, Table 51
osteitis **120–3**, 124, Tables 49–50, 106–7, Mf 1: 2, 5–6
osteoarthritis 117–8, 120, 123, Tables 47, 50, Mf 1: 2–3, 4–5, 7–10
osteomyelitis 120, Mf 1: 8
parietal foramina 116, Tables 45, 57–8, 75
pathology 41–2, 48, 117–24
periostitis 42, 120, Mf 1: 7–10
poliomyelitis 42, 69, 118, 120, 124, Figs 53, 102, Mf 1: 3, 9
sacralisation 123, Mf 1: 11, 12
septal aperture 115, **117**, Tables 45, 71–2, 75
sexing 4, 113–4, Tables 41, 75, Mf 1: 1
spina bifida 123, Mf 1: 11, 12
'squatting' facets 117, Tables 45, 73–5
sub-adults *see* separate entry
supra-orbital rim 116, Tables 45, 59–64, 75
supra-scapular border 116–7, Tables 45, 65–70, 75
survival good 32, 113
trauma/injury **118–20**, 123, Fig 103, Tables 48, 50, Mf 1: 2–7, 10–11
tuberculosis 42, 69, 120, Fig 53, Mf 1: 9
tumbled 13, 36–7, 40, 41, 47, 48, 51, 57, 69, 70, Figs 9, 39, Tables 5, 9, 15–16, 23
  distribution Fig 39, Table 15
  external 13, 36–7, 48, Figs 9, 39, 42–3, Tables 5, 10, 23
  internal 13, 36, Figs 9, 39–41, Tables 5, 10
Boothby Pagnell (first floor hall) 11
bridle bits (iron) Table 35
Burgred 67, 68
  Domesday manor 5, 67, 70
burial plots *see* graves/burials
burial rights 6
burials *see* graves/burials
burnt
  'Barnack' limestone
    block 98
    dressed stone Table 38
  layer (in first church) 18, 62, Figs 10, 69
  pottery 18, 58, 59, 79, 94, 96, Tables 26, 36
  quoin 98
  sacred refuse 61
  stones 22
  wood in graves 37
  see also charcoal
Burystead Figs 1–2
  manor 68

calcium carbonate (in pottery vessel) 58, 59, 96
candles
  in churches 58
  making 58, 61, 62

128